W9-ATE-009

Basic Skills in English

Book 6

Book 5

Book 4

Book 3

Book 2

Book 1

12

THE McDOUGAL, LITTELL ENGLISH PROGRAM

Basic Skills in English

Book 2

Joy Littell, EDITORIAL DIRECTOR

McDougal, Littell & Company
Evanston, Illinois
Sacramento, California

AUTHORS

Joy Littell, Editorial Director, McDougal, Littell & Company

Edward Hagelin Pearson, Lincoln Junior High School, Park Ridge, Illinois

Kraft and Kraft, Developers of Educational Materials, Stow, Massachusetts

CONSULTANTS

Hope Burke, Oliver Wendell Holmes Junior High School, Wheeling, Illinois

Dianne Elcook, Lynchburg-Clay School District, Lynchburg, Ohio

Editor-in-Chief: Joseph F. Littell
Project Editor: Trisha Lorange Taylor
Director of Design: William A. Seabright
Editorial Coordinator: Kathleen Laya
Design Associate: Lucy Lesiak
Assistant Editor: Mary Schafer

Acknowledgments: See page 466.

ISBN: 0-88343-768-6

Composition

These eleven pages consist of additional writing assignments. There is an exercise for each Part in the nineteen Sections. Your teacher may choose to assign each of these exercises as additional practice after each Part. The exercises will give you extra practice in improving your writing skills.

Handbook

HANDBOOK SECTION 8

Using Adjectives 313

HANDBOOK SECTION 9

Using Adverbs 327

HANDBOOK SECTION 10

Using Prepositions and Conjunctions 337

HANDBOOK SECTION 11

Using the Parts of Speech 352

Words: Developing Your Vocabulary

Part 1

Alive and Well

Using Our Language

Here's the Idea English is a living language because it is continually growing and changing. **Modern English** is different from **Middle English,** which was spoken until about 500 years ago. It is even more different from **Old English,** which was spoken until about 900 years ago. Many of the words you use today came from Middle and Old English words. For example, the number *seven* comes from the Middle English word *seoven*. *Seoven* came from the Old English word *seofon*. Words that come from older forms of English are native English words. There are also several other sources for our words.

Borrowed Words Many of our words come from other languages. English has borrowed words from the American Indian languages, from Latin, Spanish, French, and Dutch, among others. The words *moccasin, antenna, chili, coupon,* and *boss,* for example, have been borrowed from these languages.

Compound Words Two words are often put together to make a new word. Some examples are *basketball, headache,* and *liftoff*.

Blends Sometimes a part of one word and a part of another word make a new word. For example, the word *smog* comes from *smoke* and *fog*.

Acronyms An acronym is a word made from the first letters of several words. The acronym *scuba* comes from the words *self contained underwater breathing apparatus*.

Echoic Words Some words imitate sounds. *Buzz, meow,* and *zap* are examples of words that echo sounds.

English is a continually changing language. In this lesson, you have seen how some changes occur. You can now see why learning English is a continual process for everyone.

Check It Out Read the following sentences.

1. Our family spent the *day* at Hampton Beach.
2. Ken likes *pizza* with mushrooms and pepperoni.
3. The Sears Tower is Chicago's tallest *skyscraper*.
4. The Thompsons enjoy *brunch* every Sunday.
5. *NASA* officials cheered today's launching.
6. The parrot *squawked* as we neared its cage.

- Do you see how English is enriched by new words?
- Which word comes from the Old English word *daeg?* Which word is borrowed from Italian? Which word is a compound word? Which word is a blend of *breakfast* and *lunch?* Which word is an acronym for *National Aeronautics and Space Administration?* Which word echoes a sound?

Try Your Skill Using a dictionary, try to find out how each of these words came into Modern English.

boy slim snowplow UNICEF sizzle patio

Keep This in Mind

- English continually grows and changes. New words are being formed as others are no longer being used.
- Some Modern English words come from Middle and Old English. Others come from borrowed words, compound words, blends, acronyms, and echoic words.

Now Write Write four of these words: *Saturday, antenna, boss, liftoff, chortle,* and *sonar*. Using a dictionary, check the meanings of the words and find out how they came into English. Write a sentence for each of them. Label your paper **Alive and Well.** Keep your paper in your writing folder.

Part 2

Say It Again, Sam

Context: Definition and Restatement

Here's the Idea When you see an unfamiliar word, you may be able to learn its meaning from the context. **Context** means the words surrounding a word that help you figure out the meaning of that word. The most direct clues are definition and restatement.

When **definition** is used, the meaning of a new word is stated directly.

The sheets were made of *muslin*. *Muslin* is a strong, cotton cloth.

When **restatement** is used, the meaning of a new word is usually restated with key words like *or, is called, that is, which is,* or *in other words*. Sometimes the meaning of the new word is indicated by a comma or a pair of commas.

The butter had a *rancid* smell; in other words, it was spoiled.

I just want a *morsel*, a tiny piece, of that delicious cake.

When you read, look for a definition or a restatement of a new word. These clues help you learn new words more easily.

Check It Out Look at the examples below.

1. The minister stood behind a *lectern*. A lectern is a tall stand used to hold a book or notes to be read.
2. My Uncle Bob works as a *mason*, or bricklayer.
3. Al's writing is not *legible*; that is, it cannot be read easily.
4. The carpenter needed an *awl*, a small pointed tool for making holes in wood.

- What is the meaning of each italicized word?
- What is the clue in each sentence that indicates a definition or restatement?

Try Your Skill Determine from the context what the italicized word means in each of these sentences. Write a definition for each.

1. In Georgia, we saw beautiful *jasmine.* Jasmine is a plant with fragrant yellow flowers.

2. My father gave a *noncommital* answer, which was neither a yes nor a no.

3. The ring was made of *garnets,* deep red stones, set in gold.

4. New England has some of the most *fickle,* or changeable, weather in the country.

5. More than 500 American cities have *city managers.* A city manager is a person who is hired to run a city in the way a business is run.

6. The bird dog never *deviated,* or turned aside, from the trail it was following.

Keep This in Mind

- Context, the words surrounding a word, often gives clues to the meaning of that word.
- Definition and restatement are the most direct context clues.
- Several words or phrases alert you to definition or restatement. These include *or, is called, that is, which is,* or *in other words.* A definition or restatement may also be set off by commas.

Now Write On your paper, write the title of this lesson, **Say It Again, Sam.** Choose four of the following words: *chard, escalator, lease, neon, secretary, umpire.* Write a sentence for each of the four words, using definition or restatement in the context. Use a dictionary, if necessary, to help you. Check your sentences by having a reader see if your meaning is clear to him or her. When you have written and checked your sentences, put the paper into your folder.

Part 3

A Good Example

Using Context Clues: Examples

Here's the Idea An unfamiliar word is not always defined or restated. However, sometimes you may be able to understand the meaning of a word through **examples** given. By studying the examples, you can determine what the new word means.

Read this sentence:

I wrote a report on the *lynx* and other kinds of wildcats.

You may not know exactly what a lynx looks like. However, you can understand the general meaning of the word. The phrase *and other kinds* signals that a lynx is one kind of wildcat.

Many key words and phrases signal the use of examples. When an example is given, you will commonly see such key words as *especially, like, other, this, these, for example, for instance,* and *such as.*

Read the following sentence and find the key word that signals a context clue.

Some wildcats, like the *lynx*, live in North America.

The context clue here is the word *like.* This sentence also tells you that a *lynx* is one kind of wildcat.

In each of these sentences, you can tell from the context what the word *lynx* means. An example gives you the general meaning of the word.

Check It Out Read the following sentences.

1. All *citrus* fruits, especially oranges, are good sources of the Vitamin C you need.

2. Scientists are experimenting with *diesel* and other kinds of engines.

3. The music of many *composers,* Beethoven and Mozart, for example, have been used in recent movies.

4. The values of units of money such as *yen* and *francs* change almost daily.

- What is the meaning of each of the italicized words?
- Which words or phrases signal that an example is used as a context clue?

Try Your Skill Try to get the meaning of the italicized words in these sentences from the use of examples in context. Write the definition of each italicized word.

1. *Nocturnal* creatures, like bats, usually sleep during the day.

2. Dan refuses to believe in *gremlins,* or in any other imaginary creatures.

3. Some large birds, the *emu,* for instance, are unable to fly.

4. I enjoy eating all kinds of salad greens, like *endive* and *chicory.*

5. The cottage was surrounded by big clumps of *burdock* and other thorny weeds.

Keep This in Mind

- An example may be used as a context clue.
- Certain key words signal examples. Key words and phrases include *especially, like, other, this, these, for example, for instance,* and *such as.*

Now Write On your paper, write the title of this lesson, **A Good Example.** Choose three of the following words and use them in sentences: *mumps, plywood, soccer, spaghetti, tacos,* and *wool.* Make the meaning of the words clear by using an example as a context clue. Check your sentences by having a reader see if your meaning is clear to him or her. When you have checked your sentences, put your work into your folder.

Part 4

Like and Unlike

Context Clues: Comparison and Contrast

Here's the Idea Two other types of context clues can give you the meaning of an unfamiliar word. They are comparison and contrast. You can understand the meaning of a new word by learning what it is like or unlike.

When **comparison** is used, a new word is compared with a similar word that is already familiar to you. Try to determine the meaning of the word *guppy* from the context of this sentence.

Guppies, like other tiny fish, are often used in aquariums.

The words *like* and *other* signal that a guppy is a kind of tiny fish. Comparisons are usually signaled by certain key words. Those key words include *as, like, in the same way,* and *similar to.*

When **contrast** is used, a new word is compared with an opposite word that is familiar to you. If you know the opposite of an unfamiliar word, you can often understand the meaning you do not know. Read this example.

Dad found the trip *enthralling,* even though Uncle Al thought it was boring.

In the example, *enthralling* is contrasted with *boring.* The phrase *even though* suggests that Dad did not find the trip boring. *Enthralling* must mean the opposite of *boring.*

Key words that signal contrast as a context clue include *though, but, unlike, while, on the contrary,* and *on the other hand.*

Check It Out Read the sentences below.

1. *Chlorine* gas, like other dangerous chemicals, should be stored safely in a laboratory.

2. *Clove* flavors food in the same way that other spices do.

3. Unlike other forms of art, a *mural* is part of a wall.

4. Parking is *prohibited* on Sunday after 7 A.M. until noon, but it is allowed at all other times.

- What is the meaning of each italicized word?
- Which key words signal that comparison is used?
- Which key words signal that contrast is used?

Try Your Skill Write a definition for each italicized word in these sentences.

1. Unlike Jay who congratulated me, Larry *scoffed* at my prize.
2. *Merino* and other fine wools are used in making soft material.
3. *Filberts* are unlike many other nuts because they grow on bushes instead of trees.
4. Like most *extroverts*, Dot was friendly and outgoing.
5. I thought the show was exciting, but Ben said it was *tedious*.

Keep This in Mind

- Comparison and contrast provide context clues to the meanings of unfamiliar words.
- Certain key words and phrases signal that comparison is used as a context clue. These include *as*, *like*, *in the same way*, and *similar to*.
- Certain key words signal contrast as a context clue. These include *although*, *but*, *unlike*, *while*, *on the contrary*, and *on the other hand*.

Now Write On your paper, write the title of this lesson, **Like and Unlike.** Use four of these words in sentences: *book*, *breakfast*, *bus*, *cat*, *dog*, *house*. Write two sentences using comparison as a context clue. Then write two more sentences using contrast as a clue. Use key words to signal which context clue you are using. Check your sentences by having a reader see if your meaning is clear. Finally, put your paper into your folder.

Part 5 **Be Precise**

Using Synonyms and Antonyms

Here's the Idea Words with similar meanings are called **synonyms.** Synonyms do not mean exactly the same thing, however. They do mean almost the same thing.

Take the words *chuckle* and *giggle*, for instance. They mean almost the same thing, but not quite. *Chuckle* means a soft, low, laughing sound at what is mildly funny. *Giggle* means a quick, high-pitched laughing sound in what seems a silly or nervous way. You can see that one synonym would be a more accurate description than the other in a particular situation.

The word *eat*, for instance, also has many synonyms. Two of these are *gulp* and *nibble*. Which would you use to describe how a hungry person was eating? You would probably use *gulp*, since it means "to swallow greedily or in large amounts."

Antonyms are words that have almost opposite meanings. *Hot* and *cold* are antonyms. So are *fat* and *thin*. Words often have more than one antonym, just as they often have more than one synonym. Other antonyms for hot are *cool*, *chilly*, and *frozen*.

Using synonyms and antonyms carefully will help you when you write. Check to see if a synonym might be a more accurate word than one you are using. Check to see if an antonym might help you to make a comparison. If you are precise with words, you will be able to express your ideas more clearly.

Check It Out Look at the following sentences.

1. "Be quiet," *said* Tanya, "we don't want them to hear us."
   barked called shrieked whispered
2. Is your job *dull*, or is it ______?" asked Ron.
   busy exciting important valuable

- Which is the best synonym for *said?* Why?
- Which is the best antonym for *dull?* Why?
- Do the words you selected express the ideas as clearly as possible?

Try Your Skill Read each sentence below. Choose the word that best replaces the italicized word. Number your paper from 1 to 5 and write the correct word.

1. We *went* home before the storm began.
   dashed strolled walked wandered
2. Ms. Moyers said my report was *good* and deserved an A.
   fine kind nice superior
3. The library kept all of its magazines in one *big* room.
   generous giant spacious wide
4. This story is so *interesting*, I just can't put it down.
   attractive curious fascinating tantalizing

5. Carlos worked long and hard, and became quite *sad* when the radio still wouldn't work.

   dejected gloomy mournful sorrowful

Keep This in Mind

- Synonyms are words with similar meanings.
- Antonyms are words with opposite meanings.
- Choose synonyms and antonyms that are accurate and appropriate for your meaning.

Now Write On your paper, write the title of this lesson, **Be Precise.** The words *chatter*, *comment*, *recite*, and *talk* are synonyms. Use each in a sentence. Write each sentence so that the precise meaning of each synonym is clear. Check your sentences by having a reader see if your meaning is clear to him or her. When you have finished, put your work into your folder.

Part 6

Get on Base

Using Word Parts: Base Words

Here's the Idea One way to add new words to your vocabulary is to learn about base words and word parts. A **base word** is a word on which other words are based. *Trust*, for example, is a base word.

Sometimes word parts are added at the beginning of a base word. When *dis-* is added to *trust*, the new word *distrust* is formed. The new word has a different meaning from the base word. Other word parts are added at the end of base words. Add *-ful* to *trust*, and the new word *trustful* is formed. Sometimes, more than one word part is added to a base word. *Dis-* and *-ful* can both be added to *trust* to make *distrustful*.

Sometimes the spelling of a base word will be changed slightly when a word part is added. This is especially true when a word part is added at the end of a base word. When the word part *-able* is added to the base word *move*, the new word *movable* is formed. Notice that the *e* in *move* is dropped.

In the next two lessons, you will learn some word parts and their meanings. This knowledge will help you enlarge your vocabulary. You'll be able to add the meaning of the word part to the meaning of the base word. That will give you the meaning of a new word. For example, suppose that you bought a *nontaxable* item. *Non-* means "not," and *-able* means "can." The base word is *tax*. *Nontaxable* means "cannot be taxed."

Check It Out Read each group of words below.

return	adventurous	useful
returnable	misadventure	misuse
nonreturnable	unadventurous	useless

- What is the base word in each group of words?
- Which spelling of a base word was changed slightly when a word part was added at the end?
- Which words are new to you?

Try Your Skill Read the following list and write what the base word is in each word. You may want to check a dictionary for correct spelling.

1. sleepless
2. nonprofit
3. unthinkable
4. dangerous
5. illegal
6. disgraceful
7. imperfect
8. injustice
9. refillable
10. misplace
11. survivor
12. preschooler

Keep This In Mind

- Word parts may be added at the beginning or end of base words to make new words.
- Sometimes the spelling of a base word is changed slightly when a part is added.
- Knowing base words and word parts will help you to enlarge your vocabulary.

Now Write Using any one of your textbooks, find five words that have base words and word parts. The word part may be at the beginning or end of the word. Try to choose words that are unfamiliar to you.

On your paper, write the title of this lesson, **Get on Base.** Then write the words you have found. Next to each word, write the base word. If you know the meaning of the base word, write it on your paper. If not, look it up in a dictionary and then write it. Try to figure out the entire word.

Finally, put your work into your folder. You will need it for another lesson.

Part 7 # What's First?

Using Word Parts: Prefixes

Here's the Idea You know that word parts can be added to base words. A word part added at the beginning of a base word is called a **prefix.** *Pre-* means "before" and *fix* means "attach," so *prefix* means "to attach before."

The word part *un-*, for example, is a common prefix. Sometimes *un-* means "not," as it does in the word *unlike.* If you are unlike someone, you are not like her or him. Sometimes *un-* means "the opposite of," as it does in the word *unchain.* If you *unchain* the door, you can open it.

Some prefixes have one meaning. Others have two. Once you learn to recognize these prefixes, they will help you to understand many unfamiliar words. Here are some common prefixes.

Prefix	Meaning	Examples
in- (also **il-**, **im-**, and **ir-**)	"not"	indefinite, illegal immature, irregular
mis-	"wrong"	misbehave, miscount
non-	"not"	nonprofit, nonstop
pre-	"before"	prefix, prewash
re-	"again" or "back"	rebuild, recall
sub-	"under" or "less than"	subway, substandard
super-	"above" or "more than"	supernatural
un-	"not" or "opposite of"	untested, uneven

Some words seem to start with a prefix, but they really do not. At first glance, the word *region* may look as though it starts with the prefix *re.* Does it? To find out, look for the base word. If you cover the letters *re-*, you are left with *gion,* which isn't a word. Since there is no base word, the letters *re-* are not a prefix in *region.*

Check It Out Look at the words below.

immodest	disagree	misunderstand	substation
submarine	irregular	illogical	incomplete
nonfiction	repay	supermarket	preview

- What is the prefix in each word? What does each prefix mean?
- What does each word mean?

Try Your Skill Read the words below. Some of the words have prefixes. Others do not. If a word has a prefix, write the meaning of the prefix plus the base word. For example, for the word *recall*, you would write this: again + call.

1. subhuman
2. superior
3. input
4. nonviolent
5. imagine
6. improper
7. illogical
8. preflight
9. rectangle
10. unmarked
11. untie
12. invisible
13. united
14. refit
15. supertanker

Keep This in Mind

- A prefix is a word part that is added at the beginning of a word.
- Each prefix has one or more meanings. The prefix changes the meaning of the base word, making a new word.
- Some words seem to begin with a prefix, but do not. Check to see if the base word makes sense without the prefix.

Now Write On your paper, write **What's First?** Find eight words, each containing one of the eight prefixes explained in this lesson. Use a dictionary to help you. Next to each word, write its definition. Keep all your work in your folder.

Part 8

The End

Using Word Parts: Suffixes

Here's the Idea A word part added at the end of a word is called a **suffix.** One common suffix, for example, is *-less,* which means "without." If you believe that your situation is *hopeless,* it is "without a hope." Notice how the meaning of a suffix combines with the meaning of a base word to make a new word with a different meaning.

Sometimes when a suffix is added, the spelling of the base word is changed. Someone who *runs* is a *runner.* You can see that the final *n* is doubled. A person having *fame* is *famous.* A scene full of *beauty* is *beautiful.* Notice that the final *e* in fame is dropped in *famous.* Notice also that the final *y* in *beauty* is changed to *i* in *beautiful.*

Sometimes the change involves more than one letter. For example, something belonging to *Ireland* is *Irish.* You can see that when the suffix *-ish* is added, the whole word changes. Use a dictionary to check the spelling of a word if necessary.

Below are some of the more commonly used suffixes.

Suffix	Meaning	Examples
-able or **-ible**	"can be, having this quality"	likable, forcible
-er or **-or**	"a person or thing that does something"	singer, elevator
-ful	"full of, having"	graceful
-ish	"belonging to or like"	Spanish, childish
-less	"without"	homeless
-ness	"the state or quality of being"	sickness, sadness
-ous	"full of, having"	poisonous

Check It Out Look at the words below.

priceless	truthful	English
operator	carrier	movable
mysterious	gentleness	sensible

- What is the suffix in each word? What does each word mean?
- In which words is the spelling of the base word changed?

Try Your Skill Number your paper from 1 to 15. Look at the list below and find the suffix in each word. If you aren't sure about the spelling of the base word, check a dictionary. Write the base word and the meaning of the suffix for each word. For example, for the word *joyous*, you would write this: joy + full of.

1. youthful	6. Scottish	11. religious
2. avoidable	7. miner	12. sizable
3. deafness	8. pitiful	13. brightness
4. courageous	9. soundless	14. wasteful
5. trainer	10. convertible	15. devilish

Keep This in Mind

- Suffixes are word parts added at the ends of base words. A suffix changes the meaning of a base word.
- Sometimes the spelling of a base word changes when a suffix is added.
- Use a dictionary to check the spelling of a word when you add a suffix.

Now Write On your paper, write **The End.** Find one word containing each of the suffixes explained in this lesson. Next to each word write its definition. Use a dictionary to help you. Finally, put your work into your folder.

Improving Your Sentences

Part 1

One of a Kind

Writing Good Sentences

Here's the Idea A **sentence** is a group of words that expresses a complete thought. Sentences can express thoughts in many different ways. Look at the following two sentences about fog. Which sentence do you think makes a more interesting statement?

Fog doesn't make any noise. The fog comes on little cat feet.

You probably prefer the sentence on the right, which was written by the poet Carl Sandburg. It's a more interesting sentence because it states an idea in a clear and fresh way. It appeals to your senses and your imagination. It has a stronger impact.

Below are other examples of sentences that express ideas in a clear, direct, and original way.

Old friends are best. —JOHN SELDEN

What we have to learn to do, we learn by doing. —ARISTOTLE

You can never plan the future by the past. —EDMUND BURKE

The only thing we have to fear is fear itself. —FRANKLIN D. ROOSEVELT

Hopes are but the dreams of those who are awake. —PINDAR

Every sentence makes a point. No matter what point you are making in a sentence, you can make the sentence effective. Keep to one idea. Be clear and direct. Also, use your senses and imagination to express an idea in an original way.

Check It Out Read the following sentences.

1. It would be night soon, and I was afraid.
2. The waves pounded the rocky shore.

3. Do you know how to eat with chopsticks?
4. Americans should use less of the world's fuel.
5. Adobe is sun-dried clay used for building.

- Does each sentence express a single, complete thought?
- Is each sentence clear and direct?

Try Your Skill Number your paper from 1 to 5. Write a sentence in response to each of the five directions below. Make your sentences direct, lively, and original. Use details from your memory or from your imagination.

1. Describe your family.
2. Explain why you like music.
3. Tell one event from your childhood.
4. Give a definition of a good vacation.
5. Tell how you travel to school each day.

Keep This in Mind

- A sentence is a group of words that expresses a complete thought.
- Every sentence should have a meaning that is clear to the reader.
- A good sentence is clear, direct, and lively.

Now Write Write a sentence that tells something you did recently. Write a sentence that tells what your favorite possession is. Then write a sentence that describes it. Write a sentence that tells why you like your best friend. Finally, write a sentence that explains how to do something.

Read your five sentences. Are they clear and interesting? If not, rewrite your sentences.

On your paper, write the title of this lesson, **One of a Kind.** Copy your sentences and put them into your folder.

Part 2

Say Something

Avoiding Empty Sentences

Here's the Idea If sentences do not tell the reader something, they are called **empty sentences.** There are two kinds of empty sentences.

The first kind of empty sentence repeats an idea.

> Solving math problems is easy for me because I am good at math.

It is understood that a person who is good at math solves math problems easily. The idea does not need to be stated twice.

You can improve this kind of empty sentence by making it simpler. You can also improve it by adding more information.

> I have always been good at math.
>
> Solving math problems has always been easy for me, and I have always enjoyed problems with fractions.

The second kind of empty sentence gives an unsupported opinion. The writer makes a strong statement that captures a reader's attention, but leaves the reader asking "Why?"

> TV commercials should not be aimed at young children.

Such strong statements are empty of meaning for a reader unless they are supported by facts, reasons, or examples. Supporting information may be given in the same sentence or in another sentence.

> TV commercials should not be aimed at young children, who respond strongly to what they watch.
>
> TV commercials should not be aimed at young children. Studies show that children respond strongly to what they watch.

Supporting evidence might also be developed in longer pieces of writing, such as paragraphs or compositions.

You must offer readers a reason for an opinion. Otherwise, your writing will seem empty. Your readers may not agree with your opinion. However, they will know why you think as you do.

Check It Out Read the following empty sentences.

1. This book is boring, and I think it is very dull.
2. All states should have safety inspections for cars.
3. Breakfast cereals use too much sugar.
4. Many people enjoy tennis because it is an enjoyable game.
5. Reading is important for everyone.

- Which sentences repeat an idea? Which sentences give an unsupported opinion?
- How would you improve these empty sentences?

Try Your Skill Rewrite each of the empty sentences below.

1. Our refrigerator doesn't work because it is broken.
2. Don got a raise so he is making more money now.
3. Every member of a family should help with household chores.
4. The U.S. should give money to support its Olympic athletes.

Keep This in Mind

- There are two kinds of empty sentences. One kind repeats an idea. The other kind states an opinion without supporting it.
- Improve sentences that repeat an idea by making them simpler or by adding more information. Improve sentences with unsupported opinions by including reasons for your opinion.

Now Write Label your paper *Empty Sentences.* Write, or find, two examples of each kind of empty sentence. Improve the sentences by eliminating repetition or by supplying reasons. Write the improved sentences. Keep your paper in your folder.

Part 3 **Streamlining**

Avoiding Padded Sentences

Here's the Idea A **padded sentence** has useless words and phrases. The main idea is buried by unnecessary words. Look at these examples of phrases that signal padding.

on account of the fact that	what I want is
because of the fact that	the point is
due to the fact that	the reason is
what I mean is	the thing is
what I think is	

Often, you can improve a padded sentence by taking out the extra words. Sometimes, you may have to rewrite the sentence completely.

Padded What I mean is that the store manager was rude.

Improved The store manager was rude.

Padded I kept the entire group waiting due to the fact that I couldn't find my money for quite a while.

Improved I kept the entire group waiting while I looked for my money.

Many groups of words using *who, which,* or *that* may be unnecessary in a sentence. When you use them, be sure they add to the meaning of the sentence. Notice how the sentence below is improved when unnecessary words are eliminated.

Padded Our car, which is old and pink, attracts attention.

Improved Our old, pink car attracts attention.

Check It Out Read these padded sentences.

1. What I think is that the butler did it.

2. I took my shoes off on account of the fact that my feet hurt.

3. My cousin Jackie, who is older, teaches at Longmeadow High School.

- How would you improve each of these padded sentences?

Try Your Skill Improve the padded sentences below. Take out any unnecessary words or phrases or rewrite the entire sentence.

1. It took the letter two weeks to get there on account of the fact that the ZIP code was wrong.
2. My old typewriter is just fine for me due to the fact that I'm used to it.
3. The sandwiches, which were made with tuna salad, tasted good with tomato soup.
4. The reason why I couldn't lock your bicycle is because I lost the key.
5. Sam is doing all the shopping this week and the reason is that he thinks he can cut the food bill.

Keep This in Mind

- Padded sentences have unnecessary words and phrases.
- Omit any words that add nothing to the idea in a sentence. Sometimes you may have to rewrite a sentence completely.

Now Write Label your paper *Padded Sentences*. Write, or find four examples of padded sentences. Improve the sentences by eliminating any unnecessary words and phrases. Rewrite wherever necessary.

When you have finished, put your paper into your folder.

Exploring Paragraphs

Part 1

Togetherness

Defining a Paragraph

Here's the Idea A **paragraph** is a group of sentences that work together. They deal with one main idea.

See if the sentences in each of these groups work together.

1 Captain Lockwood shifted uneasily in his seat as he landed the jumbo jet. He could see nothing anywhere on this empty land. The trees and rocks were bathed in a strange pink light. Suddenly he gasped, as a sickening odor began to creep into the plane. He cleared his throat. He felt tense. He told his passengers that they had landed on an unknown planet.

2 The mist hung over the lake like a curtain. Sleepy ducks shook themselves awake to prepare for daybreak. The old rowboat skimmed across the smooth, dark surface. A baited hook made circles as it was dropped into the water. Quietly, the lone fisherman turned up his collar and settled in for a morning's fishing.

3 The next time you're looking for a healthy, crunchy snack, try sprouting beans. First, combine a few tablespoons of lentils and two cups of water in a quart jar. Second, cover the jar with cheesecloth. Then let the beans soak for three days. Rinse and drain the beans twice each day. By the fourth day, your sprouts will be ready to eat. Try them in a sandwich or in a salad.

Check It Out Look again at the three groups of sentences. The first group of sentences tells a story. The second group describes a misty morning on a lake. The third group explains a process. Are these groups of sentences paragraphs?

- Does each group of sentences deal with one idea?
- Does every sentence in each group say something about the one main idea?

Try Your Skill Read the groups of sentences below. One of them is a paragraph. Two are not. Number your paper from 1 to 3. For the group that is a paragraph, write the main idea. For each group that is not a paragraph, explain why it is not.

1 Some people always seem to do their best late in the day. Many old movies are on TV after midnight. These people are called "night people." They usually take a long time to wake up in the morning. They get more energy as the day goes on. By evening, they are usually going at full speed.

2 Once there were millions of buffalo roaming free on the Great Plains. Many Indians also lived in that part of the Old West. Now if you want to see buffalo, you have to go to a zoo or animal farm. A good zoo has healthy looking animals. Some zoos are famous for one particular animal.

3 The dog that roams our neighborhood draws a lot of attention. His eyes have a droopy, sad look. His ears are small and pointed. A curly, spotted coat of fur covers his short, stubby body. When this strange-looking creature passes by, everyone stares at him.

Keep This in Mind

- A paragraph is a group of sentences dealing with one idea.
- Every sentence in the paragraph should say something about the main idea.

Now Write On your paper, write **Togetherness.** From this lesson, choose one of the groups of sentences that is not a paragraph. Find the sentences that do not belong. Copy the remaining sentences in the form of a paragraph. Finally, read the completed paragraph to yourself. Notice how the paragraph deals with one idea.

Keep the paragraph in your folder.

Part 2

All the Same

Recognizing Paragraph Unity

Here's the Idea A paragraph deals with one main idea. All the sentences in a paragraph should relate to that main idea. When they do, a paragraph has **unity.**

Look at the following paragraph. Notice how all the sentences relate to the idea of saving a school.

The city of Chicago must not close Lakeside High School. It is true that enrollment has dropped from 1,745 students to 1,380 in the last five years. However, closing Lakeside would deal a severe blow to our North Side neighborhood. First, Lakeside has never been a problem school. Second, the thirty-year-old building is still in good condition. Most important, this experimental school offers job training programs that few other schools in the city offer. Our students deserve a good education in their own neighborhood. Keep Lakeside open.

Check It Out Now read the following paragraph.

More than one fourth of the world's population lives in a city or its surrounding area. Tokyo, Mexico City, Shanghai, New York, and Buenos Aires are the five largest city areas in the world. Tokyo, for instance, has more than eleven and a half million people who live in its city area. New York City, with almost ten million people, is the largest city area in the United States. All over the world, more and more people are living in or near cities.

- Do all of the sentences relate to one main idea? Does the paragraph have unity?

Try Your Skill Each main idea below is followed by several sentences. Some say something about the main idea. Some do not. Copy each main idea on your paper. Below it, list only those sentences that are related to the main idea.

Main Idea: The trunk of an elephant is strong and useful.

1. An elephant uses its trunk to feel and grasp objects.
2. An elephant is smart and can learn many tricks.
3. Elephants take good care of each other.
4. The trunk of an elephant is about six feet long and weighs about 300 pounds.
5. An elephant can sleep standing up.
6. An elephant smells, drinks, and feeds itself with its trunk.
7. One of the most famous elephants in this country was named Jumbo.

Main Idea: The U.S. has received more immigrants than any other country in history.

1. Most of the original colonists came from England and Ireland.
2. Many immigrants have had trouble finding jobs.
3. The largest number of immigrants has come from Germany.
4. An immigrant must pass tests before becoming a citizen.
5. Recently, many immigrants have come from Mexico and the West Indies.
6. Part of a citizenship test is written and part is spoken.

Keep This in Mind

- All of the sentences in a paragraph should relate to one main idea. Then a paragraph has unity.

Now Write On your paper, write **All the Same,** the title of this lesson. Choose a hobby, sport, or activity that interests you. List the topic you choose. Number your paper from 1 to 5. Then, write five sentences that deal with your topic.

When you have finished, put your paper into your folder.

Part 3

What's the Big Idea?

Using a Topic Sentence

Here's the Idea To control unity in a paragraph, the paragraph must have a topic sentence. A **topic sentence** states the main idea of the paragraph. Because it tells what the paragraph is about, it usually begins the paragraph.

A topic sentence serves two purposes:

First, it helps you keep your paragraph unified. A topic sentence helps you, the writer, keep your main idea in mind. Check to make sure that every sentence in a paragraph works with the topic sentence. Omit sentences that are not related to the main idea.

Second, a topic sentence acts as a guide for your readers. It tells your readers what to expect in the sentences that follow.

Check It Out Read the paragraph below.

> Is the idea of an iceberg off the coast of Saudi Arabia simply a wild mirage? Some scientists and Prince Faisal of Saudi Arabia don't think so. They believe that someday icebergs might be towed from the Antarctic to the Red Sea. There they would be melted for drinking water and irrigation. Tests are being conducted with 125-ton wooden icebergs to see if the idea will work.

- What is the topic sentence?
- What is the main idea of this paragraph?

Try Your Skill Read the three groups of sentences below. Decide which sentence is the topic sentence in each group. Number your paper from 1 to 3. Copy the topic sentences.

1. (a) Wearing rubber gloves, first remove the old finish with a varnish remover and steel wool.

(b) Then rinse the table carefully and allow it to dry.

(c) A coat of lemon oil applied with a soft rag will provide the final, gleaming touch.

(d) Next, sand the surface smooth with sandpaper.

(e) With a little know-how and a lot of energy, you can transform a dingy, old wooden table into a showpiece.

2. (a) He joined the major leagues in 1948 as a forty-two-year-old rookie for the Cleveland Indians.

(b) Seventeen years later he pitched three shutout innings for Kansas City in his final major league game.

(c) He began playing in the National Negro League where he pitched 3,000 games and won 300 of them by shutouts.

(d) Satchel Paige was a major league pitcher with an arm of steel.

(e) At an age when most ball players have retired, he pitched two shutouts in his first three games in the major leagues.

3. (a) Wolves share food with each other.

(b) Wolves are now believed to be noble and wise animals.

(c) A destructive wolf may only be ill or hungry.

(d) They are friendly and playful with their own group.

(e) Wolves protect each other.

Keep This in Mind

- A paragraph must have a topic sentence.
- A topic sentence states the main idea of the paragraph.

Now Write On your paper, write the title of this lesson, **What's the Big Idea?** Choose two topics you would like to write about. You might choose to write about a friend, a pet, or a hobby. Write a topic sentence for each of your topics. Put your work into your folder.

Part 4

Show Your Support

Developing a Paragraph

Here's the Idea The main idea of a paragraph is introduced in the topic sentence. The main idea should be developed in the sentences that follow. There are three ways to develop the main idea. You can use details. You can use examples. You can use facts and figures. One way will be more suitable than another to develop a particular main idea.

Use **details** to make your subject come alive for your reader.

The armored tank of the animal kingdom is surely the armadillo. This thick-shelled, short-legged mammal is slow-moving and might easily be caught. Because the armadillo has only small back teeth, it cannot bite in self-defense. When stopped by an enemy, the armadillo rolls itself into a tight ball. With only its armored shell exposed, the armadillo is safe from attackers.

Use **examples** to develop a general statement.

A special family tradition can make any day a holiday. Each winter after the first big snowfall, the members of my family rush outside to celebrate. For hours we toboggan down the slippery hill at the end of our street. Chilled and weary, we return home to thaw. We wrap our hands tightly around mugs of steaming chocolate. We laugh and recall our past winters.

Use **facts and figures** to prove a point or to make an idea clear.

Despite their small size, some insects are able to perform amazing feats. A tiny flea, for instance, is able to jump seven inches high and a distance of thirteen inches. The male cicada, a flylike insect, can produce a noise that can be heard over a distance of one-quarter of a mile. The speed of the great monarch butterfly has been recorded at twenty miles per hour. These tiny insects are small-scale Olympic heroes.

Whichever method or methods you decide to use, be accurate. Be sure to check any information you aren't sure of.

Check It Out Read the following paragraph.

> Coal will probably be an important fuel in the energy plans of the United States for the next twenty years. Coal represents as much as ninety percent of the total fossil-fuel reserves of the U.S. Yet it supplies less than twenty percent of the nation's energy needs. A proposal has been made to double coal production in the next ten years or so. This increase will help reduce our dependence on foreign energy supplies. It will also give the U.S. time to develop other energy sources.—*Scientific American*

- Is the topic sentence developed by details? Is it developed by an example? Is it developed by facts and figures?

Try Your Skill Find and write the topic sentence. Then write *Details*, *Examples*, or *Facts and Figures* to tell how the main idea is developed.

> Many people consider Jim Thorpe to be America's greatest athlete. In the Olympics of 1912, he won the pentathlon and the decathlon. As a major league baseball player in 1919, his batting average was .327. As a professional football player, he consistently kicked a football more than sixty yards. No other athlete has played so well in so many different sports.

Keep This in Mind

- The main idea of a paragraph may be developed by using details, examples, or facts and figures.

Now Write On your paper, write the title of this lesson, **Show Your Support.** From your folder, take out the topic sentences you wrote in the last lesson. Choose one. List three details, examples, or facts and figures that you could use to develop the topic sentence. Put your work into your folder.

Part 5

Brand Names

Recognizing Three Kinds of Paragraphs

Here's the Idea When you write, you may want to tell a story. You may want to describe something or someone. You may want to explain something or tell how to do something. For each of these times you would use one of the three main kinds of paragraphs.

A **narrative paragraph** tells a story or tells something that happened. It usually tells the story in the order that it happened.

A **descriptive paragraph** is a picture in words. It appeals to the senses. This kind of paragraph describes something so that you can see, hear, feel, smell, or taste it.

An **explanatory paragraph** explains something. It tells *how* to do something, *why* something happened, or *what* something is. A *how* paragraph explains something step by step. A *why* paragraph gives reasons or facts to support an idea or opinion. A *what* paragraph defines something.

Check It Out Read the paragraph below.

> The afternoon sun was beaming through the sheer, white curtains at the window. The delicate leaves of the fern plants rustled faintly as the cat sprang to the window seat. Its glossy patches of orange and brown fur shone like autumn leaves in the sunshine. With a lazy purr, it nestled against the well worn cushions for a midday snooze.

- Does this paragraph tell a story, describe, or explain? Is the paragraph narrative, descriptive, or explanatory?

Try Your Skill Read these paragraphs. What kind is each? On your paper, write *Narrative, Descriptive*, or *Explanatory*.

1 At last, we were off on our trip to visit Grandma and Grandpa Johnson. First, we stopped for gas. We also had the oil and tire pressure checked. Then, we checked our map to find the best route. Finally, we headed for the highway to begin the long drive to Detroit.

2 Jogging has many advantages over other sports. Unlike a tennis player, a jogger really doesn't need any special equipment, outfit, or court. Unlike baseball or football, jogging does not require a team of players. Unlike a golf game, which can take up to a whole day, jogging can be completed in a short time. Why bother with more complicated sports when jogging is so easy?

3 To fix a broken window, first remove all the broken glass from the frame. Second, remove the old putty and any bits of old wood or paint. When the frame has been cleaned out, paint it. Then, put in the new glass. Finally, put new putty around the window to seal the glass in the frame.

Keep This in Mind

- A narrative paragraph tells a story or tells something that happened.
- A descriptive paragraph describes something or someone.
- An explanatory paragraph explains *how, why* or *what.*

Now Write On your paper, write the title of this lesson, **Brand Names.** Read over your topic sentence and notes from **Now Write** in the last two lessons. Which of the three kinds of paragraphs would you use for your topic? Write the name for that kind on your paper. Explain why it is the best kind to use with your topic. Then put your work into your folder.

Writing a Paragraph

Part 1

Straight and Narrow

Narrowing a Topic

Here's the Idea Sometimes the topic you want to write about is too general or too broad to be covered in one paragraph. Telling everything you know about sports, for instance, requires more than one paragraph. The subject is too big. You need to narrow the topic so that you can write a lively, detailed paragraph.

One good way to narrow a topic is to ask questions about it. Ask questions like *who? what? when? where? why?* and *how?* Then use the specific answers to write a paragraph. For example, you could narrow the topic "sports" like this:

Who?	Aztec Indians
What?	invented basketball
When?	16th century
Where?	Mexico
How?	put ball through stone ring
Why?	to amuse spectators

These specifics can now lead you to write a detailed and interesting paragraph like this one:

> The game of basketball is more than four hundred years old. A form of the game was first played by the Aztec Indians in Mexico. The object of the game was to put a solid rubber ball through a stone ring. While this sounds very much like modern basketball, there was one important difference. The Aztecs often chopped off the head of the captain of the losing team!

You need not answer all of these questions every time you narrow a topic. Some questions will not always apply. However, answer as many as you can. Your writing will become livelier and more interesting.

Check It Out See how the topic "caves" is narrowed.

Who?	Carla Lombardo
What?	explored Mammoth Cave
When?	July, 1978
Where?	Mammoth Cave National Park, Kentucky
How?	took a walk by herself
Why?	wanted to see a big cave
Narrow Topic	Carla Lombardo's walk alone through Mammoth Cave last July

- What other details can you add?
- Can this topic now be covered in a single paragraph?

Try Your Skill These topics are too general for one paragraph. Choose two and write them on your paper. Below each topic, list *Who? What? When? Where? How?* and *Why?* Narrow the two topics by answering each question that you can.

a difficult choice	boats	hobbies	flying saucers
losing something	movies	sports	feeling scared

Keep This in Mind

- Narrow a general topic by asking *who, what, when, where, how,* or *why* questions.
- Choose a topic that you can cover in a paragraph.

Now Write In this section you will be writing a paragraph on your own. You will complete one step of the process in each lesson. At the end of the last lesson in the section, you will have a lively, well organized paragraph.

First find a topic you can write about in one paragraph. Write two general topics on your paper. Ask questions to narrow your topics. Write your narrowed topics. Label your paper **Straight and Narrow.** Put it into your folder.

Part 2

Direct Contact

Writing a Topic Sentence

Here's the Idea You have learned that a topic sentence introduces the main idea of a paragraph. It serves as a guide for the reader. A topic sentence should also make a reader want to read the rest of the paragraph.

To write lively topic sentences, follow these two guidelines:

First, make your topic sentence *direct*. Introduce the main idea clearly right away. Avoid extra words that introduce you instead of the topic. For example, avoid writing such a boring topic sentence as "I'm going to write a paragraph about how to mend socks." Write a direct statement, such as "Here's a time-saving method for mending socks."

Second, make your topic sentences *snappy* whenever it is appropriate. When you are writing about a serious topic, your topic sentence should also be serious. For many topics, however, a clever topic sentence is a way to attract your reader's attention.

You may want to use humor to make a topic sentence snappy. "Darn those darn socks" or "You can make holey socks whole again" are examples. You might use rhyme, as in "Mend those shocking stockings." You might use an unusual twist, as in "Here's how to get extra mileage out of your socks."

Check It Out Read the topic sentences below.

1. California is known as the "Golden State."
2. The Wright Brothers knew that something was wrong.
3. The North Pole is sitting on top of the world.
4. Many ancient cities had walls around them for protection against enemies.

- Do these topic sentences attract your attention? Are they direct? Are they snappy?
- Do these topic sentences avoid extra words? Which topic sentences use humor or an unusual twist?

Try Your Skill Here are five poorly written topic sentences. Decide what the topic is in each sentence. Rewrite four of them. Make them direct. Try to make them snappy.

1. In this paragraph I'm going to tell you about my first trip to Mars.
2. I think I'll make the topic of this paragraph the section of the newspaper I like best.
3. I guess if I stretch my brain I can remember what happened the night I learned to swim.
4. Would you like to know my reasons why they should serve sirloin steaks in the cafeteria?
5. What I really want to write about in this paragraph is what a true friend ______ is.

Keep This in Mind

- A topic sentence should catch the reader's attention. It should be direct.
- Avoid extra words that introduce you instead of your topic.
- When it is appropriate, use humor or an unusual twist to add interest to a topic sentence.

Now Write From your folder, take your paper titled **Straight and Narrow.** Write at least two possible topic sentences for both of your topics. On your paper, write the title of this lesson, **Direct Contact.** Copy the best topic sentence for each topic. Keep your paper in your folder.

Part 3 **The Main Road**

Developing a Paragraph

Here's the Idea Once you have written a topic sentence, how do you develop a paragraph? The best way to develop your paragraph is to use details, examples, or facts and figures.

In the lesson **Show Your Support** you learned to recognize these three main methods of paragraph development. You saw that using **details** creates a lively, realistic paragraph. You also saw that using an **example** is an effective way to develop a paragraph that begins with a general statement. Finally, you saw that using **facts and figures** helps to prove a point or to make an idea clear.

When you write your paragraph, you will have to select a method to develop your main idea. Try to relate your choice to the topic sentence. Decide which method of paragraph development will best complete the idea in your topic sentence.

Check It Out Read the following paragraph.

> The 143rd Street block my mother and father lived on was a Police Athletic League play street. That meant that the policemen put up wooden barricades at the ends of the street during the daytime. This closed the street to traffic so we could use it for a playground. One of the big games on the street was paddle tennis. I was the champion of the block. In fact, I even won some medals representing 143rd Street in competition with other Harlem play streets. I still have them, too. —ALTHEA GIBSON

- Is this paragraph developed by details? Is it developed by an example? Is it developed by facts and figures?
- Does this method of paragraph development complete the idea in the topic sentence clearly?

Try Your Skill Here are five possible topic sentences. Decide how the main idea of each topic sentence could best be developed. Write *Details, Example,* or *Facts and Figures* to show the method of paragraph development you choose. Be prepared to explain your choice.

1. In the early morning, it is cool and quiet on city streets.
2. A chimpanzee can learn to communicate with people.
3. Do you know which baseball players have the highest lifetime batting averages?
4. Some birds can fly at speeds of more than sixty miles per hour.
5. Aunt Kate tells funny stories.

Keep This in Mind

- You can use details to develop a paragraph.
- You can use an example to develop a paragraph.
- You can use facts and figures to develop a paragraph.
- Choose the method of paragraph development that will complete your topic sentence most clearly.

Now Write Review the two topic sentences you wrote in **Direct Contact.**

Select your best topic sentence. Decide which method of paragraph development will complete that topic sentence most clearly.

Now write your paragraph. Keep working until you are sure that your idea is clearly expressed.

Write the title of this lesson, **The Main Road,** on your paper. Put your paper into your folder.

Part 4
A Stop Sign

Ending a Paragraph

Here's the Idea At the end of a paragraph, you need to sum up the main idea you have developed. You also need to put a little interest into the last sentence.

A good ending works well with the other sentences in a paragraph. It ties everything together. It should not add new information. For instance, you would not end a paragraph about inventions that gave man light, by writing about the life of Thomas Edison.

A good ending is interesting. Try using humor, a catchy way of saying something, or an interesting phrase that ties everything together. If you can do this, your paragraph will have much more impact. For example, you might end the paragraph about inventions by saying, "All of these inventions have brightened people's lives."

Check It Out Read the paragraph below.

> Why did dinosaurs disappear from the earth? Some scientists think that dinosaurs died because the climate became too cold for them. Scientists also blame a change in plants, the food of some dinosaurs. Others suggest that a terrible disease killed all the dinosaurs. Many scientists believe that the development of mammals threatened the dinosaurs. Sixty-five million years ago the last dinosaurs died out, but today their disappearance is still a mystery.

- Does this paragraph have an ending?
- Does the ending work with the rest of the paragraph?
- Does the ending sum up the main idea?
- Is the ending interesting?

Try Your Skill Below are two paragraphs with poorly written endings. Rewrite each ending so that it works well with the rest of the paragraph. Try to make each ending sum up the main idea in an interesting way.

1 Niagara Falls is one of the greatest shows on earth. The water roars over the rocky ledge, plunging 167 feet below. About 200,000 tons of water a minute pour into the rocky gorge. From the gorge, the water explodes upward in a swirling curtain of spray. The United States and Canada use the falls for hydroelectric power.

2 Where would we be without wood? For thousands of years people have used it to fuel fires for heating, cooking, and keeping wild animals at bay. We use it for building homes, for furniture, and tools. Most of the paper we use comes from pulpwood. Today, many things are made of plastic.

Keep This in Mind

- A paragraph should have an ending.
- A good ending works with the rest of the paragraph. It should not add a new idea.
- A good ending sums up the main idea of a paragraph.
- A good ending is interesting.

Now Write You are ready now to write a strong ending to your own paragraph. Review what you have written.

On your paper, write the title of this lesson, **A Stop Sign.** Write an ending that works with the rest of the paragraph. Try to sum up the idea of the paragraph. Make your ending interesting. Write your entire paragraph in a final form. Then, proofread your work carefully. This is the first paragraph you have written in this book. Keep your paragraph in your folder.

A Writer's Choices

Part 1 # Who, Me?

Using a Personal Point of View

Here's the Idea As you write, you need to make several important choices. You need to choose a topic and narrow it. You need to create a lively topic sentence. You need to choose a method of paragraph development. Another decision you need to make is what point of view to use.

The phrase **point of view** means the eyes and mind through which something is written. One possible point of view is personal, or **first-person point of view.** When you use the first-person point of view, you must use the first-person pronoun *I*.

When you write about something that is imaginary, *I* can be the most important character, or any other character. This character becomes your narrator who tells what happened. Your narrator can't tell what anyone else in the story is thinking or feeling. Your narrator can tell only what he or she can see.

When you write an account of something that happened in real life, you may also want to use a personal point of view. You may want to use *I* to tell what you yourself did, thought, or felt.

Check It Out Read the following paragraph.

> I dashed into the post office just as the first drops of rain fell. Through the open doorway, I could see others racing toward shelter. I watched as the rain poured down and splashed against the warm pavement. I turned around and looked for Diana. Where was she? She had been right behind me.

- Can you tell through whose eyes this story is told?
- Which words show that this is told from first-person point of view?

Try Your Skill Read the two paragraphs below. Each paragraph has one sentence that is not written from the first-person point of view. Find the two sentences. Then rewrite or replace each sentence. Make sure that it is written from the first-person point of view.

1 The hands on the station clock approached noon. Unless Diana arrived very shortly with my ticket, I would miss the train for Altoona. I couldn't help pacing back and forth. I went to the door and looked out. I was frantic. Halfway down the block, unaware of the time, Diana sat down in a sandwich shop to rest.

2 I rushed over to the ticket counter. The attendant told me that the train would leave on time. The attendant thought to himself, If she waits for her friend she'll miss this train. I ran back to the door. Where was Diana?

Keep This in Mind

- Point of view determines through whose eyes a story is told.
- In first-person point of view, what is written is seen through the eyes of one character.

Now Write On your paper, write your name. Below your name, write three sentences about things that you yourself have done. Use first-person point of view.

Next, write the name of a famous character. You may choose a character from a book, a movie, or television. Then, imagine you are the fictional character you've chosen. As that character, write three things you have done. Use first-person point of view.

Label your paper **Who, Me?** Put your paper into your folder.

Part 2

Out of Sight

Using an Outsider's Point of View

Here's the Idea Have you ever wished that you were invisible? As an invisible observer, you could see and hear everything. When you write a paragraph from the point of view of an invisible observer, you are writing from the **third-person point of view.**

When you use third-person point of view, you can include more information than you can with the first-person point of view. From the outsider's point of view you can see and hear everything. You can report action happening in several places at once. However, only what can be seen or heard is used in this point of view. What any characters are thinking cannot be known.

The third-person pronouns *he*, *she*, and *they* are used in third person point of view. You may be writing about what is real or what is imaginary. In either situation, use the third-person pronouns to make your observations.

Check It Out Read the paragraph below.

> Ruth peered out through the rain-spattered window of the train station. She watched people leaping over puddles in their haste to get in out of the downpour. In a sandwich shop half a block away, Diana sat down in a booth to rest. She took off her dripping jacket and shook it out. Outside the rear of the train station, the loud speaker announced, "Last call for the Altoona train."

- What can you see and hear in this scene?
- Which third-person pronouns are used?

Try Your Skill Read the two paragraphs below. Each paragraph has one sentence that is not written from the third-person point of view. Find the two sentences. Then rewrite or replace each sentence. Make sure that it is written from the third-person point of view.

1 Ruth was alone in the train station, except for the ticket agent. He watched Ruth as she paced nervously back and forth. The rain continued to beat against the roof. Finally, Ruth flopped down on a bench. She stared at the floor. She was thinking about what her cousin Willie would do when she failed to get off the train in Altoona.

2 It suddenly dawned on Diana that the Altoona train was leaving at noon. She leaped up from the booth and asked the cashier for the correct time. Diana gasped when she heard that it was five minutes after twelve. She ran out the door, dragging her jacket. Through the downpour, Diana raced to the train station.

Keep This in Mind

- From the third-person point of view, you can see and hear everything. However, you cannot know what any characters feel or think.
- Use the third-person pronouns *he, she,* and *they* when you write from third-person point of view.

Now Write On your paper, write the name of a friend. Write three sentences telling about things you have actually seen the friend do. Use third-person point of view.

Next, write the name of a famous character. You may choose a character from a book, a movie, or television. Pretend that you have observed this character. Write three sentences telling about things the character has done. Use third-person point of view. Label your paper **Out of Sight.** Put it into your folder.

Part 3

To Tell the Truth

Writing About What Is Real

Here's the Idea Much of what you read each day is nonfiction. In other words, it is about what is real. Newspaper stories are about real events. Biographies describe real people. Geography books describe real places. Science books describe real things.

Much of what you write may also be about real things. You do homework, answer test questions, and write reports and letters. You may write a narration, a description, or an explanation of what is real.

Whenever you are writing about real things, it is important that you be *accurate*. Spell the names of people and places correctly. The names of famous people are listed in the dictionary. Names of places are listed in an atlas. Check any name, dates, facts, or figures you use. Look in an almanac or encyclopedia.

Check It Out Read the paragraph below. Notice that the writer uses third-person point of view.

> The genius of Henry Ford first made automobiles available to the average American. In 1896, Ford completed his first gasoline-powered automobile. Seven years later, he organized the Ford Motor Company. The company's success was based on the assembly-line method of production. Ford was able to reduce the price of each auto by making thousands of cars such as the Model T. It takes only a glance at today's busy highways to realize the impact made by Henry Ford.

- Is this a narration, a description, or an explanation of something real?
- Is the writing factual? How can its accuracy be checked?

Try Your Skill Choose as a topic a real place that you would like to visit. You might choose the Grand Canyon, New York City, or Tokyo, for example. Find and list five facts about your topic. Check your information in an encyclopedia, atlas, or other reference. Use your list to write five factual sentences.

Keep This in Mind

- You may choose to write a narration, a description, or an explanation about what is real. You may write about real people, places, events, or things.
- Make sure your information is accurate. Use references to check your facts.

Now Write You are now ready to write a paragraph about something real. Label your paper **To Tell the Truth.**

Choose a topic. It can be a person, place, object, or event. It should be a topic that you know well. Narrow your topic so that it can be covered in one paragraph.

Write your topic on your paper. List any facts, figures, dates, or other details that relate to your topic.

Next, decide on your purpose. Do you want to tell a story? Do you want to describe your subject? Do you want to explain it?

Decide whether you will use the first-person or the third-person point of view.

Write your paragraph.

Read the paragraph you have written. Do you have a direct topic sentence? Do you develop the main idea in the body of the paragraph? Does the paragraph have an ending? Do whatever rewriting you think is necessary.

Write your paragraph in a final form. Proofread your work carefully.

Keep your paragraph in your folder.

Part 4

Mind over Matter

Writing About What Is Imaginary

Here's the Idea Some of the people, places, and events that you read about are fictional. In other words, they are not real. They are created by someone's imagination.

Your own imagination is a powerful creator, too. It is always active. Close your eyes and sit quietly for a while. Allow your mind to wander. What does your imagination show you? What can you see? hear? feel? taste? smell?

Think about whatever person, place, object, or action you imagine. You may want to tell a story based on what you imagine. You may choose to describe what you imagine. You may decide to explain it.

Whether you choose narration, description, or explanation, you need to use **details** to bring your creation to life. Be specific in order to make your reader see, hear, feel, taste, or smell whatever you imagine. Make your imaginary world come alive for your reader.

Check It Out Read the paragraph below. Notice that the writer uses first-person point of view.

> I was running for my life. Gasping, I leaned against a fence to rest and get my bearings. For a few seconds the only sound in the city was the rapid pounding of my heart. Suddenly, I heard the buzz of the helicopter. I knew the chase was over.

- Is this paragraph a narration, a description, or an explanation of something imaginary?
- What details make the experience come alive for the reader?

Try Your Skill In the last lesson, you write factual sentences about a real place you'd like to visit. Now, you can create an imaginary place in which you'd like to live.

Try to picture a special imaginary place. List at least five details that will make your place come alive for a reader. Use your details to write five lively sentences.

Keep This in Mind

- You may choose to write a narration, a description, or an explanation about something imaginary. You can create imaginary people, places, objects, or events.
- Use details based on the five senses to bring your creation to life.

Now Write You are ready to write a paragraph on your own about something imaginary.

Allow your imagination to do some of the work for you. Let your mind wander awhile. Then, on your paper, write the person, place, object, or event that you imagine. List all the details you imagine. Be specific.

Next, decide whether you want to tell a story, to describe what you imagine, or to explain it. Decide which way seems most appropriate for your subject. Then select and organize the details you have listed.

Use either the first-person or the third-person point of view.

Write your paragraph.

Read what you have written. Do whatever rewriting you need to.

Write your paragraph in a final form. Proofread your work carefully. Keep your paragraph in your folder.

Part 5 **First Choice**

Choosing the Right Verb

Here's the Idea When you write, every word is important. You need to select specific words that will express your idea exactly. You especially need to choose specific verbs. Verbs are an important part of every sentence.

A verb is a word that tells what *happened* or what *is*. Some verbs, like *whisper, roar,* and *shriek,* are strong and show action. Others are weaker and are often called linking or state-of-being verbs. These are verbs like *is, seem,* and *become.* One way to strengthen your writing is to use more active verbs. It is stronger to say "David *runs,*" than "David *is* a runner."

Another way to work with verbs is to find specific substitutes for general verbs. Specific verbs can create moods.

For example, think of all the ways to say *walk* that are more interesting and specific. For pleasure, a person might *stroll, saunter,* or *ramble.* In an unhappy mood, a person might *plod,* or *trudge,* or *poke* along. In other moods, a person might *march, prance, stride, strut,* or *swagger.* Any one of these verbs is clearer and stronger than *walk.* Each verb also helps to set a mood.

Whenever you write, take time to find the right verb. Use a dictionary or thesaurus to help you.

Check It Out Notice the verbs as you read the following paragraph.

> The cab *screeched* to a stop. The passenger *threw* open the door and *leaped* to the curb. He *darted* among the pedestrians and *raced* up the steps of the train station. The cab driver *thrust* her head out the window and angrily *demanded* her fare. "*Wait* there," *shouted* the passenger. "I *will hurry* right back."

- Are the verbs active?
- Are the verbs specific rather than general ones?
- Do the verbs help to create a mood?

Try Your Skill Read the following paragraph.

Steve *said* that he was tired of raking leaves all Saturday afternoon. His friends *said* to him from across the street that they wanted to get up a ball game. Steve *said* to his father that he wanted to go. His father *said* that he could go after his work was done.

Improve this paragraph by substituting more specific verbs for the general verb *said* whenever it is necessary. Write the paragraph, using the specific verbs you have chosen.

Keep This in Mind

- Choose active verbs.
- Choose specific verbs rather than general ones.
- Choose verbs that help to create a mood.
- Use a dictionary or a thesaurus to help you find the right verb.

Now Write Start with the verb *look*. Make a list of verbs that are more specific than *look*. You might use *spy* or *stare,* for example. Use a dictionary to help you. Then choose three verbs from your list. Write one sentence containing each verb. Try to make your sentences create different moods.

Put your paper into your folder.

Part 6 # The Name Game

Writing a Title That Works

Here's the Idea You have learned about important choices that you make as a writer. You choose to write about something real or to create something imaginary. You choose to express an idea through narration or description or explanation. You choose a point of view that is appropriate for the idea. You select specific words that express the idea exactly. You will make all of these choices for most writing that you do.

For some of your writing, you will also need to decide on a title that expresses your idea. Short pieces of writing, like paragraphs, do not usually have a title. However, longer pieces of writing, like compositions and reports, need titles.

The title of your writing is the first thing a reader will see. However, it will probably be the last thing you write. A good title should catch the reader's attention. It might also indicate the main idea or even the mood of your writing. A title may be as simple and direct as "Charles." It may be as startling as "The Night the Ghost Got In."

Check It Out Read the following titles of stories you may have read:

"A Game of Catch"
"When I Am President"
"What's He Doing in There?"
"Night Drive"
"Ghost of the Lagoon"
"To Build a Fire"
"Champion's Son"
"Raymond's Run"
"The Monkey's Paw"
"The Gold Bug"

- Are these good titles? Why?

Try Your Skill Choose three of the following topics for longer pieces of writing. On your paper, write each topic you choose. Then write two possible titles for each topic. Make the titles express the idea of the topic in a simple or lively way.

1. a description of your favorite place
2. a report on the healthiest types of exercise
3. a story about a family pet that becomes invisible
4. an explanation of how to change the oil in a car
5. an explanation of why ______ is a good friend
6. an explanation of what a subway is
7. a report on the rising cost of food
8. a story about the best birthday present you ever received

Keep This in Mind

- A title should catch a reader's attention. A good title may be direct and simple, or it may be surprising.
- Use a title for longer pieces of writing, such as compositions or reports.

Now Write Choose a topic that you know about and care about. For example, you may want to choose a hobby, a sport, or a memorable event. Imagine that you are going to write something on your topic.

On your paper, write the title of this lesson, **The Name Game.** Below it, write several possible titles. Circle the one you like the best. Put your work into your folder.

The Process of Writing

The Process of Writing

From this point on you will be learning, and practicing, the skills of writing. You will be writing about what is important to you. You will also be able to practice different kinds of writing.

There will be variety in your writing experiences. Whenever you write, however, there will be something that remains the same: **the process of writing.** There are steps you can follow, **before you write, when you write,** and **after you write.** As you follow these steps, you will be learning to write.

On these four pages you can follow the process of writing from beginning to end. First, read about each step in the process. Then look at the example that shows how one person might have followed each step.

Before You Write Sometimes you write in response to an assignment. Sometimes you choose to write in order to communicate something important to you. Whatever you write, and whenever you write, you will find the beginning steps, called prewriting, very important.

Before you write, you need to focus on your subject. Take your time at this point in the process of writing. Narrow the topic so that you can handle it in a given length.

Think about your audience. Think about whether you want to use a personal point of view or an outsider's point of view. Use all of your senses to bring your subject clearly into focus.

Make a list of interesting details. Jot down any notes or ideas related to your topic. You don't have to use them all. If you need to learn more about your topic, do that, too.

Before You Write

You list possible topics.

topics

sunset at the lake
downtown at Christmas
monkey house at zoo
the county fair
school dance

You select a topic.

specifics

smells of peanuts, popcorn
sword swallower
two-headed calf
exhibits of crafts
vegetables, jams, cakes
pie-eating contest
games of chance
hot dogs,
cotton candy
side shows
ferris wheel,
roller coaster
loud music
dusty ground

You list, in any order, details about your topic.

notes

kind of paragraph? descriptive?
point of view 1st person
try to show exciting mood

You plan what you want to write.

When You Write At this point in the process of writing, you are ready to write. Simply put your pencil to paper and write. Don't fuss with the writing. Don't worry about organizing ideas. Don't fret about spelling or punctuation. Don't get trapped by trying to make anything perfect at this stage. Let whatever happens, happen. Just write.

When You Write

You write a paragraph about your topic.

We passed through the entrance gate to the county fair. The delicious smell of peanuts roasting mixed with the dust kicked up by our shoes. A man called us over to see the amazing sword swallower and the incredible two-headed calf. The huge roller coaster looked dangerous and exciting as it swung around its tracks. High above, the brave passengers on the ferris wheel looked down at us. Joey and I couldn't decide what to do first.

Notice how this paragraph *tells* about the topic.

After You Write Stop. Read what you have written. At this stage of the process you will need to work more carefully and thoughtfully. You have to check what you have written. Did you include everything you wanted to? Do you like what you've written? Is it interesting? Think about your topic.

At this point, it is possible that you may not like what you've written. It is likely, though, that you generally like your idea. Then you can rewrite whatever you need to change or want to change. Concentrate on every word: Is your idea clearly expressed? Did you *show* your reader what you want to say?

Is your writing organized logically? Is there a beginning, a middle, and an end to the development of your idea?

Is the writing lively and direct? Is each word the right word? Take time to read your writing and think about it carefully.

After You Write

You rewrite.

You express your idea in a different way.

greeted us as

We passed through the entrance gate to the county fair. ¶ The delicious smell of peanuts roasting ~~mixed with the dust kicked up by our shoes~~. A red-shirted man to our right ~~man~~ called us over to see the amazing sword swallower and the incredible two-headed calf. To our left, ~~The~~ the huge roller coaster swung ~~looked~~ dangerously ~~and exciting as it swung around~~ in its tracks. High above, the ~~brave~~ passengers on the double ferris wheel waved ~~looked~~ down at us. Joey and I stood in the middle of the crowd ~~couldn't decide what to do first~~. We didn't know where to begin.

Notice how this lively paragraph *shows* your idea clearly.

Now, you need to look at how you expressed your idea. It is important to make your writing correct as well as clear and lively. Check your spelling. Check capitalization and punctuation. Use whatever references you have available to check your work.

Finally, when you are satisfied that your writing is clear and correct, write it in its final form. Write carefully. Make your work as neat as possible.

When you have finished your final copy, proofread your work. Read your writing aloud, to yourself, one final time.

The smell of peanuts roasting greeted us as we passed through the entrance gate to the county fair. A red-shirted man to our right called us over to see the amazing sword swallower and the incredible two-headed calf. To our left, the huge roller coaster swung around dangerously in its tracks. High above, the passengers on the double ferris wheel waved at us. Joey and I stood in the middle of the crowd. We didn't know where to begin.

You can learn to write only by writing. In each writing section you will be learning an idea about writing, checking your understanding of the idea, practicing your skill, and then writing on your own. Whenever you write, try to follow the steps in the process of writing. Each time you write you will be learning something about writing, and about yourself.

The Narrative Paragraph

Part 1 # Then What?

Using Chronological Order

Here's the Idea A narrative paragraph tells a story. When you write about what you did on vacation, you are writing a narrative. When you write about what happened in an imaginary place, you are also writing a narrative. The best way to tell what happened is in the order that the events took place. This is called **chronological order.** It is in the order of time. Using chronological order is a logical way to tell a story.

A narrative paragraph is a natural way of writing. You may not always begin with a topic sentence that states the main idea. However, you should always try to begin your narrative with a strong and lively sentence.

The other events of the narrative will follow the first sentence. Use the natural time sequence to organize the events. Tell what happened first, what happened next, and so on.

Look at this true account. Notice that the events are told in the order that they happened.

> The dog stayed on the small hill until he saw Joy coming across the street toward him. I opened the window and could hear her faintly calling, "Good dog, here's some food. Have some food." As she began to cross the street, he leaped off the hill. He bounded through and over the snow into the darkened park. Joy waited for a few minutes. She called to the dog and extended her hand. Finally, she emptied the food onto the top of the hill. Then she turned and walked back to the building.
>
> —PAUL WILKES

Check It Out Now read this imaginary narrative.

> There was a farmer named Maibon. One day he was driving down the road in his horse and cart. He saw an old man hob-

bling along. The old man seemed so frail and feeble that Maibon doubted the poor soul could go many more steps. Maibon offered to take him in the cart, but the old man refused. Maibon went his way home, shaking his head over such a pitiful sight.
—LLOYD ALEXANDER

- Are the events of this narrative in chronological order?

Try Your Skill Below are two lists of events for narrative paragraphs. The lists are not in chronological order. On your paper, write the events in chronological order.

1. (a) I was given an X-ray.
   (b) The ambulance came and took me to a hospital.
   (c) I broke my arm skating.
   (d) Friends wrote on my cast.
   (e) My arm was put in a cast.

2. (a) The vase rolled off the edge of the table.
   (b) Ellen's little brother bumped into a table.
   (c) An expensive vase toppled over on its side.
   (d) Ellen dove toward the table and caught the vase in one hand.

Keep This in Mind

- In a narrative paragraph, use chronological order to organize events.

Now Write On your paper, write the title of this lesson, **Then What?** Write a narrative paragraph using chronological order. Follow all the steps in the process of writing.

Before you write, plan your idea. List and organize related details. Write your paragraph. Then read what you have written. Do any necessary rewriting. Write you paragraph in a final form. Proofread your paragraph. Then put it into your folder.

Part 2

How Time Flies!

Using Transitions in a Narrative

Here's the Idea In a narrative paragraph you are telling a story. If you tell a story as it happened, you need certain words and phrases to help you show chronological order. The words and phrases that help you show the order in time are called **transitional** words and phrases.

Good transitions make for clear writing. They almost take your readers by the hand. They show readers your thought process. Study this list of transitional words and phrases:

first	now	at the beginning	before
then	soon	in the middle	after
next	later	at the end	by the time
finally	when		at the same time

The list shows some of the transitional words and phrases you can use. There are many more. In fact, you can use any period of time to show chronological order. You can write your narrative using minutes, hours, days of the week, months, or years.

When you select transitions, don't rely too much on general transitions like *then* and *next*. They don't tell the reader how much time has passed. Try to be more specific. Use transitions like *after a few minutes, early in the week,* and *several hours later.*

There are other transitions, too. When you write, use a variety of transitions to make your idea clear. You can see that there are many ways to show time sequence.

Check It Out Notice the transitions as you read the following narrative paragraph.

When I went to bed, the whales were still circling leisurely. I slept late. I was awakened by the snarl of outboard engines, an excited shouting, and by the sound of feet pounding on my deck. When I thrust my head out of the hatch, I found what appeared to be about half the male population of St. Pierre. The crowd included a good many women and children. Everyone was closely clustered along the waterfront. —FARLEY MOWAT

- Find the transitions. Do they help make the story clear?
- Do the transitions show time order?

Try Your Skill Read the paragraph below. Then, rewrite the paragraph, adding transitions to show chronological order.

We hiked up into the White Mountains. We sat up camp in a clearing near a brook. We cooked supper over the open fire. We sat around the campfire talking. We went to sleep. We got up, broke camp, and moved on.

Keep This in Mind

- Transitional words and phrases help to make a narrative clear.
- In a narrative paragraph, use transitions that show chronological order.

Now Write Label your paper **How Time Flies!** Write a narrative paragraph. Your narrative may be real or imaginary. Use transitions to show chronological order. Underline the transitional words and phrases you use.

When you have written your paragraph in its final form, put it into your folder.

Part 3

In Detail

Developing a Narrative Paragraph

Here's the Idea How do you develop a narrative paragraph? Once you have a topic, or beginning, sentence, how do you expand it? The most effective method, almost always, is to use **details.** Details give life to your writing.

Using details can be an easy task if you ask the right questions. Newspaper reporters use questions to find the details of a story. Reporters ask *who? what? where? when? why?* and *how?* In the process of your writing, try to ask the same questions. You may not always answer all the questions. However, ask these questions about any story idea, real or imaginary. You'll see how easily the details come.

Suppose you were telling a first-person account of a real incident. You could ask a reporter's questions to develop specific details. For example, look at these possibilities:

Who? Rosa and I

What? elevator fell three floors

Where? in our apartment building, New York City

When? Tuesday afternoon

Why? Mr. Deluca, building superintendent, didn't know why it fell

How? a repair crew is checking elevator

Once you have specific details to develop your narrative fully, arrange them in chronological order. Use transitions. Then, use these notes to write a lively paragraph.

Check It Out Read this narrative about a scary fall.

On Tuesday afternoon my sister Rosa and I had a scary fall. We were riding the self-service elevator to our apartment on the sixth floor. Between the fourth and fifth floors, the elevator suddenly hesitated, and then stopped. The next moment it began to fall rapidly. Rosa threw herself against the emergency button. The elevator made a screeching sound and came to a stop just above the first floor. We were dizzy and frightened, but we were safe.

- Is this narrative developed by details?
- Does this narrative show *who, what, where, when, why,* and *how?*

Try Your Skill Imagine that you are taking a walk, enjoying a spring afternoon. You see a familiar face coming toward you. Suddenly, you recognize a good friend who moved away four years ago. You greet each other happily. You begin to catch up on lost time. Later in the day, you want to tell the story of your meeting to someone at home.

On your paper, write this topic and develop details for it by answering *who? what? where? when? why?* and *how?* Then, using your details, list the events of your meeting in chronological order.

Keep This in Mind

- Develop narrative paragraphs by using details.
- To develop specific details, answer the questions *who? what? where? when? why?* and *how?* about your topic.

Now Write On your paper, write **In Detail,** the title of this lesson. Write a narrative paragraph using vivid details. Use either real or imaginary details. Choose either first-person or third-person point of view. Follow all the steps in the process of writing. Write your story in a final form. Proofread it and put it into your folder.

The Descriptive Paragraph

Part 1

You Are There

Using Your Senses in Description

Here's the Idea To write a descriptive paragraph, use your senses—sight, hearing, touch, taste, and smell. Try to use all of your senses to provide the details of your description. These details are called **sensory details.** Choose specific words to show how each sense is affected. When you use sensory details in a description, your reader will be able to share your experience.

Read this descriptive paragraph.

> By evening, the house smelled of Christmas. In the kitchen, sweet-potato pies, custard pies, and rich butter pound cakes cooled. A choice sugar-cured ham brought from the smokehouse baked in the oven. In the heart of the house, freshly cut branches of long-needled pines lay over the fireplace. In the fireplace itself, in a black pan set on a high wire rack, peanuts roasted over the hickory fire. The fine velvet night was speckled with the first flakes of a coming snow. The warm sound of laughter mingled in tales of days past but not forgotten. —MILDRED D. TAYLOR

Notice how the use of sensory details makes you feel as if you had been there, too.

Check It Out Now read this imaginary description of a change in the weather.

> The sun was shining when Aaron left the village. Suddenly the weather changed. A large black cloud with a bluish center appeared in the east and spread itself rapidly over the sky. A cold wind blew in with it. The crows flew low, croaking. At first it looked as if it would rain, but instead it began to hail as in

summer. It was early in the day, but it became dark as dusk. After a while the hail turned to snow. —ISAAC BASHEVIS SINGER

- What sensory details does this description use?

Try Your Skill Look at the objects and places listed below. Choose two of these topics, and write them on your paper. Then, list at least five sensory details about each topic. Try to use all of your senses. Think about size, shape, color, and movement. Think about sounds and feelings. Think about tastes and smells.

a car engine	a closet at home
a bag of potato chips	your street on a hot day
a chocolate bar	inside a refrigerator
a rug	a gas station
an orange	a grocery store
a newspaper	a subway car

Keep This in Mind

- When you write a descriptive paragraph, use sensory details. Be specific. Use details of sight, hearing, touch, taste, and smell.

Now Write Imagine that you are in a real place that you know well. On your paper, write *Sight, Hearing, Touch, Taste,* and *Smell.* Thinking of your special place, list details for each of the senses. Next, decide which senses are the most important in describing your place. Then organize those details in a natural order.

Write a descriptive paragraph about your place. Read your paragraph aloud and do whatever rewriting you need to.

Write your paragraph in a final form. Label your paper **You Are There.** Proofread your work and put it into your folder.

Part 2 # The Right Mood

Using Adjectives To Create Mood

Here's the Idea Some of the most powerful words are adjectives. These are words that describe, like *small, old, happy,* or *kind.* Adjectives also help to set a feeling, or **mood.** For example, using adjectives like *silent, still, calm,* or *hushed* helps set a mood.

When you write a description, choose specific adjectives to create a particular mood. For instance, you may say that a small room is *cozy* or that it is *cramped.* You may describe a winter day as *brisk* or *raw.* You may describe a smile as *friendly* or *silly.* In these examples, you can see that *cozy, brisk,* and *friendly* are adjectives that have a pleasant, or positive, effect. *Cramped, raw,* and *silly* have an unpleasant, or negative, effect. Choose adjectives carefully so that they create the mood or feeling you want.

It is important to use adjectives carefully. If you use too many adjectives, your writing will be wordy and dull. There is no need to say "a sweet, kind, gentle person" when "a gentle person" is clear. In description, use adjectives, but use them carefully.

Check It Out Read the following description.

> November nights are long and chill and full of stars. They are full of the crisp whisper of fallen leaves skittering in the wind. November nights are good for walking down a country road. Then the world is close about you. It is a world drawn in bold charcoal strokes against the sky. —HAL BORLAND

- Which adjectives help to create a mood?
- Do all of the adjectives fit the mood?
- Are there too many adjectives?

Try Your Skill Compare the two lists of adjectives below. Words from one list might be used to write a positive description of a person. Words from the other list would produce a negative effect. Choose words from one list that fit best in the blanks in the sample paragraph about Oscar. First, read the paragraph. Then, copy it on your paper, filling in the blanks.

A		B	
honest	generous	dishonest	stingy
gentle	cheerful	rough	gloomy
handsome	thoughtful	ugly	inconsiderate
polite	funny	rude	serious
kind	friendly	mean	unfriendly

Oscar was always ______. No matter what went wrong, Oscar would say something ______ to make us laugh. He really liked people. He was ______ to strangers as well as to friends. He was always ______ with his money and his time. In his ______ way, Oscar offered whatever help he could give. Oscar was a good friend.

Keep This in Mind

- In description, use adjectives to create mood.
- Choose adjectives that fit the mood you are creating.
- Be careful not to overuse adjectives.

Now Write On your paper, write **The Right Mood.** First, decide on a mood you'd like to create. You may want to start by thinking of a place that makes you feel a special way.

Next, list a few adjectives that fit the mood. Third, list sensory details that fit the mood. When your lists are complete, try to organize them in natural order.

Write a paragraph of description that creates a mood.

Read the description aloud. Write your final description.

Proofread your work and put it into your folder.

Part 3

Look Around

Using Spatial Order

Here's the Idea Whenever you write a description, you are trying to create a picture or mood with words. You may want to tell your reader how something looks, sounds, smells, feels, or tastes.

To make ideas clear in a descriptive paragraph, you need to use a clear order. That order usually shows a relationship of space. Space relationship means how the things you describe are placed in relation to each other. This is called **spatial order.** Use spatial order to organize a description, especially descriptions of places or objects.

Suppose the topic of your description is an old apartment building. If an antenna on the roof catches your eye, you can start your description from that point. Then, have your description move down your subject. Move from the roof to the wash hanging on the fifth-floor fire escape. Next, describe the woman talking from an open window on the fourth floor. Below that, mention the flower pots on the second-floor window ledge. Finally, you might describe the store front of the ground-floor grocery.

Check It Out Read the following description.

> Three identical creatures stood in front of the doorway of the spacecraft. From behind them, a greenish light shone, creating frightening shadows. The creatures' heads were huge and covered with transparent pale orange skin. Their small, childlike bodies were clothed in shiny yellow suits. On their feet, the creatures wore slick green boots. As they squeaked a greeting, they took a step toward us.

• How does this description use spatial order?

Try Your Skill You are going to write a description of the picture on page 76. Spend some time looking at it. Look at all the details carefully. Study the relationship of the objects and people. What is in front of something else? What is behind? What is above, next to, or below?

Decide on a natural spatial order that fits this picture. The easiest way is to find the main focus. What one object first catches your eye? That's what is called the main focus. Use that object and describe other objects in relation to it. You could move from one side to the other, or up and down. You can even move in a circle.

Decide what spatial order you are going to use. Then list the five most important objects in the order you have chosen.

Keep This in Mind

- Use spatial order to organize descriptions. You may be describing people, places, or objects.

Now Write Think of a person, an object, or a place you would like to describe in a paragraph. Your subject can be real or imaginary.

List the important details. Organize the details in a natural spatial order. Decide where you will begin your description. Make sure the rest of your description follows in an organized way.

Write your description.

Read it aloud. See if someone else can picture or draw what you have described by using only your paragraph.

If your description is not clear, rewrite it.

Write your paragraph in a final form. Label your paper **Look Around.**

Proofread your work and keep it in your folder.

Part 4

Where Is It?

Using Transitions in a Description

Here's the Idea In narratives, one kind of transitional word shows chronological order. A different kind of transitional word is needed for description. Since description usually uses **spatial order,** the transitional words show relationships of some things to other things.

Here are some examples of transitional words and phrases used in description:

in	ahead of	down	to the right
on	outside	by	back and forth
above	downstairs	front	at the end of
under	upstairs	north	side by side
behind	close to	east	in back of
near	between	toward	next to
up	beneath	among	facing
over	beside	to the left of	against
below	alongside	in the center	at the top of
onto	high	in the corner	around
inside	low	on the edge	throughout

In the following paragraph, notice how the transitions show spatial order.

The orange lay atop the other pieces of fruit in the basket. I picked it up and cupped it in my hand. Its outer surface, the peel, felt rough and grainy. I tore through the peel to the smooth, white, inner covering. Inside the white layer, the orange was divided into ten, crescent-shaped sections. Each section was covered by a thin skin. I split open a section and was sprayed by the juice within. I popped the sweet tidbit into my mouth, thoroughly enjoying my snack.

Check It Out Now read this description of a ghost town.

Carol drove north down the dusty road leading into the old, Nevada mining town. She found herself standing in front of a rundown, wooden building. The front porch was enclosed with the broken stubs of what once were rails. The blistered front door was hanging by one hinge. Directly above the door hung a peeling sign. The faded letters spelled "Virginia City General Store." For a few moments Carol stood gazing at the sign. She imagined how exciting it would have been to have lived 100 years ago in this famous frontier town.

- How does this descriptive paragraph use transitions to show spatial order?

Try Your Skill Using any one of your textbooks, find a picture of something real. Study the picture. Decide what is the most important, or most striking, part of the picture. Starting from that point, list the most important items in the picture.

Next, decide which transitional words and phrases you need to show the spatial order of the picture. Beside each item you have listed, write the appropriate transition. Check to see that the order of your list is logical and clear.

Keep This in Mind

- In a descriptive paragraph, use transitional words that show spatial order.

Now Write Write a descriptive paragraph of a person, place, or object that interests you. Your description may be of something real or imaginary. When you finish writing, read your paragraph aloud. See if your description is clear. See if you have used transitions that show spatial order.

Rewrite. Make a final copy. Label your paper **Where Is It?** Proofread your work and put it into your folder.

The Explanatory Paragraph

Telling *How*

Part 1

Here's How!

Planning an Explanation

Here's the Idea Everyone knows how to do something well. Chances are that someone would like to learn something you know how to do. Can you share what you know so that someone else can learn? You can if you can write a good explanation.

An explanatory paragraph explains. Sometimes it explains *why* or *what*. Sometimes it explains *how*. Whenever you explain how to do something—how to plan a trip, use a drill, or make bread—you are writing an explanatory *how* paragraph.

To write an explanatory *how* paragraph, choose a topic that you know well. A paragraph is not very long. You will have to choose a simple process. Be clear, specific, and accurate in your explanation.

Check It Out Read the following paragraph.

> You can grow large, healthy houseplants once you learn the simple steps necessary to repot a plant. You will want to do your work outside or over a newspaper inside. The first step is to choose a new pot that is one or two inches larger in diameter. Second, for good drainage, line the bottom with a half-inch or more of small stones. Add enough potting soil to cover the stones completely. Next, spread one hand over the top of the old pot, holding the stem firmly between your fingers. Turn the pot upside down. Gently tap the pot on a hard surface until the plant slips out. Then, place the plant, roots down, into the new pot. Cover it with potting soil, filling the pot to within one inch of the top. Pat the soil down firmly all around the plant. Finally, water the plant well.

- What process is explained?
- Is this explanation simple and specific?

Try Your Skill A six-year-old child gave the following explanation of how to make stew. Could you follow the steps?

Corn beef stew

First you have to get in the wagon and drive downtown.

Then you buy:

The tall French-Italian bread
The butter
The paper towels

Then you get in the wagon and drive back home.

Then take everything out and put it away. Put the bag between the cat food—but fold it up.

Cook it in the stove in your pan. Look in the window all the time to see if it's done.

Then say a prayer and eat.

Serves for a pretty long time if there's only 3 people. (Eat out in between.)—*Smashed Potatoes*

On your paper, list at least five errors in these directions.

Keep This in Mind

- An explanatory *how* paragraph explains how to do something or how to make something.
- Write about a simple process you know well. Be clear, specific, and accurate in your explanation.

Now Write Think of one simple household task or chore that you know how to do. You may know how to cook bacon, iron a shirt, paint a ceiling, or wax a floor. List the steps you follow to complete your task. Be specific and accurate.

Use your list to write an explanatory *how* paragraph. Check your work by having a reader see if your explanation is clear and easy to follow. Write your paragraph in a final form. Label it **Here's How!** and put it into your folder.

Part 2

Get in Step

Using Step-by-Step Order

Here's the Idea In an explanatory *how* paragraph, you need to describe a process **step-by-step.** It is important to make each step in the process simple and specific. Begin with the first step and then explain each step in the natural time order of the process. If one step in the process affects another step, be sure to explain how the steps are related.

For example, if you wanted to explain how to make your own jigsaw puzzle, you might first list the steps in the process:

1. Find a magazine picture.
2. Find a sheet of cardboard. Make it the same size.
3. Spread paste on one side of the cardboard and on the back of the picture.
4. Mount the picture on the cardboard.
5. Smooth out wrinkles.
6. Cut the mounted picture into odd-shaped pieces.

Notice how simple this process seems when it is explained step-by-step.

Check It Out Now read the following paragraph.

> You can make your own jigsaw puzzle. First, select a large magazine picture and a sheet of heavy cardboard of equal size. Next, spread paste evenly on the back of the picture and on one side of the cardboard. When the paste has dried for a few minutes, lay the picture on the cardboard. Then use the sides of your hands to smooth out the wrinkles from the center of the picture outward. After the paste is completely dry, use a pair of sharp scissors to cut the mounted picture into odd-shaped pieces.

- Does this explanatory *how* paragraph explain a process step-by-step?
- Are the steps listed in a natural, logical sequence?

Try Your Skill Imagine that you want to write a paragraph explaining how a simple game is played. You could choose a card game, a board game, or a sport. Choose a game you understand and enjoy.

On your paper, write your topic. Below it, make a list of simple instructions to follow. List all the steps in the correct order. Check your work by having a reader see if your explanation is clear.

Keep This in Mind

- In an explanatory *how* paragraph, explain a process step-by-step.
- Write the steps in the natural time order of the process.

Now Write Think of a simple activity or hobby you enjoy and perform well. Make a list of the steps you take to complete the process. Be as specific as you can.

Organize your detailed list. Write an explanatory *how* paragraph.

Read your paragraph to yourself. Rewrite.

Then write it in a final form.

Label your paper **Get in Step.**

After you have proofread your work, put it into your folder.

Part 3

In Order

Using Transitions in an Explanation

Here's the Idea An explanatory paragraph that tells how to do something is ordered by the steps in the process. The explanation begins with the first step. Then it moves through the steps in the order that they happen. It tells what to do *first,* what to do *second,* what to do *next,* and so on.

There are special transitional words and phrases for an explanatory *how* paragraph. Study these examples:

first	then	at first
second	now	to start with
third	when	after that
fourth	while	at the same time
next	until	the next step
last	finally	at last

There are many variations of these transitional words and phrases. Choose whichever transitions seem to work best for the process you are describing.

Check It Out Read the paragraph below.

> The next time you are bothered by hiccups, try this unusual cure. First, fill a glass with water. Next, bend over the sink, holding the glass. Then lean forward, placing your lips against the farthest rim of the glass. Last, tilting the glass away from you, drink as much water as you can. When you finish your backwards drink, your hiccups will be gone.

- What transitional words and phrases in this explanatory *how* paragraph show step-by-step order?

Try Your Skill Read the explanatory *how* paragraph below. As it reads now, a tree can grow magically in a very short time. What transitional words and phrases are necessary to make the step-by-step order sensible and clear? On your paper, rewrite the paragraph using transitional words.

> Here's a slow but sure-fire way to gather your own firewood. Plant an acorn and water it. Support the young sapling with a stake. Chop down the mature tree. Saw up the wood and stack it.

Keep This in Mind

- In an explanatory *how* paragraph, use transitional words and phrases to show step-by-step order.

Now Write You have written about chores and hobbies that you perform well. Now use your imagination to invent a simple new activity. Imagine, for example, a new food you can cook, a new game you can play, or a new pet you can train.

First, decide what new activity you want to invent. Next, list the steps to follow in order to complete this activity. Be clear and specific.

Then use your list to write an explanatory *how* paragraph. Use transitions that show step-by-step order. Underline the transitions you use.

Write your paragraph in a final form. On your paper, write the title of this lesson, **In Order.** Then put your work into your folder.

The Explanatory Paragraph

Telling *Why*

Part 1

State Your Case

Stating an Opinion

Here's the Idea How do you feel about homework, your cousin Leona, math, McDonald's, or school dances? You would probably have no trouble expressing your opinions on these and many other subjects. Having strong feelings or beliefs about things that affect your life is only natural. Expressing your opinion is something you do often.

The purpose of an explanatory *why* paragraph is to present an opinion in writing. You may want to explain why something is so, or why something should be changed. You will want to be convincing. To do this, start by giving an opinion. Then use reasons or facts to support your opinion. Any facts you use must be checked for accuracy.

The topic sentence of an explanatory *why* paragraph should state your opinion. Be as direct and as specific as possible. For instance, if you believe that soccer belongs in a school sports program, you should write a more direct topic sentence than "Soccer is a great game." You should also write a more specific topic sentence than "We should change our fall sports program." A direct and specific sentence might be "More high schools should offer soccer."

Topics for explanatory *why* paragraphs are not difficult to find. Ask yourself what you feel strongly about. When you watch a news program or read a newspaper, which stories make you feel angry? Which make you feel happy? Why? How do you feel about your school, your neighborhood, and your town? How do you feel about what happens to you? What would you like to see changed? What should remain the same? Your answers to these questions are opinions that you can develop in your writing.

Check It Out Read the following paragraph.

Prospect School should shorten the lunch period from forty-five minutes to thirty minutes and allow students to leave the cafeteria. Most students finish eating lunch in fifteen minutes. After finishing lunch, some students become rowdy. They litter and play with food. The students need to have another activity. Choices might be study hall or exercises in the gym. Many students would benefit from these lunchtime activities.

- Does this paragraph express an opinion clearly?
- Does the topic sentence state the opinion directly?

Try Your Skill Choose two of these questions that interest you. On your paper, write a direct and specific topic sentence to express your opinion on both subjects.

1. Is watching TV educational?
2. Should all national holidays be celebrated on Mondays?
3. Is competition in sports a good thing?

Keep This in Mind

- In an explanatory *why* paragraph, you express and explain an opinion.
- State your opinion in a specific topic sentence.

Now Write Jot down several strong opinions you have. You might consider your feelings about something you do at home or at school or something that happens in your community.

Narrow one opinion to an opinion you can write about in a paragraph. State your opinion in a clear, strong sentence. Then list at least three reasons or facts to support your opinion. Label your paper **State Your Case.** Put it into your folder.

Part 2

Be Reasonable

Developing an Opinion

Here's the Idea To write a strong explanatory *why* paragraph you need convincing reasons to support your opinion. "That's how it is" and "because I say so" are not convincing reasons. Your reader will expect you to give specific reasons. Once you have good reasons, you will need to put them into some kind of order. An effective method is to save your strongest reason for last. Build your case from the weakest point to the strongest; that is, in order of importance. In that way, you leave your readers with your most convincing reason fresh in their minds. For example, below are three reasons why telephone lines should be placed underground.

1. There would be no poles and wires to clutter the landscape.
2. It would be cheaper to maintain underground lines because they would not be exposed to the weather.
3. Since lines could not be harmed by bad weather, people would be able to make emergency calls during storms.

The first reason is a good one, but it isn't as important to people as saving money. The last reason is the most important, since it affects people's safety. These reasons have been listed in order, from the least important to the most important.

Check It Out Read the following paragraph.

People should travel in car pools. First, using fewer cars helps to solve parking problems. More important, sharing rides is a way of reducing pollution. Most important, however, is the conservation of gasoline that would result from fewer people driving. Our nation's energy crisis and pollution problems would be greatly relieved if more people shared rides.

- Is an opinion supported by specific facts or reasons?
- Is the evidence given in order of importance, from the least important to the most important?

Try Your Skill This opinion has three reasons to support it. The reasons are listed in order of importance, from weakest to strongest. However, the reasons are not yet specific and convincing enough. Copy the opinion on your paper. Then, rewrite each reason so that it is convincing and specific.

Everyone should exercise regularly.

1. It's fun.
2. It helps you to relax.
3. It's healthy.

Keep This in Mind

- In an explanatory *why* paragraph, give specific reasons or facts to support an opinion.
- The most convincing way to organize an explanatory *why* paragraph is in order of importance. Start with the least important reason or fact and end with the most important.

Now Write Take out the work you did for the last lesson, **State Your Case.** You should have one opinion for an explanatory *why* paragraph and at least three specific reasons or facts to support the opinion.

Arrange the reasons or facts for each opinion in order, from the least important to the most important.

Use your notes to write a convincing, well organized explanatory *why* paragraph. Do any rewriting you feel is necessary.

Write a final copy of your paragraph. Label it **Be Reasonable.** Proofread it carefully.

Finally, put your work into your folder.

Part 3

The Defense Rests

Using Transitions

Here's the Idea Two kinds of transitions help you to develop your opinion in an explanatory *why* paragraph. One kind helps you to state the reasons or facts. The other kind of transition helps you to put your reasons or facts in order of importance.

To State Reasons or Facts:	because, so, since, therefore, as a result, if (something) . . . then (something)
To Put in Order of Importance:	the first reason, second, more important, most important, finally

Check It Out Look at these notes.

Opinion: Television can be educational.

Reasons: teaching tool, develops critical judgment, broadens experience

In a second pre-writing step, the reasons can be written with the appropriate transitions and arranged in order of importance.

teaching tool	—	*As a result of* watching educational programs, children learn math and reading skills.	=	first of all
develops critical judgment	—	*If* students watch and discuss good programs, they will learn to choose programs more wisely.	=	second
broadens experience	—	*Since* most people cannot travel world-wide, television can take them there.	=	finally

Now read the completed paragraph.

Television can be educational. First of all, as a result of watching educational programs, children can learn skills such as math and reading at home. Second, if students watch and discuss good programs, they can learn to choose TV programs more wisely. Finally, TV can broaden people's understanding of the world. By taking viewers back through history, or on adventures around the world, TV expands their knowledge. Opportunities to travel and to gain useful skills, then, are as close as the nearest television set.

- Does the topic sentence state an opinion clearly?
- What transitions show the reasons and their order of importance?
- Does the concluding sentence sum up the argument?

Try Your Skill Below is a set of notes for an explanatory *why* paragraph. First, put the reasons in the best order. Then write a good topic sentence and a good concluding sentence.

Opinion: All dogs should be kept on a leash.

Reasons: people safe from dogs, property safe from dogs, dogs safe from traffic

Keep This in Mind

- State the opinion in the topic sentence.
- Use transitions that show the reasons and their order of importance.
- Sum up your argument in the concluding sentence.

Now Write Label your paper **The Defense Rests.** Write an explanatory paragraph expressing an opinion important to you. Do whatever pre-writing, writing, and rewriting are necessary to write a convincing paragraph.

Proofread your paragraph, and put it into your folder.

The Explanatory Paragraph

Telling *What*

Part 1

What Is It?

Stating a Definition

Here's the Idea An explanatory *what* paragraph is a definition of something. What is defined may be a real object, like a *furnace,* or a term, like *democracy.* The topic sentence of the paragraph is a definition. The rest of the paragraph gives details that further show and explain the topic defined.

In many everyday situations you may be asked to explain what something is. For instance, in your classes you may be asked to explain a *veto,* a *simile,* or *gravity.* To explain an object or term clearly, you need to learn to write a good definition.

A good definition does three things. First, it gives the word to be defined. Next, it puts a subject in the general class to which it belongs. Then, it shows the particular characteristics of the subject. That is, it shows how the subject is different from all the other members of its class.

Imagine that you want to define a collie. What is a collie? First, you would write that a collie is a dog. That puts it in its general class. How is a collie different from other dogs? You could write that a collie is a large dog. That's a start. It shows how collies are different from beagles, dachshunds, and other small dogs. However, because there are many other big dogs besides collies, you might add that collies have long hair. Yet there are many other kinds of large dogs with long hair. You could add that collies have long, narrow heads. However, an Irish setter is also a large dog with long hair and a long head. You add that collies were originally bred in Scotland for herding sheep. Now you have a specific definition.

Your complete definition might be stated like this: A collie is a large, long-haired dog with a long, narrow head. It was originally bred in Scotland for herding sheep.

Check It Out Read the following explanation of a tornado.

A tornado is a violent wind storm that can be recognized by its dark, funnel-shaped cloud. Winds swirling up to 500 miles per hour are at the center of the funnel. The winds destroy everything in the path of the tornado. Tornadoes strike most often in the southern and central parts of the United States. They usually occur during late spring and early summer. Tornadoes are formed when a mass of cold air forces warm, moist air to rise rapidly. As the warm air rises, a revolving motion begins. This revolving is the basis for the name *tornado,* a Spanish word meaning "twister."

- Does the topic sentence give a definition?
- Does the definition state the general class and the particular characteristics of the subject?

Try Your Skill Choose three of the objects below. Write a good definition for each. Put each object into its class. Then, show its particular characteristics. You may want to use a dictionary or an encyclopedia.

a potato	a saxophone	a canoe	a rose
a bus	a football	Mars	a jet plane

Keep This in Mind

- Explanatory *what* paragraphs explain what something is. The topic sentence is a definition.
- A good definition puts a subject in its general class. Then it shows the particular characteristics of the subject.

Now Write On your paper, write the title of this lesson, **What Is It?** Choose a real object to explain. Write a complete definition of your object in an explanatory *what* paragraph. Keep your work in your folder.

Part 2

Be Particular

Developing a Definition

Here's the Idea There are many subjects you may choose to define in an explanatory *what* paragraph. You may define real objects, such as *Latex* paint, *chow mein, sagebrush,* or a *diesel* engine. You may also define many ideas or terms, such as *friendship, freedom, inflation,* or *progress.*

The subject you choose should be defined in the topic sentence. The rest of the paragraph should develop the definition as fully as possible. A definition is most helpful when it is developed by details, or facts and figures.

You may develop some definitions in a detailed, factual way. If you define *diesel,* for example, you will probably use facts and figures to develop your explanation. A dictionary or encyclopedia will help you to be complete and accurate.

Sometimes, you may develop a definition in a detailed, but more personal, way. If you define *friendship,* for example, you will probably use specific details from your own experience to develop your definition.

Check It Out Read the following definition of a family.

> A family is a unit of people who help one another. Members of a family stand by each other in any situation. When my best friend moved away, my family shared my sadness. When I won first prize at a craft fair, my family celebrated with me. My family always supports me. I am happy to be a member of the Graleno family.

- Does this paragraph develop the definition given in the topic sentence? Is the paragraph developed by details or facts and figures?

Try Your Skill Look at the list of ideas and terms below. Choose three. For each of your choices, write a good definition. You may want to use a dictionary or encyclopedia to help you.

a friend	a curve ball
happiness	to bake
courage	a clipping penalty
a family	a misdemeanor
freedom	a private eye
home	a fad

Keep This in Mind

- An explanatory *what* paragraph develops the definition given in the topic sentence. The paragraph is usually developed by details, or facts and figures.

Now Write On your paper, write the title of this lesson, **Be Particular.** Choose an idea or term that has special meaning for you. You may choose an idea like *loneliness* or a term like *quarterback.*

Write a definition of your topic in an explanatory *what* paragraph. Develop your topic fully by using details, or facts and figures.

Keep your paper in your folder.

Exploring Compositions

Part 1

Take a Look

Defining a Composition

Here's the Idea A **composition** is a group of paragraphs dealing with one idea. That idea can be one story, one description, or one explanation. You will want to write a composition to express ideas that require more than a few sentences.

A composition is similar in some ways to a paragraph. Like a paragraph, a composition deals with only one idea. Also, a composition is organized by using transitional words and phrases.

Compositions, however, deal with ideas that are too long or too complicated to be covered in a paragraph. For example, you could write about the climate of San Francisco in a paragraph. You would need to write a composition to tell about the climate of California, however. Because of their longer length, compositions usually have titles.

Check It Out Read the following composition.

The Block Party

Last July, the families of Hastings Street staged a block party. It was our first celebration as a neighborhood, and it involved everyone on the block. We celebrated all day long.

We gathered in front of the Murphy's house at eight o'clock for warm-up exercises, and a slow jog around the block. Barricades provided by the police had closed our block to traffic. After our run, the younger kids had a bicycle parade. Later, many families moved to the north end of the street to play volleyball. At noon, everyone gathered for sandwiches, potato chips, lemonade, and ice cream.

The afternoon was filled with more activities. Kids challenged the adults to a game of stickball in the street. To our surprise, old Miss Mackle scored the winning run for the adult team!

Scattered along the block were games of hopscotch, croquet, and checkers. Small groups of people sat along the curb, chatting and watching the games.

By evening everyone had worked up a huge appetite. Our potluck dinner was truly a feast. Those of us on the east side of the street had brought salads to share. There were tossed salads, macaroni salads, egg salads, potato salads, and fruit salads. Our neighbors on the west side of the street had provided desserts. There were brownies, cookies, and huge cakes of all shapes and flavors. Each family had brought hotdogs and hamburgers. We cooked them on barbecue grills set up in the middle of the block.

After dark, the block party ended with a short display of colorful fireworks. It had been a busy, but very special, day for all of us. From now on, the Hastings Street neighbors plan to celebrate together every year.

- What is the main idea of this composition?

Try Your Skill Read these topics. Number your paper from 1 to 6. Write *P* next to the number if the topic could be covered in a paragraph. Write *C* if the topic requires a composition.

1. a description of an apple
2. how to build a house
3. a story about people lost in a blizzard
4. how to eat an ear of corn
5. what a skyscraper is
6. why a good education is important

Keep This in Mind

- A composition is a group of paragraphs dealing with one main idea.

Now Write Think of five topics that you can write about in compositions. Choose topics that you know about and care about. On your paper, list the topics. Label your paper **Take a Look.** Keep your list in your folder. You will need it later.

Part 2

Triple Play

Developing a Composition

Here's the Idea There are three parts to a composition: an **introduction,** a **body,** and a **conclusion.** The introduction is the part that tells what the composition will be about. The introduction is similar to the topic sentence of a paragraph.

The body of a composition is the part that develops the main idea. In a narrative, the body develops the events of the story. In a description, the body gives the details that make up the word picture. In an explanatory composition, the body presents steps in a process, reasons, or facts.

A composition needs a conclusion, or ending. Your reader must know that it is over. Sometimes the conclusion may be a summary of the story, description, or explanation. Sometimes the conclusion may be a group of sentences that clearly signals an ending to the idea you have developed.

As a last step, you may want to add a title. The title will tell your readers what the composition is about.

Check It Out Read the composition below.

My Special Day

Shortly after Thanksgiving, the downtown area begins to undergo a great change. Decorations are added to each street and store. Wreaths, ribbons, and sparkling lights appear. The sights and sounds of the holiday season are everywhere. At this time of year, my favorite adventure is a day of shopping.

The adventure begins when the subway train hisses to a stop. The doors open, spilling crowds of people into the dark underground station. Eager shoppers climb the stairs to the street. Snow is falling softly. The air is cold. On the busy street, the crowd scatters in all directions.

All day long, we parade past store windows with holiday displays. In one window an electric train chugs around a mountain of gifts. In another window shiny copper skillets and kettles are displayed. My favorite window holds fancy cakes, cookies, and candies decorated for the holidays.

In the square, a red-cheeked Santa Claus stands next to a black, iron kettle. He nods a greeting to passers-by as he clangs his big bell. Across the square, children are singing carols.

At dusk, the lights on the huge fir trees in the nearby park are turned on. The lights shine brightly through the lightly falling snow. We cross through the park as we head home. My arms are full of packages. My mind is full of my holiday in the city.

- Which part is the introduction, which is the body, and which is the conclusion?

Try Your Skill Write the name of the part of the composition in which this paragraph belongs. Write your reasons.

Her next task was to reach the zoo before David did. Pam raced up the street toward the taxi stand. Jumping into the lead cab, she shouted, "The zoo, driver, and quickly!" Five minutes later, they pulled up at the main entrance. Pam caught sight of David just as he was entering the main gate.

Keep This in Mind

- A composition should have three parts: an introduction, a body, and a conclusion.

Now Write Take out the topics you selected in the last lesson. On your paper, write the title of this lesson, **Triple Play.** Write the headings *Introduction*, *Body*, and *Conclusion*. Choose one of your topics. Decide what you would include in each part of a composition on this topic. Jot down one or two sentences of notes for each part. Put your work into your folder.

Part 3

Name Tags

Recognizing Three Kinds of Compositions

Here's the Idea When you write a paragraph, you may want to tell a story, to describe, or to explain. Whenever you write a composition, you may also do these same things.

Narrative compositions tell stories. Sometimes a narrative is an account of something that really happened. Sometimes a narrative is an imaginary story. In either a true account or a story, the events are told in the order in which they happened.

Descriptive compositions are word pictures. They may describe an object, a place, a scene, or a person. Sensory details are used to make the word picture vivid and lively.

Explanatory compositions explain *how* something should be done or *why* something should be so. This kind of composition uses steps in a process, reasons, or facts.

Check It Out Read the composition below.

City Birds

One city creature is usually considered a nuisance. The cause of the trouble is the pigeon. Some city residents insist that the pigeon population should be strictly controlled. People argue that pigeons are the cause of too much damage to property. However, I believe that pigeons add much to city life.

The simplest reason in support of pigeons is that they are a natural part of the city environment. There are more than 300 kinds of pigeons in the world, but only eleven species live in the United States. In fact, one native species, called passenger pigeons, was totally destroyed by American hunters in the 1800's. Pigeons eat fruit, grains, and insects. However, many birds need help from people during the winter in order to find enough food to survive.

More importantly, pigeons add a touch of beauty to the city. Although a pigeon is usually covered with gray feathers, its neck shimmers with purple, green, and blue in the sunlight. Pigeons are also strong, swift fliers. Pigeons gliding gracefully down from building ledges are a pleasant sight to city dwellers. In addition, their soft cooing is a peaceful sound.

The most important reason for allowing pigeons in the city is simply that they do give people pleasure. Young and old alike enjoy feeding them and watching them fly.

People should put the pigeon issue to rest. Pigeons have a natural right to be in the city. They add beauty. They give people pleasure. Pigeons are an important part of city life.

- What kind of composition is this? How do you know?

Try Your Skill On your paper, identify the two kinds of compositions given as models in the last two lessons, **Take a Look** and and **Triple Play.** Write your reasons for your answers.

Keep This in Mind

- There are three kinds of compositions. Narrative compositions tell a story. Descriptive compositions create a word picture. Explanatory compositions explain how to do something or *why* something should be so.

Now Write Take out the topics that you listed in **Take a Look.** Which topic would make a good narrative composition? Which topic would make a good descriptive composition? Which topic would make a good explanatory composition?

On your paper, write the title of this lesson, **Name Tags.** List *Narrative, Descriptive,* and *Explanatory*. Below each heading, write the topic you have chosen. Then write a sentence or two telling what you would include in each composition. When you are finished, put your work into your folder.

The Narrative Composition

Part 1

True or False?

Planning a Narrative Composition

Here's the Idea How can you find a topic for a narrative composition? One source for topics is your own memory. What unusual or funny things have actually happened to you? What real people, places, or events from your own past have made a strong impression on you? Use your memory to find a real life topic. Then write a **true account.**

Another source of topics is your own imagination. Can you recall any interesting dreams? What kinds of imaginary places or characters would you like to create? In what kinds of situations can you imagine your characters? Use your imagination to create an unusual, new idea. Then you can write a **story.**

Once you have a topic—real or imaginary—make sure it is broad enough for a composition. Answer the questions *who? what? when? where? how?* and *why?* about your topic. Jot down all the details that you plan to include in the introduction, the body, and the conclusion of your composition. If you find that you have too few notes, your topic is too narrow. Use details to develop your topic more fully or choose a different topic.

Plan a true account by *recalling* details about people, places, and events. Plan a story by *inventing* details about people, called **characters.** Invent details about time and place, called the **setting.** Invent details about events, called the **plot.**

Check It Out Look at these notes for a narrative composition.

Topic a great game

Introduction—our Bedford High School baseball team tied for first place with the Landis High team

—tie-breaking game at end of regular season

Body—our pitcher, Frank West, gave up a home run
—scoreless game for next 7 innings
—great catch by our shortstop, injury
—our coach brought in Marion Reed, the first girl to play on our team

Conclusion—Marion hit a double
—both runners scored, crowd went wild

- Are these notes for a true account or for an imaginary story?
- Are these notes complete and detailed?
- Are details about people and events included in these notes?

Try Your Skill Below is a list of topics for narratives. Choose one topic that interests you. Make a set of notes. Supply details from your memory or your imagination.

a first meeting	a wild chase	built it myself
a summer vacation	going to the store	trouble at school

Keep This in Mind

- You may choose to write a narrative composition that is a true account or an imaginary story.
- List details for a real or imaginary topic. Make sure the topic will be developed in the introduction, body, and conclusion of the composition.
- Recall or invent details about people and events.

Now Write Choose a topic for a narrative composition. Try to choose a situation in which there is a problem to be solved, a difficulty to be overcome, or a hard choice to be made.

On your paper, write the title of this lesson, **True or False?** Write your topic and make a list of details to develop the topic.

Keep your work in your folder.

Part 2 # What Do You Know?

Using Point of View

Here's the Idea When you write a narrative composition, you decide whether to write a true account or an imaginary story. You also must decide who will tell the narrative for you. In a true account, you will probably want to tell the events yourself from the first-person point of view. For a story, it may be more difficult to know which point of view is best.

If you were writing a story about a party, for instance, which point of view would you use? When you use the **first-person point of view,** a story is told by the character identified as *I*.

When you use the **third-person point of view,** a story is told by a character who sees and hears everything that happens. The pronouns *he* and *she* are usually used.

There is also another point of view. It is called **omniscient** (om•ní•shunt), which means "knowing all things." From this point of view, a story is told by a character who sees and hears everything. In addition, a character also knows what every other character thinks and feels. The pronouns *he* and *she* are used.

When you write a story, try to decide which point of view will work best.

Check It Out Read these two paragraphs.

1 I watched nervously as Marion came to bat. However, on the first pitch, she hit a double to center field. Both runners scrambled around the bases and scored. The excitement brought me to my feet cheering. I saw Marion smile as the other cheering players lifted her onto their shoulders.

2 Marion hit a double to center field. Both runners scrambled around the bases and scored. In the stands, the fans from

Bedford High jumped up and cheered wildly. On the field, the Bedford players lifted Marion onto their shoulders. Marion laughed happily. She felt proud of her part in the team's victory.

- What is the point of view of each paragraph? How do you know?

Try Your Skill Number your paper from 1 to 6. Identify the point of view from which each sentence is written.

1. Later in the morning I tried to telephone Carol.
2. Carol was in the shower when the phone started ringing.
3. Jan wished that Carol would hurry up and answer.
4. Carol was nervous as she raced to reach the phone.
5. When the phone had rung for the tenth time, I groaned and hung up.
6. When Carol picked up the phone and found no one there, she slammed down the receiver.

Keep This in Mind

- In the first-person point of view, the reader knows only what the main character sees and feels.
- In the third-person point of view, the reader can see and hear everything.
- In the omiscient point of view, the reader knows everything—thoughts, feelings, and actions.

Now Write Label your paper **What Do You Know?** From your folder, take out the topic you chose in the last lesson, **True or False?** Review the topic and details you have chosen for your narrative composition. Decide which point of view is best for the true account or the story you will write. Revise your notes so that all the details listed fit the point of view you choose. Put your work into your folder.

Part 3

Best Foot Forward

Writing an Introduction

Here's the Idea The first paragraph of a narrative composition is the **introduction.** In your introduction, you want to capture your reader's interest. You also want to introduce to the reader the most important element of your account or story.

In a true account, you need to decide whether the people, the place, or the events are the most important. Are the people who were involved the most important element? Are the time and place of the action the most important? Are the events themselves the most important? Decide which is the most important element, and present that in your introduction.

In an imaginary narrative, your introduction also depends on the emphasis of your story. You may want to begin with the setting, if it is unusual or if it is important to the events of the story. You may want to begin with a description of the main character, if an unusual character is at the center of your story.

No matter what you decide to begin with, you must get your narrative started. Prepare your reader for what is to follow. By the end of the introduction, your reader should feel the mood of the narrative.

How do you feel as you read the following introduction?

> The water was dark and still at the far end of Wolf Lake. No birds sang from the shore. Here and there a fallen tree jutted out into the water. Old-timers had told me that there was a huge muskie lurking in that part of the lake. On that drizzly Saturday morning, I had come to look for the huge fish. I leaned over the edge of my old skiff and slowly lowered my line.

Check It Out Now read the introduction to the baseball narrative that was planned in **True or False?**

The air was charged with suspense. Two teams, Bedford High and Landis High, were about to take the field. Each had identical records of nine wins and one loss. The teams were tied for first place in Division One. They had met twice before and each had managed a narrow victory. The day of the tie-breaker had arrived, the University Stadium was jammed.

- Which words and phrases introduce the people, places, and events of this narrative?
- What kind of story do you expect will follow this introduction?

Try Your Skill Read the following introduction to a narrative composition. You will notice that it is not interesting. Use your imagination to add details, and rewrite it so that it is a lively introduction. Save your work. You will need it for **Try Your Skill** in the next lesson.

One day in gym class we were told to climb to the top of a rope. The rope was hooked up to the ceiling. I usually like gym class. That day I got a funny feeling about climbing that rope. Everyone else had done it, but I just stood there.

Keep This in Mind

- Try to present an important element of the narrative in your introduction.
- The introduction should make readers curious enough to read on.

Now Write From your folder, take out your notes from the previous lesson, **What Do You Know?** Use your notes to write an introduction for your narrative. Read your introduction to yourself, to be sure you have made it as vivid and strong as you can. Make revisions, if necessary. Label your paper **Best Foot Forward.** Keep your introduction in your folder.

Part 4

Let's Have Action!

Developing a Narrative Composition

Here's the Idea The **body** of a narrative composition—real or imaginary—tells what happened. The body of the narrative usually tells how a problem was solved or a choice was made. In either an account or a story, the sequence of these events is developed with details.

When you are relating a true account, you must be sure that your details are accurate. Check your facts. Use reliable sources.

When you are creating an imaginary story, use specific details that develop the plot and give it life. The **plot** of a story means the events that happen from a beginning action, through conflict, to an ending. These actions are presented in the order in which they happen.

What controls the plot is the conflict. **Conflict** means the main problem troubling the characters in a story. A conflict may exist between certain characters. It may result from something that happens naturally, such as a fire or a flood. The conflict may even be within one character who is struggling to make an important decision.

Every interesting narrative has an unusual, frightening, or dramatic conflict. Conflict creates suspense. If you involve your readers in your narrative, they will be eager to find out the result of the conflict.

Check It Out Notice how this conflict is presented.

> In the first inning, our ace pitcher, Frank West, was on the mound. We were rooting for him with every pitch he made. Suddenly, Al Wright belted a home run over the left field wall. The Landis team was immediately ahead! As Wright trotted around the bases, the Landis High fans screamed and cheered.

For the next few innings, Frank had excellent control and threw nothing but strikes. At the same time, however, the Landis pitcher was shutting out our batters. We were desperate.

In the top of the eighth inning, the score was still 1 to 0. Then, our shortstop, Dave Baxter, lunged for a streaking line drive and saved a run. When Dave got up, he was limping.

At shortstop, we needed a strong, steady player. The coach decided to put in Marion Reed. The entire stadium fell quiet. Marion was the first girl ever to play on our high school team. Although she was my friend, I couldn't help feeling nervous. Would Marion be able to help us win?

- What details develop the body of this narrative?
- What conflict is presented?
- How could the accuracy of these details be checked?

Try Your Skill Below are some incomplete notes for the body of the narrative about climbing the gym rope. Write three or four paragraphs developing the plot.

I grabbed the rope.
I slowly pulled myself up.
I was nearly to the top.
I grabbed the ceiling rafter.
I lost control of the rope.
I was afraid.

Keep This in Mind

- Develop the action of a narrative with details.
- Make sure that the action arises out of a conflict.
- When writing about a real event, be sure that the details of your account are accurate.

Now Write Now write the body of your composition. Develop the action and conflict of your narrative.

Label your paper **Let's Have Action!** and put it into your folder.

Part 5 **Let's Talk**

Using Dialogue in a Narrative

Here's the Idea A **dialogue** is a conversation between two or more persons. Sometimes you may want to include dialogue in a narrative composition. Using dialogue is one way to break up long sections of straight narration. Using dialogue is also a direct way to bring people, or characters, to life.

Whenever you write dialogue, follow these rules:

1. Use quotation marks to show that you are using the exact words of a speaker. This is called a **direct quotation.**

   "Oh no, I've lost my wallet!" cried Susan.

2. Only the speaker's exact words are placed inside the quotation marks. Explaining words like *cried Susan* are placed outside.

   "Where did you lose it?" **John asked.**

3. Separate the direct quotation from the explaining words by using a comma or other appropriate punctuation.

   "I must have lost the money on the bus**,**" said Susan.

   "Do you think we can find it**?**" John asked.

Notice that the punctuation is placed inside the quotation marks.

4. A direct quotation may be placed at the beginning of a sentence or at the end. It may also be divided into two parts.

   "How can I pay for the trip home?" Susan wailed.

   Susan wailed, **"How can I pay for the trip home?"**

   "How," Susan wailed, **"can I pay for the trip home?"**

5. Use explaining words for each line of dialogue. Try to vary the explaining words you use. Use *asked, answered, cried,* or *laughed,* for example, as well as *said.*

   "Don't worry," **said** John. "I'll lend you the money."

   "Oh, thank you so much," **replied** Susan.

6. Begin a new paragraph every time a different person speaks.

7. If you do not use the exact words of a speaker, do not use quotation marks. This is called an **indirect quotation.**

   Susan said that she hoped that they would find her wallet.

Check It Out Read the following dialogue that continues the baseball narrative you have been reading.

> "Is that girl going in to play shortstop now?" shouted Paul, sitting beside me.
>
> "That's Marion Reed," I replied. "She's a good player."
>
> "It's not a good idea to put a girl in at a time like this," Paul insisted.
>
> I asked him what he thought was wrong with the idea of girls playing baseball.
>
> "Girls can't take the pressure," he answered.
>
> "Sure they can," I said. "Wait until you see Marion play."

- What are the narrator's exact words? What are Paul's exact words? What explaining words are used? How can you tell when the speaker changes?

Try Your Skill You were left hanging from the rafters in **Try Your Skill** in the last lesson, **Let's Have Action!** Write a short dialogue between you and your friend on the gym floor. Use the dialogue to keep up the suspense.

Keep This in Mind

- In a narrative, use dialogue as a change of pace. Use dialogue also to express the feelings of people or characters in your story.
- Follow the rules for punctuating quotations.

Now Write Review what you have written thus far for your own composition. Find a place where a dialogue would be effective. Have the people or characters in your narrative tell what they are doing, feeling, or thinking. Try to make the dialogue fit in smoothly with your plot or sequence of events. Write the dialogue. Follow the rules for punctuating quotations. Label your paper **Let's Talk** and put it into your folder.

Part 6 **Other Voices**

Using Dialogue To Reveal Character

Here's the Idea Compare the examples below. Which speaker is polite and which is not?

"Pardon me, sir," said the man, "but your umbrella is sticking into my back."
"Hey, mister," said the man, "watch where you shove that umbrella!"

From these examples, you can see that dialogue is an excellent way to reveal character.

When you write dialogue, try to make the dialogue sound right for the character who is speaking. The character should talk like himself or herself.

The explaining words you choose also help to reveal character. The word *grumble* suggests a different way of speaking from the word *shout.* A speaker may *comment, gasp, snap, snicker,* or *whine,* for example.

Read the following dialogue. Identify the character or attitude of each speaker.

"What a great day to be alive!" Ben said. "Isn't this just a terrific morning?

"Only if you like spring," muttered Carl.

"Look at the sunlight on those flowers! Smell those flowers!" Ben exclaimed.

"It means nothing to me," growled Carl.

Check It Out Read the dialogue below. It is similar to the sample dialogue from the baseball narrative in **Check It Out** in the last lesson. However, the dialogue has been revised so that it clearly reveals the characters of the speakers.

> "Oh no!" groaned Paul beside me. "They're bringing in a girl to play shortstop."
> "She happens to be a great shortstop," I insisted.
> "The coach must be daffy!" Paul exclaimed.
> "You don't need to worry about Marion," I assured Paul.

- What does this dialogue reveal about the people speaking?
- What explaining words have been used?

Try Your Skill In **Try Your Skill** in the last lesson, you wrote a dialogue between yourself and a friend holding the gym rope. Rewrite the dialogue so that it reveals each character. Imagine that your friend is trying to calm you. Imagine, on the other hand, that you are close to panic.

Keep This in Mind

- Using dialogue is a good way to reveal character. Try to make your dialogue match the character's personality and feelings.
- Choose explaining words that also help you reveal character.

Now Write Think about the characters or people in the narrative composition you are writing. Decide what kind of people they are. From your folder, take out the paper labeled **Let's Talk.** Reread it. How could you revise your dialogue to reveal the characters more clearly? Make whatever revisions are necessary.

On your paper, write the title of this lesson, **Other Voices.** Neatly copy your revised dialogue and put it into your folder.

Part 7

Moving On

Using Transitions in a Narrative

Here's the Idea The events of a narrative are usually told in the order in which they happened; that is, in **chronological order.** To make the order clear, you need to use transitional words and phrases. In narrative paragraphs, you have used such transitions as *first, next, later,* and *finally.* You have seen that transitions are important within a paragraph.

It is also important to use transitions between paragraphs. The topic sentence of each paragraph should connect that paragraph to the one before it. These transitions also show how much time has passed between events. Examples of paragraph transitions are *two years later, last week, yesterday, after dinner,* and *next summer.*

Notice the transitions within the following paragraph:

> *While* waiting for Dave to swim out of my way, I stood at the end of the diving board. *For several minutes,* I stared down at the choppy water. *When* the surface was calm again, I crouched forward. *After* taking a deep breath, I made my dive.

Check It Out Now read this paragraph that continues the baseball narrative.

> In the bottom of the ninth inning, our leadoff batter grounded out. After the next batter struck out on three pitches, the home fans nearly lost hope. However, the next two batters reached base on a walk and a single to right field. Marion came to the plate with the winning run on second base. Suddenly, the tense crowd fell silent.

- What phrase shows the transition from the previous paragraphs to this one?
- What transitional words and phrases help to make clear the time sequence within the paragraph?

Try Your Skill It's time to get yourself down from the rafters where you were left in **Try Your Skill** in the last lesson. Read the paragraph below. Rewrite the paragraph, adding transitional words and phrases to help make the time sequence clear. Try to choose transitions that help add to the feeling of suspense.

> I let go of the rafter with one hand. I grabbed the rope tightly. I froze. I let go with my other hand and caught the rope. I took a deep breath and slowly came down the rope.

Keep This in Mind

- Transitional words and phrases make a sequence of events clear. Transitions also show how much time has passed between events.
- In a paragraph, transitions show time sequence from sentence to sentence.
- In a composition, transitions show time sequence from paragraph to paragraph.

Now Write From your folder, take out what you have written thus far in this section on your narrative composition. Review your work. Is the sequence of events clear? Have you used a variety of transitional words and phrases? Could they be more specific? Consider any problems your readers might have in following your story. Make whatever revisions are necessary.

Label your paper **Moving On** and put it into your folder.

Part 8 **The Finale**

Completing a Narrative Composition

Here's the Idea The final paragraph of your narrative is the **conclusion.** A good conclusion fits naturally with the rest of a narrative composition. The characters, or people, in the narrative shouldn't suddenly develop new personalities. The point of view shouldn't change. Nothing new should be added.

In the conclusion, you should tie up any loose ends in the sequence of events. In the conclusion, you should also resolve any conflicts. How was your problem solved or a difficult decision made? How have the people or characters reacted?

Your conclusion should be interesting. It is the last impression you leave with your reader. You want to make it a good one.

Finally, you need to write a title for your narrative composition. The **title** of your story is the first thing the reader will see. However, it will probably be the last thing you write. A good title should catch the reader's attention. It might also point toward the main idea of your narrative.

Check It Out Read the conclusion and title for the baseball narrative.

> I was hoping that Marion wasn't as nervous as I was. However, she couldn't have been, because she slammed the first pitch over the second baseman into center field. The two runs scored, and Marion had rounded second. Suddenly, the dugout emptied onto the field. The players lifted Marion onto their shoulders. Every one of us felt as though we were on the field, too, sharing Marion's pride and the team's wild joy.
>
> **Title:** Marion Makes a Hit

- Does this conclusion tie all the elements of the narrative together?
- Does the title fit the story?

Try Your Skill Write a conclusion for the story about how you conquered the gym rope. Tell how the conflict was resolved. Have the characters reveal their feelings. When you finish the conclusion, write a good title.

Keep This in Mind

- Write a conclusion that ties all the elements of the narrative together. It should leave a strong, last impression.
- Write an interesting title that fits the story.

Now Write From your folder, take out your narrative composition. Write a conclusion. Check to be sure you have tied up all the loose ends. Have you resolved a conflict? Have you described the reactions of the people or characters?

Read over all that you have written for your composition. Do you like what you've written? Is your writing lively? Does it say what you want it to say? Make any necessary revisions.

Write a title for your narrative.

On your paper, write the title of this lesson, **The Finale.** Write the final copy of your narrative composition. Put your completed narrative composition into your folder.

WRITING SECTION 14

The Descriptive Composition

Part 1

What Do You See?

Planning a Descriptive Composition

Here's the Idea A descriptive composition paints a detailed picture with words. It may describe a scene, like a park in the city. It may also describe an object, such as a taxi. When you write a description, select a topic that appeals to most of your senses. Also, be sure to narrow your topic.

After you have chosen a topic, make your pre-writing **notes.** Use your senses to find and list details. Ask yourself how your subject looks, sounds, smells, tastes, and feels.

Next, organize your notes using spatial order. Show how the objects in the scene or background are placed in relation to each other. You may want to use such transitions as *above, near, next to, in front of,* and *in the center.*

Finally, organize your notes into three parts: the introduction, the body, and the conclusion. In the **introduction,** plan to show your reader what the entire composition is about. In the **body,** plan to develop your description with details. In the **conclusion,** plan to summarize your ideas and feelings about your subject.

Check It Out Look at the pre-writing notes below.

Topic Grandma Sarah's apartment

Introduction Grandma Sarah and the sea
- lives in New Bedford, apartment near harbor
- treasures from Grandfather's sailing days

Body bedroom
- four-poster bed (center), Chinese clock
- oval mirror, sea chests (opposite wall)

favorite corner
- window facing sea, seashells, rocking chair

special treasure, Popeye, the noisy parrot

Conclusion I like visiting Grandma Sarah
laugh at Popeye, listen to stories, watch the sea

- What will be the main idea of this description?
- What main ideas will be developed in the composition? What details will help to describe the apartment?
- Are these notes in a natural, logical order?

Try Your Skill Below are some disorganized notes for a descriptive composition about a pizza parlor. Decide which group of ideas and details belongs in the introduction. Then decide which groups of ideas belong in the body of the description. Finally, decide which group of ideas belongs in the conclusion. Copy the notes in the correct order on your paper. Label them *Introduction*, *Body*, and *Conclusion*.

Regina's Pizzeria (outside)
small, old building
neon sign
long lines

Pizza
favorite meal
which is best?
Regina's Pizzeria

Regina's (inside)
10 plain, wooden tables
huge refrigerator for soda
cardboard menu on walls

Regina's is best pizza
mushrooms, pepperoni
crispy crust
worth a long wait

Keep This in Mind

- Choose and narrow a topic for a description.
- List the main ideas and details you will use.
- Use a natural, logical order to organize your notes.

Now Write Write the title of this lesson, **What Do You See?** Choose and narrow a topic for a descriptive composition. Write and organize notes for your composition. Label your paper *Notes* and put it into your folder.

Part 2

A Wider View

Using Sensory Details

Here's the Idea After planning your description, you are ready to write the introduction. The **introduction** usually describes the setting of your subject. This paragraph should be interesting enough to make the reader want to continue reading.

One sentence of the introduction must serve as the topic sentence for the whole composition. It tells the reader of the specific object or area that you are going to describe.

The **body** of a descriptive composition should present a clear word picture to the reader. The more specific your details are, the more vivid your word picture will be. To find and create interesting **details,** use each of your senses.

Not every object or scene affects all the senses. However, you should try to use as many of your senses as possible. What is the size, shape, or color of your subject? How does it sound? Are there special tastes or smells connected with your subject? Is there an unusual surface or texture? Use all the details you can to describe your subject fully.

Check It Out Here are the introduction and the body of the description of the apartment planned in the last lesson.

> Grandma Sarah has always loved the sea. From her second-floor apartment that overlooks the New Bedford harbor, my grandmother can watch the fishing boats in the busy port. The apartment itself is filled with reminders of the sea, and of the long ago days of my grandfather's sailing voyages.
>
> Against the wall in the center of the bedroom is a tall, maple, four-poster bed from England. On the table sits a Chinese clock painted with red dragons. On the wall by the door hangs an oval mirror from India. Against the opposite wall stand two wooden

sea chests. They are scratched and worn now, but they are filled with letters and souvenirs sent home by Grandfather.

In the far corner of the room is my grandmother's favorite place. In this small alcove, there is a window facing the sea. The windowsill is lined with colorful sea shells. In the mornings, Grandma Sarah sits near the window, watching the boats.

Also in the alcove is one very noisy reminder of the sea. On a perch that Grandfather carved from whalebone, sits a pale green parrot named Popeye. From his stand, Popeye squawks, "Come aboard, mate! You old sea dog!"

- Does the introduction describe the location of the scene?
- What is the topic sentence in the introduction?
- Point out the sensory details in these paragraphs.

Try Your Skill Do you remember the pizza parlor described in **Try Your Skill** in the last lesson? Think about how each of your senses would be affected if you were there. Write *Sight Sound, Smell, Taste,* and *Feel* on your paper. Use your imagination to list at least two details for each of the senses.

Keep This in Mind

- In the introduction for a descriptive composition, describe the location of the scene or object.
- One sentence of the introduction should serve as the topic sentence for the whole composition.
- Use sensory details to develop the body of the descriptive composition.

Now Write Take out the notes for the description you planned in the last lesson. Write the introduction to your description. Make sure you present your subject in an interesting way. Next, write the body of your composition. Use vivid details.

Label your paper **A Wider View** and put it into your folder.

Part 3

How Do You Feel?

Organizing a Description

Here's the Idea Use a natural, logical order to organize a descriptive composition. Sometimes you may want to use **spatial order** to organize your description. There are many spatial patterns you can follow. You can describe your subject from top to bottom, for example, or from left to right.

Using transitions will help to make your pattern clear. They are useful for organizing the details within a paragraph. They are also useful between paragraphs. They show how the parts of a scene or object appear in relation to one another.

You need to write a strong, clear conclusion to your descriptive composition. Think about how you can pull your ideas together to summarize the main idea. Try to say it in a different way.

Also, think about why you are telling the reader about your topic. Why is it interesting to you? You can share your feelings so that the reader will feel closer to your subject.

As a final step, you may want to add a title for your description.

Check It Out Review the descriptive composition shown in the last lesson. Notice how the description is organized. Then read the conclusion.

> I always love to visit Grandma Sarah. We sit together in her special room. We laugh at the noisy Popeye. We talk of times past and places far away. Best of all, we watch the sea that she has always loved.
>
> **Title:** A View of the Sea

- In what order is the description of the apartment organized? Point out the transitional words and phrases.

- Does the conclusion pull all the main ideas in the composition together?
- Does the title fit the description?

Try Your Skill Look at the notes below for a description of a hot dog stand. Imagine what the stand would look like. Arrange the details in a logical order. Add details, if you'd like. Then, use clear transitional words to write a paragraph of description.

small, wooden shack	napkins, salt and pepper
painted sign	grill
long counter with red stools	cook
bags of chips on rack	cash register
jars of mustard, ketchup	soft drink machine

Keep This in Mind

- Use a natural, logical order to organize a description. Use transitions that show spatial order.
- The conclusion of a descriptive composition should pull all the main ideas together.
- In the conclusion, tell how you feel about what you are describing.
- You may want to add a title for the description.

Now Write Read over the composition you have been writing in the last two lessons. Is your description organized in a clear, logical way? Do you need to add transitions? Make revisions, if necessary. Then write the conclusion. Make sure that the conclusion fits smoothly with the rest of your description.

Proofread your work for spelling and punctuation. Write a title for your composition.

Make a final copy of your description. Label your paper **How Do You Feel?** and put it into your folder.

The Explanatory Composition

Telling *How*

Part 1

How Do You Do?

Planning an Explanation

Here's the Idea An explanatory *how* composition explains the steps in a process. You might explain how to do something, such as fly a model airplane. You might explain how to make something, like a kite.

When you are looking for a **topic,** choose a subject that you know about and care about. Think of your hobbies, of sports you enjoy, or of any area of study that you take a special interest in.

Once you have a topic, jot down your pre-writing **notes.** In your notes, list the steps involved in the process. Also, list any materials and tools required. Organizing your notes this way will tell you whether you have enough details for a composition.

The **title** of an explanatory *how* composition should state the topic clearly. You may want to use the words *how to.* The reader will know right away what the composition is about.

Check It Out Read these pre-writing notes.

How To Tie-Dye a T-shirt

1. Collect materials.
   plain, light T-shirt
   string or rubber bands
   stick, bucket, salt, dye, rubber gloves
2. Prepare T-shirt.
   wash
   fold, twist, tie
3. Dye T-shirt.
   mix solution, soak shirt
   hang to dry

- What process do these steps explain?

- Do these notes list the steps involved and the materials needed?
- Is the title clear?

Try Your Skill Below is a jumbled set of instructions for making a pair of stilts. On your paper, rearrange the notes into two lists: the steps in the process, and the materials needed. Keep these notes in your folder.

two 2-inch × 4-inch × 6-foot boards
attach footholds
measure boards for footholds
one 4-inch square piece of wood, 2-inches thick
mark wood for footholds
screwdriver, pencil, saw
wipe off excess stain
cut wood cube diagonally for footholds
one pint of maple stain
six 3-inch wood screws
one 2-inch wide paintbrush
sand wood
stain wood
rags
measuring tape
sandpaper
hammer

Keep This in Mind

- Explanatory *how* compositions explain the steps in a process. They explain how to do something or how to make something.
- In your notes, list the steps in the process and the materials and tools required.
- The title should state the topic clearly.

Now Write On your paper, list two processes you could explain in a composition. One should be about how to do something. One should be about how to make something. Also, write a possible title for each topic.

Label your paper **How Do You Do?** and put it into your folder.

Part 2

Step It Up

Using Step-by-Step Order

Here's the Idea An explanatory *how* composition can be organized this way: introduction, steps in the process, and conclusion.

In your first paragraph you must introduce your topic. One sentence of the introduction should serve as the topic sentence for the composition. If your topic is tie-dyeing, the topic sentence may be "Tie-dyeing is a clever way to create a new look, especially for T-shirts."

In the body of the composition, give a step-by-step explanation. For example, you might divide the process of tie-dyeing into collecting the materials, tying the design, and dyeing the T-shirt. Each of these steps would be discussed in separate paragraphs. Make sure they are complete and accurate.

Develop the concluding paragraph from the final step. For instance, you may want to write about dyeing, using many different designs and colors. Make sure your reader knows your composition is ended.

Check It Out Read the body of an explanatory *how* composition about tie-dyeing.

> First of all, you will need a few things to get started. Find a plain T-shirt that is white or light colored. Also collect some string or rubber bands, a stick, a bucket, and salt. You need to buy a package of colored dye and a pair of rubber gloves to protect your hands.
>
> Next, wash the T-shirt. Then fold or twist several bunches of the material. Tie the string or elastics around those areas that you want to be free of dye. These folds and twists are what will create the final patterns on your shirt.

Now you are ready to dye the shirt. Before you begin, put on the rubber gloves. Then mix the dye, water, and salt in the bucket, following the package instructions. Next, dampen the T-shirt. Then dip the parts of the T-shirt to be dyed into the dye solution. Use the stick to stir the solution often. Keep checking the color of the shirt. Remove it when it is the shade you want and hang it up to dry. Be sure to place plenty of newspaper under the drying T-shirt.

- What are the steps explained in the body of this composition?

Try Your Skill Here are some jumbled notes for the body of the composition on how to make stilts. List the steps below in the correct step-by-step order. Add any details you think might be necessary. Keep your work in your folder.

—Wipe off excess stain.
—Attach footholds with screws.
—Measure boards for footholds two feet from one end.
—Sand stilts.
—Saw cube of wood diagonally to make two footholds.
—Brush stain on sanded stilts.

Keep This in Mind

- In the introduction, present your topic. Make one sentence serve as the topic sentence for the composition.
- Develop the body with a step-by-step explanation.
- Develop the concluding paragraph from the final step of the process.

Now Write Look at the processes you listed in **Now Write** in **How Do You Do?** Choose one process you could explain easily. List details for each step in the process. Write the body of an explanatory *how* composition. Label your paper **Step It Up.** Put your work into your folder.

Part 3

The Final Step

Using Transitions

Here's the Idea Use transitions to make the step-by-step order clear in an explanatory *how* composition. Transitional words and phrases show the time order of the steps. Use transitions similar to the transitions used for narratives. Here are some examples:

first	to begin with	before	before
second	the first step	to start	during this time
third	the next step	when	at the same time
next	after that	finally	as soon as
then	at last	last	afterwards

Transitions help make clear the order within a paragraph. Transitions also help to link paragraphs. They work like a bridge to carry the reader from the main idea of one paragraph to the main idea of the next paragraph.

Check It Out Here are the introduction and conclusion of the composition on tie-dying. First, review the body of the explanation in the last lesson. Find the transitions used within each paragraph. Find the transitions that link the three paragraphs. How are the introduction and conclusion linked to the body of the composition?

Introduction

Nowadays, buying new clothes is very expensive. Fortunately, there are a couple of ways for you to improve your wardrobe without spending much money. One method is to make your own clothes. Another is to change some of the clothes you already own. Tie-dyeing, for example, is a clever way to create a new look, especially for old T-shirts.

Conclusion

You will probably be pleased with your colorful new T-shirt. Later on, you may want to experiment again. Next time, try different designs and colors to match other clothes. Tie-dyed shirts can become a practical and creative addition to your wardrobe.

- Are there any transitions used within the introduction or the conclusion? What are they?
- Are there any transitions that link the introduction or the conclusion to the body? What are they?

Try Your Skill From your folder, take out the work you did in **Try Your Skill** in the last lesson, **Step It Up.** Reread the steps in the process of making stilts. What transitional words and phrases would make the order clear? On your paper, rewrite each step, adding transitions.

Keep This in Mind

- Time transitions help make the order of each paragraph clear in explanatory *how* compositions.
- Some time transitions link the main idea of one paragraph with the main idea of the next paragraph.

Now Write From your folder, take out the body of the composition you wrote in **Now Write** in **Step It Up.** Add the transitional words you will need within each paragraph.

Write an introduction and a conclusion to your explanatory *how* composition. Add transitions between paragraphs.

Rewrite, if necessary.

Make a final copy of your composition. Proofread it carefully.

Label your paper **The Final Step.** Put your work into your folder.

The Explanatory Composition

Telling *Why*

Part 1

For or Against?

Stating an Opinion

Here's the Idea An explanatory *why* composition presents an opinion. You may want to explain why something is so, or why something should be changed. Suppose you believe that the automobile industry should produce electric cars. You can write an explanatory *why* composition that presents a convincing argument.

To find **topics** for explanatory *why* compositions, ask yourself what issues you feel strongly about. For instance, how do you feel about pets, work-study programs, or solar energy? What is your school, your community, or the United States doing right? What are they doing wrong? What should be changed? Choose a topic that is important to you.

Once you have chosen a topic, jot down **notes** for your composition. Think about why you feel as you do. In your **introduction,** plan to present your opinion. In the **body** of your composition, plan to support your opinion with reasons or facts. In the **conclusion,** plan to sum up your argument.

Check It Out Read these notes for an explanatory *why* composition.

Topic: Deposits should be required on soft drink bottles.

Introduction: people litter with bottles
deposits discourage littering, solve problems

Body: reasons

1. save money
   less for bottles, beverages, litter cleanup
2. save energy
   materials, making bottles, recycling

3. save environment
less litter, today's cities, future generations

Conclusion bottle deposits save money, energy, environment

- Is this topic suitable for an explanatory *why* composition?
- Is an opinion stated clearly and directly?
- Can these notes be developed into a composition?

Try Your Skill Below are some topics too general for explanatory *why* compositions. Choose three of them. Then narrow each topic and state your opinion about it. Be as clear, direct, and forceful as you can. Circle the opinion that you feel strongest about. Keep your work in your folder.

television	equal rights for women	dress codes
education	movie ratings	the environment
curfews	legal driving age	

Keep This in Mind

- An explanatory *why* composition presents an opinion.
- State your opinion clearly and directly.
- In your notes, jot down your opinion and the supporting reasons or facts. Organize your notes for the introduction, the body, and the conclusion.

Now Write Think of several strong opinions that you have. List them on your paper. Choose one opinion that can be developed in an explanatory *why* compositon.

State your topic in one clear, forceful sentence.

Plan your composition by making your pre-writing notes. List the reasons you will use to support your opinion. Organize your notes into the introduction, the body, and the conclusion. Label your paper **For or Against?** and put it into your folder.

Part 2 # With Good Reasons

Supporting an Opinion

Here's the Idea An opinion without strong supporting evidence is like a boat without a bottom. There's nothing to keep it afloat. To convince people that your opinion is sound, you need to present strong, specific reasons or facts.

Whether your opinion is convincing or not depends on how well you present supporting evidence. The most effective way to organize your supporting evidence is to give the weakest reason or fact first and the strongest reason or fact last; that is, **in order of importance.** In this way, readers are left with the most convincing evidence fresh in their minds.

The **body** of an explanatory *why* composition should present the supporting evidence you have organized. Develop each important reason or fact in a separate paragraph. Make sure that your reasons or facts are presented in order of their importance, from the least important to the most important.

Check It Out Read the body of the composition about requiring deposits for soft drink bottles.

> The first reason for requiring a deposit is that we could save money. Since returnable bottles can be recycled, the costs of making bottles would be less. As a result, beverages themselves would cost less. Because of the deposit, people would return empty bottles. This would also lower the cost of cleaning up litter everywhere.
>
> A more important reason for requiring deposits on bottles is that we would save energy. Glass bottles are made mostly by melting sand, soda, and lime. Since the heating furnaces must be at temperatures of about 3000° F. (1649° C), the process of making glass bottles requires huge amounts of energy. There are

more than 100 bottling plants located in thirty states. These plants produce about forty billion bottles a year. By recycling returnable bottles, we could save much energy.

The most important reason for requiring bottle deposits is that we would save our environment. Two billion tons of solid wastes pollute the environment each year. A large part of the pollution we see is the litter of bottles. Sidewalks and roadsides, especially in cities, are spoiled by litter. We could lessen that, too.

- Is the opinion supported by specific facts or reasons?
- Is the evidence given in order of importance, from the least important to the most important?

Try Your Skill In your folder, turn back to your work in **Try Your Skill** in the last lesson, **For or Against?** Find the topic that you circled. On your paper, copy your opinion. List three specific reasons or facts to support your opinion. Then arrange your evidence in order of importance, from the least important to the most important. Keep your work in your folder.

Keep This in Mind

- In the body of an explanatory *why* composition, give specific reasons to support your opinion.
- The most convincing way to organize supporting evidence is in order of importance. Start with the least important and end with the most important.

Now Write From your folder, take out your paper labeled **For or Against?** Review the notes you have written for an explanatory *why* composition.

Reread the reasons or facts you have listed to support your opinion. Arrange them in order of importance. Then write the body of your composition, using the reasons or facts. Label your paper **With Good Reasons.** Keep it in your folder.

Part 3 # Furthermore

Using Transitions

Here's the Idea In an explanatory *why* composition, two kinds of transitional words and phrases are useful. One kind of transition helps you to present reasons or facts in order of importance. It includes such words as *the first reason, second, most important,* and *finally*. This kind of transition is most useful in the body of your composition.

The other kind of transition helps you to state your reasons or facts. It includes such words as *because, so, since, therefore,* and *as a result*. This kind of transition is most useful in the introduction and conclusion where you must state your opinion in a direct and convincing way.

In your **introduction,** it is most important to state your opinion clearly. One sentence should serve as the topic sentence for the whole composition. Be as direct and specific as possible.

In your **conclusion,** it is important to restate your opinion. You need to sum up your argument in an effective way. It is your final chance to convince your readers.

Check It Out Read the introduction and the conclusion to the composition about bottle deposits.

Introduction

Americans love soft drinks. In fact, we consume about 250 bottles of soda per person each year in the U.S. What happens to all those bottles? Unfortunately, many of them end up on the ground. However, if a deposit were required on all soft drink bottles, we could solve several major problems.

Conclusion

If a deposit were required on all soft drink bottles, we Americans could still continue to enjoy our favorite sodas. However, we would also be helping to save money, our supply of energy, and our environment.

- Does the introduction state an opinion clearly?
- Which transitions help to state the reasons?
- Does the conclusion sum up the argument?

Try Your Skill Write the transitions in this paragraph.

Our city should install a special express lane for car pools on the freeway. The first reason for this change is that it would encourage more people to share rides. As a result, there would be less traffic on the road. More important, fewer cars being driven would help save gasoline. Finally, fewer rush hour traffic jams would result in fewer accidents. Creating an express lane would have a major effect on everyone in White Plains.

Keep This in Mind

- State your opinion clearly in your introduction. Write one sentence that serves as the topic sentence for the whole composition.
- Use transitions that state the reasons and their order of importance.
- Sum up your argument in the conclusion.

Now Write Review the notes you wrote for an explanatory *why* composition in **For or Against?** Think about how you feel about your topic. Write an introduction for your composition.

Read the body of the composition you wrote in **With Good Reasons.** Now write a conclusion that sums up your argument.

Read your entire composition. Have you used transitions that show your reasons and their order of importance? Rewrite, if necessary. Make a final copy of your composition. Proofread. Label your paper **Furthermore.** Keep your work in your folder.

Writing Letters

Part 1

Write Soon

Writing a Friendly Letter

Here's the Idea Do you write many letters? A **friendly letter** is one that you write to someone you know. It should be interesting and easy to read. A friendly letter gives you the chance to write about what is important to you and interesting to a friend. Make your letter detailed and lively.

The form for a friendly letter has five main parts: the *heading*, the *salutation* or the greeting, the *body* or main part, the *closing*, and the *signature*.

The **heading** tells where you are. When you are writing, the heading appears in the upper right corner of the page. It usually includes two lines for the address and one for the date.

The **salutation** is the way you greet your friend. It is written on the next line and begins at the left margin.

The **body,** the main part of the letter, starts on the next line. It is in this part of your letter that you talk to your friend. You want to make your friend feel as though you were there in person. The first word of the body is indented. Each new paragraph of the body is indented, too.

The **closing** is the way you leave your friend. It is written on the line below the last sentence of the body. The closing should line up with the first line of the heading.

The **signature** is the last part of your letter. Skip a line after the closing and sign your name in line with the first word of the closing. Use your first name as your signature whenever you are writing a friendly letter to someone you know well. Otherwise, sign your full name.

Begin every main part of your letter with a capitalized word. Put a comma after the salutation and the closing.

Check It Out Read the following friendly letter.

1321 Hillcrest Avenue
Boulder, Colorado 80309
June 3, 1979

Dear Donna,

Your letter arrived this morning. It was good hearing from you. You certainly sound excited about astronomy, your new hobby. I've always wanted to know more about the stars. You can see quite a few tonight because the sky is so clear.

I'm reading up on amateur radio. There's certainly a lot to know in order to get a license! I think I'll start out with just a short-wave receiver. I hope to buy a kit and make it myself. It should be quite a challenge.

Please let me know when you've finished building your telescope. Can you bring it with you when your family comes to visit? Write again soon.

Yours truly,
Mark

- What details make this letter interesting?
- Identify the five parts of this letter.

Try Your Skill Think of one event that has happened during the last week that you would enjoy telling a friend about. Try to recall as many details as you can, including how you felt about it. Imagine that you are writing a friendly letter. Write three or four sentences describing the event.

Keep This in Mind

- Friendly letters should be detailed, interesting, and easy to read.
- Friendly letters should follow the correct form. The heading, salutation, body, closing, and signature should each be written correctly.

Now Write Write the title of this lesson, **Write Soon,** on your paper. Then write a friendly letter to a friend or relative. Try to include interesting details. Use the correct form.

When you have finished, put the letter into your folder. You may want to copy the letter so that you can mail it.

Part 2

Handle with Care

Preparing Letters for the Mail

Here's the Idea When you have written your letter, fold it neatly. Use an envelope that matches the width of the stationery. Insert the letter into the envelope and seal the envelope.

Follow these steps for preparing your envelope:

1. Address the envelope. Add your return address.
2. Check all numbers to make sure they are in the proper order.
3. Include the correct ZIP code and state abbreviation.
4. Put a stamp on your envelope.

Taking time to prepare the envelope correctly is an important step in letter writing. Always check letters and packages for accuracy. If you need more information, call your post office.

Check It Out Look at the envelope below.

Nora Barnes
18 Watson Place
Wichita, KS 67211

Joe Delgado
85 Elm Street
Philadelphia, PA 19116

- To whom is the letter being sent? Who sent the letter?
- How could you check to be sure that the state abbreviations and ZIP codes are correct?

Try Your Skill On your paper, draw an envelope in the shape of a rectangle. Address it as though Louise Holmes were sending it to Peter Kaufman. Peter's address is 16 Wilson Street in San Francisco, California. Peter's ZIP code is 94105. Louise is writing from her home at 231 Sayers Place, Palo Alto, California. Her ZIP code is 94303.

Keep This in Mind

- Prepare your letters correctly. Fold your letter neatly, and use an envelope that matches the width of the stationery.
- Check addresses for neatness and accuracy. Check abbreviations of states and correct ZIP codes.
- Put your return address on the envelope.

Now Write Write the title of this lesson, **Handle with Care,** on your paper. Draw a rectangle about the size of an envelope. Address it to the friend you wrote to in the last lesson. Make sure you include your return address.

Put your work into your folder when you are done. You may want to copy the information onto a real envelope and mail it.

Special Occasions

Writing Social Notes

Here's the Idea Social notes are written for specific reasons on special occasions. Invitations and thank-you notes are social notes. They are both short forms of friendly letters. They have the same five-part form. The heading may be shortened, however, to include only the date.

If you send an **invitation,** you must include details about *what, when,* and *where.* Make sure you include any special information a guest might need to know about the occasion. If you receive an invitation, you should reply as soon as possible. Tell whether or not you will attend.

You may also send thank-you notes. One kind of **thank-you** note is usually written after you have received a gift. If your gift was sent by mail, a thank-you note tells the sender that the gift arrived. If you liked the gift, tell the sender. In any case, always thank someone for his or her kindness.

A second kind of thank-you note is a **bread-and-butter** note. This social note is written to thank someone for his or her hospitality. If you stayed overnight at someone's house, you would write a thank-you note.

When you write either of these kinds of social notes, show your appreciation to the other person. Also be sure to write your notes as soon as you receive a gift or someone's hospitality.

Check It Out Read the social note on page 166. Then answer these questions.

- What kind of social note is this? How is the form of this letter different from the friendly letter shown on page 161?
- What words and phrases are used to show appreciation?

April 12, 1979

Dear Aunt May,

Many thanks for the leather wallet you sent. I really appreciate your thinking of me each birthday. As you know, I often carry money around for lunch, busfare, and school supplies. Having a wallet will help to keep me from losing everything.

Thanks again for your present.

Love,
Jean

Try Your Skill Your best friend Reuben gave you a gift certificate good for one record album at a local store. Write a note to Reuben thanking him for the gift certificate.

Keep This in Mind

- Social notes, like invitations and thank-you notes, are short forms of friendly letters.
- An invitation should tell *what, when,* and *where.*
- Thank-you notes thank people for the thoughtfulness of their gifts and their hospitality.

Now Write Write the title of this lesson, **Special Occasions,** on your paper. Now write an invitation, a thank-you note, or a bread-and-butter note to someone you know. Make up details. Use the correct form. Put your work into your folder.

Part 4

Dear Sir or Madam:

Writing a Business Letter

Here's the Idea If you want to request information, order a product by mail, or complain about a product to the manufacturer, you will be writing a **business letter.**

The two types of business letter forms are *modified block form* and *block form*. In the modified block form the paragraphs are indented, and the closing and signature are in line with the heading, just as in a friendly letter. This form may be used for both handwritten and typed business letters.

The *block* form for a business letter is used only when the letter is typewritten. All the parts of the letter begin at the left margin. The paragraphs are not indented. Instead, there is a double space between paragraphs.

In both forms, the address you are writing to is placed above the salutation. Begin this address at the left margin. If you are writing to a specific person, use *Dear* and the person's name in the salutation. Otherwise, use a general greeting such as *Dear Sir or Madam*. All salutations begin two lines after the inside address and end with a colon (:).

It is important to be brief and to the point in a business letter. It is also a good idea to make a copy of business letters for your records. If you make a copy, be sure to mail the original.

Check It Out Look at the letter on page 168. Then answer these questions.

- What is the purpose of this business letter?
- Identify the six parts of the letter.
- In what form is this letter written?

90 Robinson Avenue
New Orleans, Louisiana 70118
March 9, 1980

The Greylock Company
1570 Washington Street
Columbus, Ohio 43209

Dear Sir or Madam:

In this month's issue of Sky World I read your advertisement for model airplane kits. The ad also offered a free catalog. I would like you to send me the free catalog. Please send it to me at the address given above.

Sincerely yours,

Mario Rizzo

Try Your Skill On your paper, write a short letter of complaint to the following imaginary company: Colorful Clothes Company, 35 Wildwood Drive, Atlanta, Georgia 30333. Tell them that the personalized T-shirt you ordered two months ago has not arrived. In your letter, be sure to mention the size, color, and style of T-shirt you requested. Also, be sure to mention the exact spelling of your name as you wanted it to be printed. Use today's date and your own name and address.

Keep This in Mind

- Business letters are written to request information, order products, or complain about a product. They should be brief and to the point. Keep a copy for yourself.
- There are six parts to the form of a business letter. They are *heading, inside address, salutation, body, closing,* and *signature.*
- *Block* and *modified block* are two forms for a business letter.

Now Write Find an advertisement in a magazine or newspaper for free information or a free booklet. On your paper, write the title of this lesson, **Dear Sir or Madam:** Write a business letter asking for the advertised item. Write the letter in one of the correct forms for a business letter.

Put your work into your folder. You may want to copy the letter and send it later.

Part 5

Information, Please

Writing Letters of Request

Here's the Idea You can receive valuable information by writing a business **letter of request.** Companies are usually pleased to send information about their products. Schools and camps will send catalogs. Local officials in most towns will send maps, brochures, and sightseeing information, if you ask.

A well written letter will usually receive a quick reply. Remember that you are asking someone to do something for you. Therefore, make sure your letter is polite and neat.

Make sure that your letter contains all the information that the company or person needs in order to send you what you request. If you are writing to a local chamber of commerce for information, tell them why you want to know about the town. Explain your request briefly and clearly. Be specific.

Also, make sure the letter is sent to the right place. Many times you will find the name and address in an advertisement. Sometimes, though, you may have to do a little detective work. If you received a radio and want a parts list or wiring diagram, where should you write? Look carefully on the box and on the radio itself. Somewhere you will find the name and address of the company. If you write to *Customer Service* at that address, you should hear from someone. Other good places to find the right address are at the end of instruction manuals, on tags, or in the yellow pages of a telephone book.

Check It Out Read the letter of request on the next page.

- Is this letter of request brief and polite?
- Is all the necessary information requested?

21 Clark Street
Chicago, Illinois 60611
October 10, 1978

Guide Dog Foundation for the Blind
109-19 72nd Avenue
Forest Hills, New York 11375

Dear Sir or Madam:

I am writing a report on Labrador retrievers and I understand that they are often used as guide dogs for the blind. Please send me information telling where you get the dogs, how they are trained, and how a blind person gets a guide dog. It is necessary that I receive the information by November 1 for my report.

Very truly yours,
Jessica Gould

Try Your Skill Write a letter to the Lefthander's League, P.O. Box 89, New Milford, New Jersey 07646. Tell them that you would like information about joining their society. Find out what dues, if any, are charged, and what you need to do in order to join. Use the modified block form for this letter.

Keep This in Mind

- Letters of request should be brief and polite.
- Ask only for the information you need. Be specific.

Now Write Label your paper **Information, Please.** Plan a letter of request that you will actually mail. Write your letter. Make a copy. Keep one copy in your folder. Mail the other.

WRITING SECTION 18

Using a Dictionary

Part 1

Word for Word

Using a Dictionary

Here's the Idea A **dictionary** is a reference book containing both a list of words and information about those words. The listing itself is valuable because it shows you that a word exists. The information shows you how to use words correctly.

In a dictionary, the words are listed in alphabetical order. Words that begin with *a* come before words that begin with *b*, and so on. If two words begin with the same letter, they are alphabetized by the second letter. If the first and second letters are the same, look at the next letter. These words are in alphabetical order: *on, once, one, tea, teach,* and *team.*

Dictionaries are not all alike. Some list words for special fields. For example, you can find a dictionary of medical terms or a crossword puzzle dictionary. Some dictionaries list the words in one language and the explanations in another.

Some of the biggest dictionaries are unabridged. That means they contain nearly all the words of the language. Most of the time a desk or pocket-size dictionary, which is abridged, will contain the information you need.

The abbreviations, symbols, and organization may be different in different dictionaries. For this reason, you need to become familiar with the dictionary you use. Study the explanations in the front of the dictionary that tell you what the abbreviations and symbols stand for.

Check It Out Look at the bottom portion of a dictionary page on page 175. Answer these questions.

- How are the words listed?
- What special symbols are used?
- What words are new to you?

☆**chic·le** (chik′'l) ***n.*** [AmSp. < Nahuatl *chictli*] a gumlike substance made from the milky juice of the sapodilla tree, used in making chewing gum
Chic·o·pee (chik′ə pē) [< AmInd., lit., swift river] city in SW Mass.: pop. 67,000
chic·o·ry (chik′ə rē) ***n., pl.*** **-ries** [< OFr. < L. < Gr. *kichora*] **1.** a weedy plant of the composite family, with blue flowers: the leaves are used in salads **2.** its root, roasted and ground for mixing with coffee or for use as a coffee substitute
chide (chīd) ***vt., vi.*** **chid′ed** or **chid** (chid), **chid′ed** or **chid** or **chid·den** (chid′'n), **chid′ing** [OE. *cidan*] to scold, esp. in a mild way —**chid′ing·ly** ***adv.***
chief (chēf) ***n.*** [< OFr. < L. *caput*, the head: for IE. base see HEAD] **1.** the head or leader of a group, organization, etc. **2.** *Heraldry* the upper third of a shield —***adj.*** **1.** highest in rank, office, etc. [the *chief* executive] **2.** main; principal [the *chief* advantages] —**in chief** in the chief position [commander *in chief*]

CHICORY

☆**Chief Executive** the President of the U.S.
chief justice the presiding judge of a court made up of several judges
chief·ly (chēf′lē) ***adv.*** **1.** most of all; above all [*chiefly* interested in science] **2.** mainly; mostly [a melon is *chiefly* water] —***adj.*** of or like a chief
child·ish (-ish) ***adj.*** **1.** of or like a child **2.** not fit for an adult; immature; silly —see ***SYN.*** at CHILDLIKE —**child′ish·ly** ***adv.*** —**child′ish·ness** ***n.***
child labor the regular, full-time employment in factories, stores, offices, etc. of children who are less than a legally defined age: in the U.S., it is against Federal law to employ children under the age of 16 (or under 18 in occupations that are dangerous)
child·like (-līk′) ***adj.*** like a child, esp. in being innocent, trusting, etc. —**child′like′ness** ***n.***
SYN.—**childlike** and **childish** are both applied to persons of any age in referring to qualities considered typical of a child, **childlike** suggesting the favorable qualities such as innocence, honesty, curiosity, zest, etc., and **childish** the unfavorable ones such as immaturity, foolishness, lack of self-control, self-centeredness, etc.
chil·dren (chil′drən) ***n.*** *pl. of* CHILD
children of Israel the Jews; Hebrews
child's play (chīldz) anything simple to do
Chil·e (chil′ē; *Sp.* chē′le) country on the SW coast of S. America: 286,397 sq. mi.; pop. 9,780,000; cap. Santiago —**Chil′e·an** ***adj., n.***
☆**chil·e** (chil′ē) ***n.*** *same as* CHILI
☆**chil·e con car·ne** (chil′ē kən kär′nē, kän′) *same as* CHILI CON CARNE
Chile saltpeter native sodium nitrate, esp. as found naturally in Chile and Peru
☆**chil·i** (chil′ē) ***n., pl.*** **chil′ies** [MexSp. < Nahuatl *chilli*] **1.** the dried pod of red pepper, a very hot seasoning **2.** the tropical American plant, of the nightshade family, that bears this pod **3.** *same as* CHILI CON CARNE

fat, āpe, cär; ten, ēven; is, bīte; gō, hôrn, tōōl, look; oil, out; up, fur; get; joy; yet; chin; she; thin, *th*en; zh, leisure; ŋ, ring; ə for *a* in *ago*, *e* in *agent*, *i* in *sanity*, *o* in *comply*, *u* in *focus*; ' as in *able* (ā′b'l); Fr. bàl; ë, Fr. coeur; ö, Fr. feu; Fr. mo*n*; ô, Fr. coq; ü, Fr. duc; *r*, Fr. cri; H, G. ich; kh, G. doch; ‡foreign; ☆ Americanism; < derived from. See inside front cover.

Try Your Skill Write each group of words in alphabetical order. Then, use a dictionary to find a word to add to each list.

1. turn, tape, teeth, tile, toe, try
2. thank, there, the, thaw, theater, thin
3. throw, throat, three, thread, through, throne

Keep This in Mind

- Dictionaries are reference books that list words alphabetically and give explanations for each word.
- Use a dictionary when you're reading and writing.
- Become familiar with the abbreviations, symbols, and organization of the dictionaries you use.

Now Write Label your paper **Word for Word.** Find ten words that begin with the same letter. Alphabetize them and write a definition for each. Use a dictionary.

Part 2

Follow the Signs

Using Guide Words

Here's the Idea Open a dictionary and look at the top of any page. You will see two words written in large, bold print. They are **guide words.** The guide word on the left is the same as the first entry word on the page. The guide word on the right is the same as the last entry word on the page. All the other words on the page are arranged alphabetically between the guide words. Look at the top portion of this dictionary page.

mushroom 632 **musty**

to start or to go faster —*vi.* to travel on foot over snow, usually with a dog sled —*n.* a journey by mushing

mush·room (mush′rōōm′, -room′) *n.* [OFr. *moisseron* < LL. *mussirio*] **1.** any of various rapid-growing, fleshy fungi having a stalk with an umbrellalike top; popularly, any edible variety, as distinguished from the poisonous ones (*toadstools*) **2.** anything like a mushroom in shape or rapid growth —*adj.* **1.** of or made with mushrooms **2.** like a mushroom in shape or rapid growth —*vi.* **1.** to grow or spread rapidly **2.** to flatten out at the end so as to resemble a mushroom

mush·y (mush′ē) *adj.* **mush′i·er, mush′i·est** **1.** like mush; thick and soft **2.** [Colloq.] affectionate or sentimental in a way that seems silly or overdone —**mush′i·ly** *adv.* —**mush′i·ness** *n.*

mu·sic (myōō′zik) *n.* [< OFr. < L. < Gr. *mousikē* (*technē*), musical (art) < *mousa*, a Muse] **1.** the art of putting tones together in various melodies, rhythms, and harmonies to form compositions for singing or for playing on instruments **2.** the tones so arranged, or their arrangement **3.** any rhythmic sequence of pleasing sounds [the *music* of the birds] **4.** *a*) a musical composition, esp. in the form of a written or printed score *b*) the musical compositions of a particular style, period, or composer **5.** ability to respond to or take pleasure in music —☆**face the music** [Colloq.] to accept the consequences, however unpleasant —**set to music** to compose music for (a poem, etc.)

mu·si·cal (myōō′zi k'l) *adj.* **1.** of or for the creation or performance of music **2.** melodious or harmonious **3.** fond of or skilled in music **4.** set to music —*n.* ☆a theatrical or film production with dialogue and a musical score with popular songs and dances: in full, **musical comedy** (or **play**, or **drama**) —**mu′si·cal′i·ty** (-kal′ə tē) *n.* —**mu′si·cal·ly** *adv.*

☆**musk·rat** (musk′rat′) *n., pl.* **-rats′, -rat′**: see PLURAL, II, D, 1 **1.** a N. American rodent living in water and having glossy brown fur, webbed hind feet, and a musklike odor **2.** its fur

MUSKRAT (body 9–13 in. long; tail 7–11 in. long)

musk·y (mus′kē) *adj.* **musk′i·er, musk′i·est** of, like, or smelling of musk —**musk′i·ness** *n.*

Mus·lim (muz′ləm, mooz′-) *n., adj. same as* MOSLEM

mus·lin (muz′lin) *n.* [< Fr. < It. *mussolino* < *Mussolo*, Mosul, city in Iraq] a strong, often sheer cotton cloth of plain weave; esp., a heavy variety used for sheets, pillowcases, etc.

muss (mus) *n.* [prob. var. of MESS] **1.** [Now Rare] a mess **2.** [Old Slang or Dial.] a squabble —*vt.* to make messy or untidy; disarrange (often with *up*)

mus·sel (mus′'l) *n.* [< OE., ult. < L. *musculus*, mussel, MUSCLE] any of various bivalve mollusks; specif., *a*) an edible saltwater variety *b*) a large freshwater variety with a pearly shell formerly made into buttons

Mus·set (mü se′), **(Louis Charles) Al·fred de** (ȧl fred′ də) 1810–57; Fr. poet & writer

Mus·so·li·ni (mōōs′sô lē′nē; *E.* moos′ə lē′nē, mus′-), **Be·ni·to** (be nē′tô) 1883–1945; It. dictator; Fascist prime minister of Italy (1922–43): executed

Mus·sorg·sky (moo sôrg′skē), **Mo·dest Pe·tro·vich** (mô dyest′ pyi trô′vich) 1839–81; Russ. composer

Mus·sul·man (mus′'l mən) *n., pl.* **-mans** [< Per. < Ar. *muslim*] [Now Rare] a Moslem

Guide words tell you at a glance the range of words that appear on the page. They make it quicker and easier to find words. Refer to them as you flip the dictionary pages in search of your word. Keep looking for guide words that are more and more like the word you want.

Check It Out Look at the portion of a dictionary page at the left.

- What are the guide words for this page? Would you find the word *museum* on this page? Which way would you turn the pages to find *muscle?*

Try Your Skill Write the following sets of guide words on your paper: *dinner/dirty, disagree/discover, few/figure,* and *file/fire.* Write each word below under the appropriate set of guide words. Then put your lists in alphabetical order.

fight	disc	discomfort	fiction
discover	diploma	direct	fiddle
direction	field	film	dinosaur
final	discount	dirt	disconnect
fine	fifth	directory	filter
disaster	fill	fierce	finish

Keep This in Mind

- Dictionary guide words show the alphabetical range of words on each page. The left guide word is the same as the first word on the page. The right guide word is the same as the last word on the page.

Now Write If you were writing a composition about outer space, you would need to look up the following words: *astronaut, galaxy, meteor, nebula, plant,* and *satellite.* On your paper, write the title of this lesson, **Follow the Signs.** List the words above. Find each word in the dictionary. Next to each word, write the guide words that appear at the top of the page where the word is found. Then write six sentences. Use one of the words in each sentence.

Put your work into your folder.

Part 3 **Read All About It**

Reading a Dictionary Entry

Here's the Idea A dictionary entry explains the meaning of a word. An entry also shows a great deal of other helpful information about a word. Not every entry will include all information. Not every dictionary will arrange the information in the same order. However, most dictionaries will give you the following information in a single entry:

The **entry word** itself is in bold type and divided into syllables. For example, *neighborhood* is entered as **neigh·bor·hood.**

The **pronunciation** of the word often appears inside parentheses. Symbols help you to sound out the word. An accent mark tells you which syllable to stress.

The **part of speech** is given by an abbreviation in bold print. For example, *noun* is abbreviated ***n.,*** *adverb* is abbreviated ***adv.***

If a word has **special forms** or **endings,** they will be included next in the entry. For example, the entry for the irregular verb *run* includes the forms **ran, run,** and **running.**

The **origin,** or **history,** of a word is given next, often in brackets. Symbols and abbreviations are used. The symbol < means "came from." Look up unfamiliar abbreviations in the complete list at the front of the dictionary.

Definitions are given in a numbered list. Usually the most common definition is given first.

A word may have a meaning that is informal. This is a colloquial meaning. The dictionary also indicates slang, which is very informal, popular language.

Synonyms and **antonyms** may also be listed. Some entries may include a *synonymy*—a group of synonyms and their shades of meaning. Or, the notation "**SYN.** *see*" may refer you to a synonymy in another entry.

Check It Out Look at the dictionary entry below.

> **gar•den** (gär′d'n) ***n.*** [< ONormFr. *gardin* < Frank.: for IE. base see GIRD] **1.** a piece of ground, usually close to a house, for the growing of fruits, flowers, or vegetables **2.** an area of fertile, well-cultivated land: also **garden spot** **3.** [*often pl.*] a parklike place for public enjoyment, sometimes having special displays of animals or plants **—*vi.*** to work in or take care of a garden, lawn, etc.**—*vt.*** to make a garden of **—*adj.*** **1.** of, for, or grown in a garden **2.** ordinary; commonplace *[a garden* variety of poet*]* **—lead (someone) down the garden path** to mislead or deceive (someone)— **gar′den•er *n.***

- How many syllables are there in *garden?* Where is the pronunciation given? What part of speech is *garden?* Is it used as any other part of speech? From what languages did the word come? What is the most common definition?

Try Your Skill Turn back to the sample dictionary page in the last lesson, **Follow the Signs.** Answer the following questions.

1. How do you pronounce *mussel?*
2. What are the parts of speech of *mushroom?*
3. What are the other forms of the adjective *mushy?*
4. Where does the word *muslin* come from?
5. What is the most common definition of *mushroom?*
6. What is an informal meaning of *mushy?*

Keep This in Mind

- A dictionary entry contains the meanings of a word and other helpful information.
- Dictionary entries may differ from book to book.

Now Write Label your paper **Read All About It.** Using a dictionary, find examples of words with these characteristics:

1. four syllables
2. two pronunciations
3. three parts of speech
4. have come from France

Write the examples on your paper. Keep your work in your folder.

Part 4

A Good Fit

Finding the Meaning of a Word

Here's the Idea What would you do if a word has several meanings listed in a dictionary? How can you tell which is the right one? In most cases, the sentence in which you found the word, the context, will help you out.

In each sentence below, the context helps you to determine the meaning of the word *eyes*.

1. Close your *eyes* and count to ten. (In this context, *eyes* means "organs of sight.")

2. The *eyes* of three hurricanes have passed over our house. (In this context, eyes means "calm centers.")

3. Can you thread the *eyes* of needles? (In this context *eyes* means "holes.")

First read through the definitions given in the dictionary. Then try to find the meaning that fits the particular context.

Check It Out Read this sentence and dictionary entry.

Will your bicycle fit in this *space?*

space (spas) ***n.*** [< OFr. < L. *spatium*] **1.** *a*) the area that stretches in all directions, has no limits, and contains all things in the universe *b*) *same as* OUTER SPACE **2.** *a*) the distance, expanse, or area between, over, or within things [the *space* between desks] *b*) area or room for something [parking *space*; advertising *space* in a newspaper, etc.] **3.** length or period of time [the *space* of a week] ☆**4.** accommodations that can be had or reserved on a train, airplane, etc. **5.** *Math.* a set of points or elements that can be represented in a coordinate system by a single real number, a pair of numbers, etc. **6.** *Music* the open area between any two lines of a staff **7.** *Printing* *a*) a blank piece of type metal used to separate words, letters, etc. *b*) the area left vacant by this in a printed or typed line —***adj.*** of space, esp. outer space —***vt.*** **spaced, spac′ing** to arrange with spaces in between [trees *spaced* evenly; concerts *spaced* throughout the season] —**space′less** ***adj.*** —**spac′er** ***n.***

- Which definition of *space* fits the context of this sentence?

Try Your Skill Look at this dictionary entry for the word *grade*. You can see that there are many meanings. Some meanings are for *grade* as a noun, and some are for *grade* as a verb.

Each of the meanings is used in one of the sentences that follows. Write the number of each sentence. After it, write the meaning that matches the use of the word *grade*.

> **grade** (grad) ***n.*** [Fr. < L. *gradus*, a step < *gradi*, to step < IE. base *ghredh-*, to stride] **1.** any of the stages in a series; step; degree *[*civil service jobs arranged in *grades]* **2.** *a*) a degree in a scale of quality, rank, etc. *[grade* A eggs*]* *b*) any of the official ranks or ratings of officers or enlisted men *[*an army colonel and a navy captain are in *grade* 0-6*]* *c*) an accepted standard or level *[*up to *grade]* *d*) a group of the same rank, merit, etc. ☆**3.** *a*) the degree of rise or descent of a slope, as of a road *b*) the slope itself *[*climbing a steep *grade]* **4.** the ground level around a building ☆**5.** a division in a school curriculum, usually equal to one year ☆**6.** a mark or rating on an examination, in a school course, etc. —***vt.*** **grad′ed, grad′ing** **1.** to arrange in grades; sort *[*to *grade* apples*]* ☆**2.** to give a grade (sense 6) to **3.** to gradate ☆**4.** to level or slope (ground) evenly for a road, etc. —***vi.*** **1.** to be of a certain grade **2.** to change gradually *[*green *grading* into blue*]* —☆**make the grade** **1.** to get to the top of a steep incline **2.** to overcome obstacles and succeed

1. Ronnie's grade on the math quiz was 88.
2. Mom bought one dozen extra large grade A eggs.
3. The driver slowed down as she approached the steep grade.
4. My sister Bonnie is in the ninth grade.
5. The sunset you painted is realistic, especially where the yellow grades into orange.

Keep This in Mind

- If you are not sure what a word means, look it up. Read all the definitions of this word. Use the context of the sentence to help you find the appropriate definition.

Now Write Look up the word *run* in the dictionary. Copy five different meanings of *run*. For each meaning, write a sentence. Label your paper **A Good Fit** and put it in your folder.

AUDUBON
CERAMICS MONTHLY

Using the Library

Part 1

A Good Place To Visit

Using the Library

Here's the Idea A library can help you in two ways. It's a good place to find an enjoyable book to read. It's also a good place to find information.

Library books are divided into two groups, **fiction** and **non-fiction.** Fiction books have their own section of shelves. They are arranged alphabetically according to the author's last name. For example, *Old Yeller*, written by Fred Gipson, would be shelved under **G.**

Nonfiction books are arranged according to their subjects. Most libraries use the **Dewey Decimal System.** This system puts nonfiction books into ten major categories, or classes. Each category has its own range of numbers. Each nonfiction book is assigned a number within one of the categories. The ten categories are listed below.

000–099	**General Works**	(encyclopedias, almanacs)
100–199	**Philosophy**	(ethics, psychology, occult)
200–299	**Religion**	(the Bible, mythology)
300–399	**Social Science**	(economics, law, education, government)
400–499	**Language**	(languages, grammars, dictionaries)
500–599	**Science**	(math, biology, astronomy)
600–699	**Useful Arts**	(cooking, sewing, carpentry, television, business)
700–799	**Fine Arts**	(music, sports, paintings, dance)
800–899	**Literature**	(poetry, plays)
900–999	**History**	(biography, travel, geography)

On the spine of each nonfiction book is its **call number.** This number includes the Dewey Decimal number and other information. Look at this example.

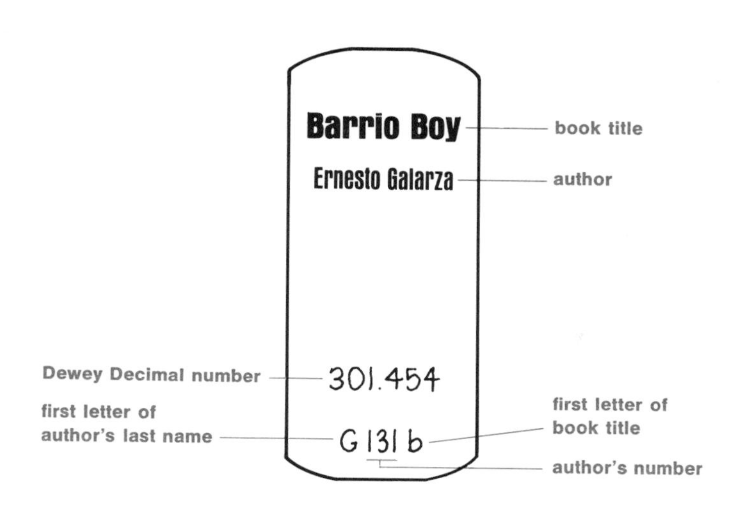

Check It Out Look at the spines of the books represented below.

True Tales of Bold Escapes
Theodore Roscoe
904
R719t

The City Rose
Ruth White Miller

Nina Baker
Ten American Cities Then and Now
917.3
B175t

Fireweed
Jill Paton Walsh

William Hopke
The Encyclopedia of Careers and Vocational Guidance
R
371.42
En 19
1975

Racing Cars
Raymond Francis Yates
629.2
Y27s

In Nueva York
Nicholasa Mohr

The Columbia Encyclopedia
R
031
C723
1963

- How can you tell which books are fiction and which are nonfiction?
- How can you tell what the general category of each nonfiction book is?
- How can the call numbers and authors' names on the spines help you find these books?

Try Your Skill On your paper, make two groups, one for fiction and one for nonfiction. Then, list the books in the appropriate group. Be prepared to explain where they would appear on the shelves.

1. *The Legend of Dr. J.*, Marty Bell 796.32309 Er93zB
2. *Light a Single Candle,* Beverly Butler
3. *Five Were Missing,* Lois Duncan
4. *The Jazz Book,* Joachim Berendt, 785.42BER
5. *Black Like Me,* John Howard Griffin, 326G875b
6. *The Great Gilly Hopkins,* Katherine Paterson

Keep This in Mind

- Library books are divided into two groups, fiction and nonfiction.
- Fiction books are filed alphabetically by the author's last name.
- Nonfiction books are classified in ten major categories. Each nonfiction book has its own call number to show where it can be found on the shelves.

Now Write If you have a favorite author, write his or her name on your paper. If not, find the name of an author. You may want to ask your teacher or a librarian for some help. Write the author's name on your paper.

Next, think of a subject you're interested in. It might be a place, a career, or a hobby. Write it on your paper.

Use your school or public library to find books by the author you have chosen and on the subject you have chosen. Try to find at least three fiction books and three nonfiction books. Write their titles on your paper.

Label your paper **A Good Place To Visit** and put it into your folder.

Part 2 **Card Tricks**

Using the Card Catalog

Here's the Idea The card catalog in the library can help you locate the books you want. You will find every book in the library listed there—three times.

Every book is recorded on an **author card,** a **title card,** and a **subject card.** All three cards give the call number of nonfiction books in the upper left corner. The same number appears on the binding of the book. The number determines where the book is located on the shelves.

Although the information is arranged differently, all three cards contain the same information. All three cards tell the publisher, the date of publication, and the number of pages in the book. A notation tells whether the book has illustrations. Sometimes, there is a short description of the book or mention of other books on the same topic.

On an **author card,** the author's name is at the top. The author's name is written with the last name first. Author cards are arranged alphabetically by the author's last name.

791.45013 **Winn, Marie**
WIN

The plug-in drug, by Marie Winn.
New York: Viking Press, 1977.
xii, 231 p.: ill.; 22 cm.
Includes bibliographical references
and index.

On a **title card,** the title comes first. Title cards are alphabetized according to the first word of the title. If A, *An,* or *The* appear as the first word in a title, look for the title card under the first letter of the second word in the title. The title card for *The Plug-in Drug* would be filed under *P.*

791.45013
WIN

The plug-in drug

The plug-in drug, by Marie Winn. New York: Viking Press, 1977.
xii, 231 p.: ill.; 22 cm.
Includes bibliographical references and index.

On a **subject card,** the subject is at the top. In the card catalog, the subject card is arranged alphabetically by the first word of the subject. The subject may be written in capital letters or in red.

791.45013
WIN

TELEVISION AND CHILDREN

The plug-in drug, by Marie Winn. New York: Viking Press, 1977.
xii, 231 p.: ill.; 22 cm.
Includes bibliographical references and index.

Check It Out Look at the three sample cards shown. Answer the following questions.

- Under what letter of the alphabet would each card be filed?
- Where could you look for more books by Marie Winn?
- Where would you find more books on television?

Try Your Skill Here are the title, author, and call number for a book about television. On your paper, draw three rectangles to represent file cards. Use the information below to make an author card, a title card, and a subject card.

About Television, by Martin Mayer, 338.5544 M452a

Keep This in Mind

- Every book in a library is listed in the card catalog on three different cards—author, title, and subject.
- Each card records the call number, the author, the title, and other important information about the book.

Now Write On your paper, write the title of this lesson, **Card Tricks.** Draw three rectangles to represent file cards. Think of a job that interests you. It might be related to medicine, cars, art, or the military.

In the library, go to the card catalog and find a subject card, an author card, and a title card for books related to your job. Copy the information from the cards onto your paper. Keep your work in your folder.

Part 3

It's All There

Using an Encyclopedia

Here's the Idea One of the most useful sources of general information is an **encyclopedia.** An encyclopedia consists of a set of numbered volumes containing articles on a wide variety of subjects. The subjects of the articles are arranged alphabetically from the first volume through the last. On the spine of each volume, you will find a single letter or guide letters that tell you what subjects are in it. Look at the set of encyclopedias in your school library or public library.

Suppose that you were planning a composition on the effects of television. You might use the *World Book Encyclopedia, Collier's Encyclopedia,* or the *Britannica Junior Encyclopaedia.* Find the appropriate volume and look up "Television." You will find that the pages are marked with guide words, like a dictionary, to help you find your topic quickly.

An encyclopedia article on a major subject is usually organized into parts with subtitles. The article on television might include such parts as "Television in the Home," "The Television Industry," "How Television Works," and "Effects of Television." You may want to read only the parts related to your specific topic. You may also want to look at the end of the article for a list of other related articles in the encyclopedia or for a list of books for further reading.

Different encyclopedias have different reading levels. To find the one that is easiest for you to understand, choose a topic and look it up in several encyclopedias. You may want to ask the librarian for an encyclopedia that would be best for you.

Check It Out Look at the encyclopedia in your school library or public library. Answer the following questions.

- In what volume would you find information about Mexican food? space travel? folk music? Mark Twain?

Try Your Skill Number your paper from 1 to 5. Write the key word in each question below that tells you where to look in the encyclopedia.

1. What factors are important in choosing a career?
2. What unusual forms of transportation are used in other parts of the world?
3. In what state does the Mississippi River begin?
4. Did Edgar Allan Poe write a story called "The Black Cat"?
5. What first-aid treatment is recommended for burns?

Keep This in Mind

- An encyclopedia contains articles on many different subjects. Articles are arranged alphabetically in numbered volumes.
- Use key words to help find articles on your topic. Refer to the appropriate subtitle in an article to find specific information about your topic.
- Use an encyclopedia that you can read easily.

Now Write On your paper, write the title of this lesson, **It's All There.** Find an encyclopedia article on the job you chose in **Now Write** in the last lesson. List the following information: the name of the encyclopedia where you found the article, the number and guide letters of the volume, the guide words on the page, any related articles, and the title of any books on the subject. Put your work into your folder.

Write Again

In the preceding lessons, each Part taught you a new skill. In the following eleven pages you will find additional exercises to help you improve those skills. As you finish each lesson, your teacher may assign one of these additional exercises to give you more practice in writing. The exercises are interesting and you will most likely enjoy them. Give them your best effort.

Words: Developing Your Vocabulary

Part 1 **Alive and Well** What is your favorite sport? List the names of five sports you enjoy. Use a dictionary to find out how each word came into English. Write a sentence using each word.

Part 2 **Say It Again, Sam** List four words related to your favorite sport. They might name equipment or skills. Write a sentence for each word, using definition or restatement in the context. Use a key phrase or punctuation to alert the reader to the context clue.

Part 3 **A Good Example** Choose three of these unusual words: *caftan, furze, koto, papaw, sloop, tautog.* Look them up in the dictionary. Use them in sentences. Make the meaning of the words clear by using example as a context clue.

Part 4 **Like and Unlike** Use three of these words in sentences: *lemonade, radio, skateboard, tent, whale.* Write two sentences using comparison as a context clue. Then write two more sentences using contrast as a context clue.

Part 5 **Be Precise** List three synonyms for the word *nice.* Use a dictionary or thesaurus to help you. For each synonym, write a sentence that fits the special meaning of that synonym.

Part 6 **Get on Base** Using a magazine, find five words that contain base words and word parts. Choose words that are unfamiliar to you. Copy each word and write the base word. Try to figure out the meaning of the entire word.

Part 7 **What's First?** List the prefixes *in-, il-, im-, ir-, mis-, non-, pre-, re-, sub-, super-,* and *un-.* Make a new word for each by adding the prefix to a base word. Write the new words. Choose five of them and write a sentence for each word.

Part 8 **The End** List the suffixes *-able, -ible, -er, -or, -ful, -ish, -less, -ness,* and *-ous.* Make a new word for each by adding the suffix to a base word. Write the new words. Choose five of them and write a sentence for each word.

Improving Your Sentences

Section 2

Part 1 **One of a Kind** What is your favorite time of day? Write a sentence explaining what that time of day is. Write a sentence describing where you are then. Write a sentence explaining why you like it. Write a sentence explaining how you usually spend that part of your day. Write one telling about something unusual that happened at that time of day. Make your sentences clear and interesting.

Part 2 **Say Something** Find, or write, two examples of each kind of empty sentence. Improve the sentences by eliminating repetition or by supplying reasons. Write the improved sentences.

Part 3 **Streamlining** Find, or write, four examples of padded sentences. Improve the sentences by omitting any unnecessary words. Rewrite, if necessary. Write the new sentences.

Exploring Paragraphs

Section 3

Part 1 **Togetherness** Find a short paragraph in a newspaper article. Decide what the main idea of the paragraph is. Now add one more sentence to the paragraph. Be certain that it says something about the main idea. Copy the paragraph, including the sentence you added.

Part 2 **All the Same** Find a short paragraph in a newspaper article. Decide what the main idea of the paragraph is. Be certain that the paragraph has unity. Write one sentence that is on the same topic as the paragraph, but that does not relate to the main idea. Write another sentence that does relate to the main idea.

Part 3 **What's the Big Idea?** Choose a person you know well. Think about ways that you could write about him or her. Write two possible topic sentences for paragraphs about the person.

Part 4 Show Your Support Choose a person you admire. Write this topic sentence on your paper: (Name) is a talented person. List three details, examples, or facts and figures to develop the topic sentence.

Part 5 Brand Names In a book or magazine, find one paragraph of each kind: narrative, explanatory, and descriptive. Copy and label each paragraph.

Section 4 Writing a Paragraph

Part 1 Straight and Narrow What city do you live in or near? Suppose that city were the topic for a paragraph. Write the name of the city. Narrow the topic by asking *Who? What? When? Where? Why?* and *How?* Write the narrowed topic.

Part 2 Direct Contact Think of your city. Write a topic sentence that expresses your main idea about the city. Make your topic sentence direct. Make it snappy.

Part 3 The Main Road Write a paragraph about your city. Choose a method of paragraph development that completes your topic sentence clearly.

Part 4 A Stop Sign Write a concluding sentence for a paragraph about your city. Make sure the concluding sentence sums up the main idea. Make sure it is an interesting ending.

Section 5 A Writer's Choices

Part 1 Who, Me? Imagine that you are the first human being to live on Mars. Use first-person point of view to write four sentences about what your life is like.

Part 2 Out of Sight Imagine that you are a being who has lived on Mars for centuries. Use third-person point of view to write four sentences about what you observe about the human beings who have come to your planet.

Part 3 **To Tell the Truth** Choose any simple machine that you know how to use. Decide whether to write a narration, description, or explanation. In a narrative you will tell how you used the machine recently. In a description you will describe the machine. In an explanation you will tell how to use it. Write your topic and list details, facts, figures, or dates. Organize and check your information. Write your paragraph. Read it, and rewrite as necessary.

Part 4 **Mind over Matter** Think about a machine that the world could use, if it existed. Decide whether to write a narration, description, or explanation. In a narrative you will tell how the machine was invented. In a description you will describe the machine. In an explanation you will tell how to operate it. Invent and organize details about your machine. Write the paragraph. Read it, and rewrite as necessary.

Part 5 **First Choice** Start with the verb *break*. List three verbs that are more specific than *break*. You might use *snap* or *smash*, for example. Write a sentence with each verb. Try to make your sentences create different moods.

Part 6 **The Name Game** Suppose that it has been raining for eight days. You have decided to write about rain. Write several possible titles for your work.

The Narrative Paragraph

Section 7

Part 1 **Then What?** Think about yesterday. List things that you did. Organize your list in chronological order. Write a narrative paragraph based on your list of details. Do whatever rewriting you think is necessary.

Part 2 **How Time Flies!** Write a narrative paragraph telling what you think you might be doing ten years from today. Follow yourself through that day. Use transitions to show chronological order and underline them.

Part 3 In Detail What has happened this year that frightened you? Write a narrative paragraph about your experience. Use vivid details. Follow the steps in the process of writing.

Section 8 The Descriptive Paragraph

Part 1 You Are There Get to know your school. Choose one part of your school to describe in a paragraph. On your paper, write *sight, hearing, touch, taste,* and *smell.* Taking a close look at part of your school, list details for each of the senses. Then organize the details in a logical order. Write a descriptive paragraph. Do whatever rewriting is necessary.

Part 2 The Right Mood Suppose that a summer festival were taking place in your neighborhood. What would it be like? List adjectives and sensory details that fit the mood. Organize your lists in a logical order. Write a descriptive paragraph.

Part 3 Look Around How do you enter your home? Describe the entrance. List and organize important details. Decide where to begin your description. The rest of your description should follow in a natural way. Write your description. Rewrite as necessary.

Part 4 Where Is It? Using the kitchen as the starting point, write a paragraph describing the arrangement of the rooms in your home. Make sure your description is in a clear and understandable order. Rewrite as necessary.

Section 9 The Explanatory Paragraph Telling *How*

Part 1 Here's How! Make a list of the steps you follow to make your favorite breakfast. Be specific. Organize your detailed list. Write an explanatory *how* paragraph. Read the paragraph, and rewrite as necessary.

Part 2 Get in Step Think of a dance step or sports activity that you do well. Write an explanatory *how* paragraph explaining how to do it. Before you write, list the steps, using specific details. When you write the paragraph, underline the transitional words and phrases that you use.

Part 3 In Order Invent a new dance step or sports activity. List the steps to follow in order to do it. Be clear and specific. Use your list to write an explanatory *how* paragraph. Use transitions that show step-by-step order. Underline the transitions.

The Explanatory Paragraph Telling *Why*

Section 10

Part 1 State Your Case Read the headlines in today's paper. Find an issue that you have an opinion on. Narrow your opinion so that you can write about it in a paragraph. State your opinion in a clear, strong topic sentence. Then list at least three specific reasons or facts that support your opinion.

Part 2 Be Reasonable What change would you like to see in your neighborhood? List three reasons why this change would be useful to you and others. Arrange the reasons in order, from least important to most important. Use your list to write a convincing, well organized explanatory *why* paragraph.

Part 3 The Defense Rests How do you feel about living in a city? Write a convincing paragraph expressing your opinion. Follow all the steps in the process of writing.

The Explanatory Paragraph Telling *What*

Section 11

Part 1 What Is It? The television is something most people use. What is a television? Write a complete definition of a television in an explanatory *what* paragraph.

Part 2 Be Particular Choose a job you would like to do. Write a definition of your job in an explanatory *what* paragraph. Develop your topic by using details or facts and figures.

Section 12 Exploring Compositions

Part 1 Take a Look Think about the things that have happened to you since this school year began. From these events, list five topics that would be suitable for compositions.

Part 2 Triple Play From the events that have happened since this school year began, choose one topic and think about how you would write a composition about it. On your paper, write three headings: *Introduction, Body,* and *Conclusion.* Write notes that tell what you would include in each part.

Part 3 Name Tags From the events that have happened since this school year began, choose a topic for a composition. You could write a narrative composition telling how the event happened. You could write a descriptive composition about yourself when it happened. You could write an explanatory composition about why the event was important. In a few sentences, write what you would include in each composition.

Section 13 The Narrative Composition

Part 1 True or False? Think of the last sports event you participated in, saw in person, or watched on television. Using this event as your topic, list specific details. You may need to use other sources to check the accuracy of some details.

Part 2 What Do You Know? Think about the last sports event you saw or participated in. Think about it from the first-person point of view of a participant. Think about it from the third-person point of view of an outsider in the stands. Make notes for two compositions, one from each point of view.

Part 3 **Best Foot Forward** Think about that recent sports event. What was most important or exciting about it? List details of the event. Use your notes to write an introduction for a narrative about it.

Part 4 **Let's Have Action!** Recall that recent sports event. Using the most important actions, write the body of a composition about this event. Include the details and conflict of the event. Try to create suspense.

Part 5 **Let's Talk** Think about the talk among the players or among the spectators at the last sports event you saw or participated in. Write a dialogue about the event, using at least three speakers. Follow the rules for punctuation of quotations.

Part 6 **Other Voices** Imagine a dialogue between two fans of the opposing sides at the last sports event you saw or participated in. Decide what each fan is like. Write a sentence describing each one. Then write a dialogue between the two fans. Use the dialogue to reveal each of them.

Part 7 **Moving On** List the major events in that recent sports event. Arrange them in chronological order. Then add transitional words and phrases that link the events and make the sequence clear. Review the transitions you have used. Is the sequence of events clear?

Part 8 **The Finale** Write a conclusion for the narrative composition you are writing about a recent sports event. Make sure the conflict is resolved. Then write a title for the composition.

The Descriptive Composition

Section 14

Part 1 **What Do You See?** Look out one window of your favorite room. Use what you see as the topic for a descriptive composition. Write and organize notes for the composition. Include sensory details.

Part 2 **A Wider View** Carefully observe the scene you see from your favorite room. Using your notes, write the introduction and body of a composition about the scene.

Part 3 **How Do You Feel?** Decide how you feel about the scene you watched from your favorite room. Then write a conclusion for your descriptive composition. Try to make your readers feel what you feel. Write a title for the composition.

Section 15 The Explanatory Composition Telling *How*

Part 1 **How Do You Do?** What do you do well that young children cannot do? It might be a hobby or a job you enjoy. Make a list of things you can do that a young child would want to learn to do. Choose one. Write a possible title for a composition on this skill.

Part 2 **Step It Up** What do you do best? Do you build models well or play a musical instrument? Choose something you know how to do well. List the steps involved in the process. Write the body of an explanatory *how* composition. Give a step-by-step explanation.

Part 3 **The Final Step** Write the steps involved in doing something you do well. Add the transitions you will need within each paragraph and between paragraphs.

Section 16 The Explanatory Composition Telling *Why*

Part 1 **For or Against?** From today's newspaper or television newscast, find a topic for an explanatory *why* composition. Narrow the topic and state your opinion about it. Plan a composition on this topic by making pre-writing notes. List the reasons or facts you will use to support your opinion.

Part 2 **With Good Reasons** In one sentence, state your opinion on a topic that affects you and your family. Then list three specific reasons or facts to support your opinion. Arrange your evidence in order of importance, from the least important to the most important. Then write the body of a composition on this topic.

Part 3 **Furthermore** Review the body of your composition on the topic that affects you and your family. Write an introduction for the composition. Write a conclusion for the composition in which you sum up your argument. Then write a title that expresses your topic.

Writing Letters

Section 17

Part 1 **Write Soon** Jot down notes on what you have been doing recently. Use these notes to write a friendly letter to a friend or relative. Use the correct form. Use vivid details. Label the five parts of the letter.

Part 2 **Handle with Care** Draw a rectangle to represent an envelope. Address the envelope as if it were a letter you were going to send to yourself.

Part 3 **Special Occasions** Imagine that a friend of yours threw a surprise party for you on your birthday. Write a thank-you note to this friend.

Part 4 **Dear Sir or Madam:** Write a business letter to an organization whose good works you admire. Request information about volunteering to help this cause. Label the six parts of this letter.

Part 5 **Information, Please** Find an advertisement in a magazine. Write a business letter requesting more information about a product advertised. Invent any details you need to complete your letter.

Section 18 Using a Dictionary

Part 1 **Word for Word** Write ten words that begin with the first letter of the name of your town. Put the words into alphabetical order. Write a short definition for each word. Check your work in a dictionary.

Part 2 **Follow the Signs** Imagine that you are writing a composition about radio. You need to look up the following words: *antenna*, *frequency*, *transmitter*, and *receiver*. List the words on your paper. Find each word in a dictionary. Next to each word, write the guide words that appear at the top of the page where you found the word.

Part 3 **Read All About It** Find the word *surface* in a dictionary. Copy the following information about the word: its pronunciation, the language it came from, and its possible parts of speech.

Part 4 **A Good Fit** Look up the word *spot* in your dictionary. Copy four different meanings of *spot*. For each different meaning, write a sentence using *spot*.

Section 19 Using the Library

Part 1 **A Good Place To Visit** Think of a machine. Use your school or public library to find at least three nonfiction books about that machine. Write their titles and call numbers.

Part 2 **Card Tricks** Write the title of a book you enjoyed reading or a book that someone has recommended. In your school or public library, find a title card and an author card for the book. Copy the information from the cards.

Part 3 **It's All There** Find an encyclopedia article on your city or a city near you. List the following information: the name of the encyclopedia where you found the article, the number and guide letters of the volume, and any related articles.

Handbook

A detailed Table of Contents for the Handbook appears in the front of this book.

Learning About Sentences

When you learned to talk, you began slowly. You probably started out by saying the names of people around you. Then you added some action words to let others know what you wanted. Still later, you learned words to describe things you saw.

Now you know thousands of words. You know how to put many of them together to express your needs and ideas. Nevertheless, you may still have trouble, now and then, in making others understand you. You can still grow in your ability to use your language.

This section will describe the rules for arranging words into good sentences. Learning these rules will help you understand more of the sentences you hear or read. It will also help you to express yourself to others, in speaking or in writing.

Part 1 Complete Sentences

A sentence is a group of words that expresses a complete thought.

If people do not understand you when you talk, they can ask you questions. However, if they are reading a report, or a letter, or a story you wrote, they cannot ask your paper any questions. Your report, letter, or story must make your thoughts clear.

When you are writing, make sure your sentences answer such basic questions as these: *Who* or *what* did it? and *What happened?* If a group of words doesn't answer these questions, that group is not a complete sentence.

Example	The loud racket in the alley

What happened? What about the racket? The example does not give you enough information to answer the questions. It is only part of a sentence, or a **fragment.**

By adding words to a fragment, you can change it into a complete sentence. Here are two complete sentences.

The loud racket in the alley kept us awake all night.
The loud racket in the alley scared the pup.

Sometimes a group of words does not answer the question *who?* or *what?*

Example	Played in the water

Who played in the water? Or *what* played? Again, the group of words does not express a complete thought. Here are two ways you might complete this fragment.

Kristen and Gene played tag in the water.
The seals played in the water.

Can you add words to the two fragments below to make them complete thoughts?

Threw out the first ball of the season
The TV special yesterday

Exercises Recognize complete sentences.

A. Number your paper from 1 to 10. For each word group, write *Sentence* or *Fragment.*

1. A pocket of my jeans
2. Sold ten tickets
3. Two trucks blocked the intersection
4. The day before the school races
5. We visited Mount Rushmore
6. Between the laundromat and the corner
7. Carefully climbed out on the roof
8. Louis was asleep
9. A fountain in Lincoln Park
10. Three pounds of hamburger

B. All but one of the groups of words below are sentence fragments. Add words of your own to make complete sentences. Write the sentences.

1. On Friday
2. All the bus drivers
3. Jill came home at six o'clock
4. Half the night
5. The automatic door at the supermarket
6. Across the bridge
7. Exploded in midair
8. Cautiously tried the ice on the pond
9. Too much water
10. A block from school

Part 2 Four Kinds of Sentences

You use sentences for several different reasons. Sometimes you want to tell something. Sometimes you want to ask something. Sometimes you want to tell someone to do something. Other times you want to show how strongly you feel about something. There is a different kind of sentence for each of these four purposes.

1. A **declarative sentence** tells or states something. It ends with a period (.).

   Gwen bought a basketball. These radishes are hot.

2. An **interrogative sentence** asks something. It ends with a question mark (?).

   Are you positive? Where are the forks?

3. An **imperative sentence** requests, instructs, or orders. It ends with a period.

   Count your change carefully. Return your books on time.

4. An **exclamatory sentence** expresses joy, surprise, anger, excitement, or other strong feeling. It ends with an exclamation point (!).

   What a great cook you are! How dark the sky is!

Begin every sentence with a capital letter.

Exercises Identify the kinds of sentences.

A. These sentences do not have punctuation marks at the end. On your paper, write *Declarative, Interrogative, Imperative,* or *Exclamatory* to show what kind each sentence is.

1. Measure the length of the table
2. May we watch Channel 11
3. Birds' bones have air pockets
4. Take a ten-minute break

5. What a scary feeling I got
6. Do you have an eraser
7. Is there enough pressure in the tires
8. Ms. Minden had a flu shot
9. Does a chipmunk have a white stripe down its back
10. Tell me all about your problem

B. Follow the directions for Exercise A.

1. John Singleton Copley painted portraits of Americans
2. Turn off the water, please
3. The watermelon rolled down the steps
4. Can you lift the 100-pound weight
5. May I go to the movies, too
6. What a fast runner Barbara is
7. The dancer wore a colorful costume
8. Wait for the next elevator, please
9. Are you rooting for Peggy
10. Guava is a tropical fruit

Punctuating Sentences

The kind of punctuation mark you put at the end of your sentence helps the reader figure out your meaning. Remember these rules:

1. Use a period after a declarative sentence.
2. Use a question mark after an interrogative sentence.
3. Use a period after an imperative sentence.
4. Use an exclamation point after an exclamatory sentence.

Exercises **Use correct punctuation.**

A. Copy and punctuate these sentences.

1. Which seats are ours

2. Remember to bring a sweater tonight
3. Call Debbie to the phone, please
4. The leaves floated on the top of the water
5. Have you ever visited the Everglades
6. Write your name in the upper right-hand corner
7. How far can you swim underwater
8. The Swiss flag is red with a white cross
9. Oil slicks kill hundreds of birds
10. What a lot of questions you ask

B. Follow the directions for Exercise A.

1. Proceed to gate G-7
2. What a great time we had at Disney World
3. Please follow the rules of the game
4. Now, which tooth is loose
5. Elvis Presley Boulevard is a street in Memphis
6. Do twenty push-ups
7. Laura practices the tuba in the den
8. Does Michael wear glasses
9. Whales are guided by tiny pilot fish
10. What is the Continental Divide

Part 3 Every Sentence Has Two Parts

Every sentence has a **subject** and a **predicate.**

1. The old car lost its tailpipe.

The old car	lost its tailpipe.
This part is the subject. It tells what the sentence is about.	This is the predicate. It tells what happened.

2. Our team won the pennant.

Our team	**won the pennant.**
This is the subject. It tells whom the sentence is about.	This is the predicate. It tells what happened.

3. My friend Sue hit a home run.

My friend Sue	**hit a home run.**
Subject	Predicate

Finding the Subject and the Predicate

Every sentence states a complete thought. A complete thought has two parts: the subject and the predicate.

The subject of a sentence tells what or whom the sentence is about.

The predicate of a sentence tells what the subject did or what happened.

An easy way to understand the parts of a sentence is to think of the sentence as telling who did something or what happened. The subject tells *who* or *what*. The predicate tells *did* or *happened*. You can divide a sentence, then, in this way:

Who or What (Subject)	**Did or Happened** (Predicate)
All my friends	came to my party.
The old elm	was destroyed by the storm.

Exercises **Find subjects and predicates.**

A. Copy these sentences. Draw a vertical line between the subject and the predicate.

Example: The yellow car | was going too fast.

1. Dad locked the keys in the house.
2. Thanksgiving will fall on November 28 this year.
3. The first batter struck out.
4. My socks have shrunk.
5. A robin's nest was in the pear tree.
6. Jay's cat eats beetles.
7. The second-string players watched from the bench.
8. We could not see through the curtains.
9. Lisa took her bathing suit with her.
10. The team can count on Mandy.

B. Follow the directions for Exercise A.

1. Maria found a gold pocket watch.
2. My little brother swallowed a dime.
3. We bought three pounds of apples.
4. My sister's Chevy uses unleaded gas.
5. The sunlight sparkled on the water.
6. Terry's cookies taste best.
7. The final whistle blew.
8. A butterfly struggled in the spider's web.
9. The inventor experimented with the wooden gears.
10. The air conditioner in the office needs a new filter.

C. Write an interesting predicate for each of these subjects. Begin each sentence with the words given.

1. The pizza

2. The black limousine
3. My dog
4. Our front door
5. Stacy's science project

D. Write a suitable subject for each of these predicates.

1. knows all the latest dances
2. is jumping next
3. are going camping
4. has twin engines
5. is allergic to peanuts

Part 4 The Verb

The subjects and predicates you have been studying so far are called **complete subjects** and **complete predicates.** The complete subject includes all of the words that tell *who* or *what.* The complete predicate includes all of the words that tell what was *done* or what *happened.*

There is one part of every complete predicate that is more important than the rest. This part is the **verb.** It is sometimes called the **simple predicate.** In the rest of this book, we will speak of it as the **verb.**

Finding the Verb

The words in *italics* in these sentences are the verbs.

We *ran* to the beach. The tall girl *is* the winner.

Some verbs tell of an **action.**

The boys *ran* home. Charlene *hit* the ball.

Other verbs state that **something is:**

That doctor *is* a surgeon. You *are* so nervous.

A verb is a word that tells of an action or a state of being.

Exercises **Find the verb.**

A. Read these sentences. Write the verb in each sentence.

Example: The tornado carried Dorothy to Oz.
carried

1. Nobody believed Esther's story.
2. Reggie does terrific stunts on his skateboard.
3. Diana Ross is a singer and movie star.
4. In the spring, northern farmers boil maple sap into syrup.
5. The bike marathon lasts all day.
6. The guide told our tour group about the state capitol.
7. One of my cousins writes for *Newsweek*.
8. A worm was in that apple.
9. Sacagawea guided Lewis and Clark in their exploration of the Northwest Territory.
10. A pack of dogs runs loose on my street.

B. Follow the directions for Exercise A.

1. Queen Elizabeth I ruled England for forty-five years.
2. Water freezes at 0°C or 32°F.
3. All the students went home half an hour ago.
4. The mail arrived early today.
5. Barry rode his bike to school today.
6. The baby eats nothing but cereal.
7. Medicine Hat is the name of a town in Canada.
8. My mother met Pearl Bailey backstage once.
9. Alex found a dollar bill in the mall parking lot.
10. The lightning storm caused static on the radio.

Main Verbs and Helping Verbs

The verb is often only a single word. Read each sentence below and notice the verb.

Eddie **laughed** at the joke. Georgia **whistled** a tune.

Other verbs are made up of more than word. Notice how you can build a one-word verb into a verb with several words:

Beth and David **collect** shells.

The verb *collect* tells what Beth and David do.

Beth and David **will collect** shells.

The verb *collect* now has another verb, *will,* before it. *Collect* is the **main verb,** and *will* is the **helping verb.** The helping verb changes the meaning of the sentence slightly.

Beth and David **were collecting** shells.

The verb *collect* has changed its form to *collecting,* but it is still the main verb. The helping verb is *were*. This helping verb changes the meaning of the sentence, too.

Beth and David **have collected** shells.

Here, the main verb is *collected,* another form of the verb *collect*. The helping verb is *have*.

As you can see in these examples, the main verb may change forms when helping verbs are added to a one-word verb. The endings *-ing, -ed,* and *-en* are frequently used on main verbs. Adding helping verbs and changing the ending do not change the basic action of the main verb. However, these changes do change the meaning slightly.

In the following examples, decide which word is the main verb and which word or words are helping verbs. Then look at the chart to see if you were right.

Grace *was skating*.
The old Ford *has been making* strange noises.
The back door *should have been locked*.

Helping Verbs +	Main Verb =	Verb
was	skating	was skating
has been	making	has been making
should have been	locked	should have been locked

Some verbs can be used by themselves or as helping verbs:

is	am	were	has	do	did
are	was	have	had	does	

Examples: Tomorrow *is* a holiday. (verb)
The pump *is working*. (helping verb)

Some words can be used only as helping verbs.

can	will	should	may	might
shall	could	would	must	

When you are finding verbs, keep these things in mind:

Some verbs are made up of a main verb and one or more helping verbs.
Some words can be used either as verbs by themselves or as helping verbs.
Some words can be used only as helping verbs.

Exercises Find the main verb and helping verbs.

A. Label two columns *Helping Verb* and *Main Verb.* Find all the parts of the verb in each sentence. Write each part in the proper column.

Examples: We have enough food for the picnic.
Eighteen customers have demanded a refund.

Helping Verb	Main Verb
	have
have	demanded

1. I have seen the dinosaur bones in the museum.
2. The blizzard stopped all traffic in the city.

3. The Cubs might beat the Braves.
4. Pennsylvania is the Keystone State.
5. Chris has completed four passes in this quarter.
6. Rick should be waiting for you.
7. Terri can do a somersault on the trampoline.
8. The chemical had poisoned the fish.
9. McDonald's invented the Egg McMuffin.
10. The fireworks in Candlestick Park will begin at eight.

B. Follow the directions for Exercise A.

1. You should have seen the game last Thursday.
2. Those hot peppers may burn your tongue.
3. The water was 26°C in the pool.
4. On Saturday the rides will cost a quarter.
5. Seattle was named for an Indian chief, Seathl.
6. The whole house would shake with each new tremor.
7. The Grand Canyon is a mile deep.
8. My sister has moved to Cleveland.
9. I might go to the pet show tomorrow.
10. You must have taped that noise at the basketball game.

Separated Parts of the Verb

The words that make up a verb are not always together in a sentence, like *could have been* and *might have seen*. Sometimes the helping verbs and the main verb are separated by other words that are not verbs:

can hardly **wait**	**could** not **have come**
has always **been**	**did**n't **understand**
is usually **found**	**must have** already **gone**

Notice that *not* and the ending *n't* in contractions are not parts of the verb even though they do change the meaning of the verb.

Exercises Find separated parts of the verb.

A. Label two columns *Helping Verb* and *Main Verb*. Find all the parts of the verb in each sentence. Write each part in the proper column.

Example: Did the kitten scratch you?

Helping Verb	Main Verb
did	scratch

1. Jenny has always been my friend.
2. Bruce would often take the bus.
3. Jeans are usually found in the sportswear department.
4. Players are sometimes traded from one team to another.
5. We will probably see the movie this weekend.
6. Judy had just cut the lawn.
7. Lynn is always whistling that song.
8. The carpet is usually vacuumed once a week.
9. Sandy didn't understand the instructions in the booklet.
10. Maurice may have already finished his lunch.

B. Follow the directions for Exercise A.

1. My mother is still looking for a new car.
2. The hot days of July and August are sometimes called dog days.
3. That catbird is always mimicking all the other birds.
4. Ms. Washington doesn't assign homework often.
5. Valerie can really walk a tightrope.
6. Mr. Lang must not have called very loudly.
7. A Venus' flytrap can really catch flies.
8. Greg would rather have a hamburger.
9. In Australia, badgers are sometimes called bandicoots.
10. New York was originally named New Amsterdam.

Part 5 The Simple Subject

In a complete sentence, every verb has a subject.

Subject	Verb
Ginny	ran.
The chocolate	will melt.
I	laughed.

The subject of the verb is sometimes called the **simple subject** of the sentence.

The simple subjects in the sentences above are *Ginny, chocolate,* and *I*. From here on in this book, the simple subject will be called the *subject of the verb*.

To find the subject of the verb, first find the verb. Then ask *who?* or *what?* before the verb.

Examples: The crowd at the concert cheered loudly.
Verb: *cheered*
Who or what cheered? The **crowd**
Crowd is the subject of *cheered*.

The tall, red-haired boy is the best goalie.
Verb: *is*
Who or what is? The tall, red-haired **boy**
Boy is the subject of *is*.

Exercises Find the verb and its subject.

A. Copy each sentence. Draw two lines under the verb. Then draw one line under the subject of the verb.

1. Ms. Carroll coached our team.
2. The spaceship has landed safely.
3. The clock struck twelve.
4. The hornets under the window buzzed angrily.

5. The cows didn't even look at the train.
6. Joel is our next-door neighbor.
7. The treasures of King Tutankhamen were found in Egypt.
8. We circled the airport for an hour.
9. All three boys could play the guitar well.
10. The cat's eyes shone in the dark.

B. Follow the directions for Exercise A.

1. Aretha worked the problem easily.
2. In July and August, the Dog Star rises with the sun.
3. Heavy traffic frequently jams the Holland Tunnel.
4. Everyone in the audience cheered.
5. The steer in that pen was branded at Lazy T Ranch.
6. The fragrance of popcorn filled the theater.
7. Now Carl can dry the dishes.
8. The hedge behind the tennis court was loaded with tennis balls.
9. My older sister must have dropped the vase.
10. The lettuce in that salad is not fresh.

Part 6 The Subject in Unusual Positions

In nearly all the sentences you have studied so far, the subject comes at the start of the sentence. There are many sentences, however, in which the subject comes later.

The *shark* lingered off the shore.
(The subject is at the beginning of the sentence.)

Off the shore the *shark* lingered.
(The subject is in the middle of the sentence.)

Off the shore lingered the *shark*.
(The subject is at the end of the sentence.)

Sometimes you can find the subject more easily if you turn the sentence around.

Through the cloud shot the *missile*.
The *missile* shot through the cloud.

Always find the verb first. Then ask *who?* or *what?* before the verb.

The subject always follows the verb in sentences that begin in these ways:

Here is	There is	Where is
Here are	There are	Where are

Here is your *guitar*. (*guitar* is the subject of *is*.)
There is our *boat*. (*boat* is the subject of *is*.)
Where are the *keys*? (*keys* is the subject of *are*.)

Exercises Find the subject in unusual positions.

A. Copy each sentence. Draw two lines under the verb. Then draw one line under the subject of the verb.

1. There is a cloud in the distance.
2. Into the pool plunged the diver.
3. Before the storm, the girls closed the windows.
4. Where is the key to your locker?
5. Over the haunted house floated strange shapes.
6. There are many irritating commercials on that program.
7. Across the street darted Mr. Walter's cat.
8. Slowly Roger understood.
9. Up the bank scrambled Patti.
10. Three hours after dark, Kevin crept from his tent.

B. Follow the directions for Exercise A.

1. Here is my idea.

2. Overhead were our helium balloons.
3. Down the river glided the barge.
4. Suddenly the rocket backfired.
5. In the tropical waters are many unusual creatures.
6. There is room for Mickey, too.
7. In last year's competition, Al's team won easily.
8. Over the plains thundered the herd.
9. Here is my bracelet.
10. Where is a public telephone?

Part 7 Subjects and Verbs in Interrogative and Exclamatory Sentences

You may have to rethink or rewrite some interrogative and exclamatory sentences to find the subject. First, put the sentence in normal order. Here are examples:

Interrogative Sentence: Did you see that interception?
You did see that interception?

Exclamatory Sentence: Was that movie boring!
That movie was boring.

Sometimes you need to omit some words to make a sentence sound normal.

Exclamatory Sentence: What terrible weather we're having!

Awkward: We're having what terrible weather.

Smooth: We're having terrible weather.

Exercises **Find the subjects and verbs in interrogative and exclamatory sentences.**

A. Change the word order in each sentence below. (You may need to omit some words to make your sentence smooth.) Then write the new sentence. Underline each subject.

Example: Did you clean your room?
You did clean your room?

1. Were you the winner?
2. What a long time you took! (Omit *What*.)
3. Has the dog been fed?
4. How orange the moon looks! (Omit *How*.)
5. Have they painted the library?
6. Did your friend win the calculator?
7. What a dark cave we saw! (Omit *What*.)
8. May I help you?
9. How fast the baby has grown! (Omit *How*.)
10. Won't this snow ever melt!

B. Copy the sentences below. Draw two lines under the verb in each sentence. Draw one line under the subject of the verb. (If you need to, change the word order mentally to find the subject and verb.)

1. Does that hamburger have onions on it?
2. How did you find the right answer?
3. What a noisy bird that crow is!
4. Did you write any poetry?
5. Have the Indians played in the World Series since 1970?
6. How funny you look in that costume!
7. Did Angel Cordero ride Affirmed?
8. What a feast we had at Thanksgiving!
9. Has Marcia read today's newspaper already?
10. Am I hungry!

Part 8 When the Subject Is Not Given

Imperative sentences (commands) usually begin with a verb. For example, in the command *Close the door,* the verb is the first word, *Close.* What is the subject? There doesn't seem to be any, does there? The subject in the sentence is *you,* even though it is not expressed. *You* is the person or group spoken to. The subject *you* is said to be understood.

Examples: (*You*) Keep off the grass. (*You*) Stop!
(*You*) Do not feed the animals. (*You*) Hurry up.

Exercises **Tell the subject.**

A. Copy the following sentences. Draw two lines under the verb in each sentence. Draw one line under the subject of the verb. If the subject is not given in the sentence, write it in parentheses in the place where it is understood.

Example: Memorize this poem.

(You) memorize this poem.

1. Play ball.
2. Marianne almost forgot her umbrella.
3. Take another turn.
4. Finish your game before supper.
5. Did Joe bring the net?
6. Give me your autograph, please.
7. How bumpy this road is!
8. Is the story true?
9. Proceed with caution.
10. Do you know Steve Fowler?

B. Follow the directions for Exercise A.

1. Wait a minute.

2. Does Rosalie speak Spanish?
3. The violin players were not quite ready.
4. Did the explorers come from Portugal or Spain?
5. Listen to that rain.
6. Can everyone hear me?
7. How many legs do insects have?
8. Shop at Safeway.
9. Turn left at the first stop light.
10. Some of my friends play handball every afternoon.

Part 9 Compound Subjects

Look at these two sentences:

Subject	Predicate
Tom	saw a traffic accident.
I	saw a traffic accident.

Since the predicates are the same, we can join the two sentences together. The new sentence will be:

Subject	Predicate
Tom and I	saw a traffic accident.

Now the subject has two parts. When two or more subjects are used with the same predicate, they are called a **compound subject.** The word *compound* means having more than one part.

In the third sentence, the word *and* joins the two parts of the subject. The word *or* is also used to join parts of a subject. A word that is used to join words or groups of words is called a **conjunction.**

Simple subject: **Darren** may win.
Simple subject: **Alicia** may win.
Compound subject: **Darren** *or* **Alicia** may win.

When three or more subjects are combined in a compound subject, use commas to separate them. The conjunction is placed before the last subject.

Example: The *trees*, the *bushes*, and the *flowers* were ruined by insects.

Exercises Write compound subjects.

A. Find the verb and its compound subject in each of the following sentences. Write the subjects and verb. Draw a vertical line between them.

Example: The wind and the sudden rain ruined the picnic.

wind, rain | ruined

1. Emily, Charlotte, and Ann Brontë wrote novels.
2. The Knicks or the Celtics may win the playoffs.
3. Shirley, Della, and Pat are best friends.
4. In *Star Wars*, C3Po and R2D2 aid in the fight against the evil Darth Vader.
5. Radishes, carrots, and potatoes grow underground.
6. That stuffed dog or the rubber duck would be a good gift for the baby.
7. John Lennon, Paul McCartney, George Harrison, and Ringo Starr became famous as the Beatles.
8. Marisa and Jorge tied for first place in the essay contest.
9. Cereal, milk, and toast make a nutritious breakfast.
10. The Mohawks and four other Indian tribes joined forces as the powerful Five Nations.

B. Think of a compound subject for each predicate listed below. Then write the complete sentence. In some sentences, try to use a compound subject with three parts.

1. suddenly rounded the corner
2. are waiting outside
3. were my best subjects
4. have never been afraid of spiders
5. covered the ground
6. were not ready yet
7. ran for the last bus
8. are in the tool kit
9. were blocking the driveway
10. tied down the trunk of the car

Part 10 Compound Predicates

When two or more predicates are used with the same subject, they are called a **compound predicate.**

By using a compound predicate and a conjunction you are often able to combine two or more sentences.

Subject	Predicate
The dog	growled.
The dog	bit the paperboy.

Subject	Predicate
The dog	growled and bit the paperboy.

When three or more predicates are combined in a compound predicate, commas are used to separate them. The conjunction is placed before the last predicate.

Example: Katherine *saw* the bear, *dropped* the camera, and *ran* off.

Exercises Write compound predicates.

A. Find the compound predicates in each of the following sentences. Number your paper from 1 to 10. Write the subject and the verbs. Draw a vertical line between them.

Example: Chris Evert practiced long hours and became a champion tennis player.

Chris Evert | practiced, became

1. I left the cake in the oven too long and burned it.
2. Ice covered the streets and caused many accidents.
3. Lydia's family went to the Grand Canyon, rode burros down the trail, and spent the night at the bottom of the Canyon.
4. The Angels lost one game but won the next three.
5. Frederick Douglass escaped from slavery and became a speaker for anti-slavery groups.
6. Our class rented a bus and visited the Natural History Museum.
7. King Kong escaped in New York City, climbed the Empire State Building, and battled planes.
8. Bring your lunch or buy a hot dog at the cafeteria.
9. Mary Pickford starred in silent movies and was called "America's Sweetheart."
10. Ed came to the plate, ignored three wide pitches, and smashed the fourth pitch into the stands.

B. Think of a compound predicate for each subject listed below. Then write the complete sentence. In some of your sentences, try to use a compound predicate with three parts.

1. The catcher
2. A clever detective
3. The Statue of Liberty
4. The school band
5. Stars and planets
6. The ice cream
7. An old house
8. Forest fires
9. A dolphin
10. The snowstorm

Sentence Patterns Word Order and Meaning

Sentences are made up of words. To make sense, the words must be put together in a special order. Look at the groups of words below. Which group makes sense?

Ralph jumped up.

Jumped Ralph up.

The first group makes sense. The words are in the right order for an English sentence. The second group does not make sense. Our experience tells us that the words are not in the right order.

Sometimes there is more than one right order for a group of words. Each order makes sense and expresses a message, but the messages are not always the same. Read this pair of sentences.

Elaine saw Hugh.

Hugh saw Elaine.

The words are the same in each sentence. Only the order of the words makes the sentences different. But the difference in order makes an important difference in meaning.

Exercise Change the word order and meaning.

Read each sentence. Then change the order of the words to change the meaning. Write each new sentence on your paper.

1. Tom spotted Phyllis.
2. Cake crumbs covered the dish.
3. The Tigers beat the Lions.
4. Carol knows my best friend.
5. Some insects eat plants.
6. Some men are nurses.
7. Donna heard the cat.
8. That boy is a dancer.

REVIEW Learning About Sentences

The Parts of a Sentence Write the verb and its simple subject for each of the following sentences.

Example: An expert studied the rare stamps.

expert | studied

1. The newspaper reported our track meet.
2. The boiler exploded into shreds.
3. Jessica should have kept her promise.
4. We will have a Halloween party.
5. The workers should have stayed.
6. A mirror is coated with silver paint.
7. A magnet will not attract plastic.
8. Out of the closet tumbled the boxes.
9. There is our helper.
10. Where are my shoes?
11. What a wild outfit that is!
12. Listen for the echo.
13. Keep your dog on a leash.
14. Ramona and Susan transferred to a new school.
15. Cal lifted the boxes and loaded them onto a truck.

Kinds of Sentences For each of the following sentences, write *Declarative, Interrogative, Imperative,* or *Exclamatory* to show what kind it is. Add the punctuation mark that should be used at the end of each sentence.

16. Are all fables about animals
17. Try this new puzzle
18. The trout is a freshwater fish
19. What a troublemaker he is
20. Watch this last race

Using Sentences Correctly

There are many ways in which sentences are different from each other. They may have different purposes and express different ideas.

All sentences, however, have one thing in common. Every sentence expresses a complete thought.

Carol's sister works at Sears.
Are you going to the John Denver concert?

Some groups of words do not express a complete thought. They express only part of a thought. These groups of words are called sentence **fragments.**

Works at Sears
Going to the John Denver concert

Sometimes two or more sentences are written incorrectly as only one sentence. These sentences are called **run-on sentences.**

Carol's sister works at Sears she is a department manager.
Are you going to the John Denver concert do you have a ride?

You can see that sentence fragments and run-on sentences do not express ideas clearly. They are confusing to you when you read them.

When you write sentences, you should try to avoid confusion. You can see that you should avoid fragments and run-on sentences. In this section, you will be able to practice writing sentences correctly.

Part 1 Avoiding Sentence Fragments

A sentence fragment may express any part of a thought.
A fragment may tell only *who* or *what*.

Examples: My family
A gorilla named Otto

Or a fragment might tell only what *happened* or what *is*.

Examples: Lived in Vermont
Is a star attraction

Or a fragment might tell any other part of a thought.

Examples: Which is a beautiful state
At the Lincoln Park Zoo

You can see that all these sentence fragments express only part of an idea. Sentence fragments do not make sense.

A sentence that is clear and correct does make sense. A sentence expresses a complete thought.

Examples: My family lived in Vermont.

My family lived in Vermont, which is a beautiful state.

Otto is the star attraction.

At the Lincoln Park Zoo, a gorilla named Otto is the star attraction.

Exercises Recognize sentence fragments.

A. Read each of the following groups of words. Write *Sentence* or *Fragment* to tell what each group is.

1. A horse named Misty
2. Firefighters climbed onto the roof
3. Matching stocking cap and waterproof mittens
4. I'll fix the salad
5. The outer layer of the tooth is enamel
6. Nomads often live in tents
7. Carrie smiled as she walked away
8. Red, yellow, and blue are primary colors
9. Because it is a familiar place
10. Watched the Grammy Awards show on TV

B. Follow the directions for Exercise A.

1. Stopped at a shady picnic spot
2. Mom had a toothache
3. Flash floods eroded the soil
4. Drove the tractor and plowed the fields
5. Vanessa read the message with a magnifying glass
6. Under the pile of firewood
7. The badly dented bicycle
8. The girls followed the map
9. Elizabeth Blackwell became the first woman doctor
10. The helicopter landed on the roof

C. All of the following groups of words are fragments. Number your paper from 1 to 10. Change the fragments to sentences by adding whatever is needed. Write each sentence on your paper.

1. The revolving door
2. The artist at her easel
3. A team of doctors
4. Planted a vegetable garden
5. Celebrated her birthday
6. Have twenty cousins
7. A sudden bolt of lightning
8. Building a model railroad
9. Traveled by train
10. A Spiderman comic book

Part 2 Avoiding Run-on Sentences

A run-on sentence has two or more sentences written as one. Sometimes the sentences are written without using capital letters and punctuation to show where each new idea begins. See how confusing these run-on sentences are.

It was a lonely foggy night everything was still.
The group climbed up the hill they camped for the night.

Now see how clear the ideas are when each sentence expresses a single thought.

It was a lonely, foggy night. Everything was still.
The group climbed up the hill. They camped for the night.

Sometimes a run-on sentence contains two or more ideas that are not related, but are joined together by the word *and*. Read this example:

Amy likes photography and she took a picture of the children, *and* she will develop the film in her own darkroom.

See how clear the ideas are when separate sentences are used.

Amy likes photography. She took a picture of the children. She will develop the film in her own darkroom.

Whenever you write, be careful to put one complete idea in each sentence. Mark the end of each sentence with a period, question mark, or exclamation point. Begin each new sentence with a capital letter. Do not use *and* where it is not needed.

Exercises **Recognize run-on sentences.**

A. Some of the following sentences are run-on sentences. Some are complete sentences. Number your paper from 1 to 10. Read each sentence aloud. Then write either *Run-on* or *Complete.*

1. We had art today it is my favorite subject.
2. All of the books in that part of the library are nonfiction.
3. Lou and Bruce went to the game there was a huge crowd.
4. May I use your scissors I lost mine.
5. Scientists are developing ways to predict earthquakes.
6. Brazil is a very big country people speak Portuguese there.
7. Terry has his own calculator he got it for his birthday.
8. During Colonial times, children did not go to school very long.
9. Valerie and Susan took lessons in ballet and tap dancing.
10. Anita got an A on the science test she studied for it all weekend.

B. Follow the directions for Exercise A.

1. John bought a sandwich it had beef, pickles, and tomatoes in it.
2. Last summer I went swimming it's too cold now.
3. Vasco de Balboa discovered the Pacific Ocean and claimed it for Spain.
4. Betsy has a garden she grows flowers.
5. The strong wind across the deck made my eyes water.
6. Have you ever read this book by Madeleine L'Engle I liked it.

7. Tammy kept careful records of all her experiments.

8. Two companies of firefighters fought the fire on my street.

9. Edith and her family visited Idaho they went in a camper.

10. Bill "Bojangles" Robinson was a popular dancer he also appeared in movies.

C. Number your paper from 1 to 10. Correct each of the following run-on sentences. Read each run-on aloud. Then rewrite each one, adding the correct capitalization and punctuation.

1. Gordon replaced a tube in the TV set now it works fine.

2. The waterfall splashed down the rocks it sprayed us.

3. The bricklayer applied mortar then she stacked another brick.

4. Chuck read *Freaky Friday* it's a funny book.

5. Pam dove into the pool she swam six laps.

6. Annie likes to play Royal Rummy Evan likes Monopoly.

7. The jury gave its verdict the man was guilty.

8. Have you ever seen this program is it good?

9. In that bakery, a machine kneads the bread dough the baker makes the cookies.

10 This soil has too much clay plants don't grow well here.

REVIEW Using Sentences Correctly

Sentences, Sentence Fragments, and Run-on Sentences Number your paper from 1 to 20. Write *Fragment, Sentence,* or *Run-on* for each of the following groups of words to show what each group is.

1. The menu with cartoon drawings on it
2. Adam studied hard for the math test
3. Advisors met with the President they discussed energy
4. A hydroplane skims the water
5. Glowed red at sunset
6. A tornado thirty miles away
7. With a two-party system of government
8. There are volcanos in Mexico one erupted in 1943
9. Wearing brightly striped socks
10. The Feldmans got a new video game
11. Scared by a sudden blast
12. Peter aimed his arrow at the target
13. Kate took her first piano lesson she learned to play a short song
14. Figure skaters glided and twirled on the smooth ice
15. A package from Nome, Alaska
16. Jupiter was a Roman god Zeus was a Greek god
17. Sarah's bicycle tire went flat on the bumpy road
18. Sheila played ringtoss at the carnival she won a prize
19. People call the radio show they talk to the disc jockey
20. An undercover agent for a foreign country

Using Nouns

Part 1 What Are Nouns?

Who are you?

You are a person, a human being, a student. You are a girl or a boy, a daughter or a son, perhaps a sister or a brother. You may be a cyclist, a chess-player, a cook. You are a friend.

All of these answers are different names for you. They are all **nouns.**

Nouns are words that are used to name persons, places, or things. Here are a few examples of nouns:

Naming Persons

child painter Max Lois Lane

Naming Places

city home Australia North Dakota

Naming Things

fence spinach dinosaur International Peace Bridge

A noun is a word that names a person, place or thing.

Nouns may name things you can see, such as *desk* and *bicycle.* They may also name things you talk about that you cannot see or touch—such as *kindness, honesty, skill,* and *courage.*

Exercises **Find the nouns.**

A. Number your paper from 1 to 10. Write the nouns in each sentence below.

1. Texas is the second largest state.
2. The rules for this game are easy.
3. The heel of my boot is caught on a nail.
4. Mrs. Holmes kept her promise to the class.
5. Which contest did the twins win?
6. An alert lifeguard sat on the platform at the beach.
7. Detroit has a problem with pollution.
8. My older sister moved to Massachusetts because of her job.
9. Three porpoises jumped out of the pool.
10. Does Betty know the title of that song?

B. Follow the directions for Exercise A.

1. The cheese on this cracker tastes funny.
2. Alaska and Hawaii are the newest states.
3. Pepper is a little dog with black spots.
4. A foil is a sword with a button on the point.
5. The prices of the coats are marked on the tags.
6. Sally was in Frontierland, looking at the old streets and houses.
7. People from Cuba speak Spanish.
8. Buttercups and daisies were growing in the field.
9. That baby has a cute smile.
10. Mr. Martin won't take any nonsense or excuses.

c. In this exercise, you will write only nouns.

a. Write the names of four persons you know.

b. Write the names of four places you have visited.

c. Write the names of four things you can see at this moment.

d. Write the names of four things you cannot see or touch, such as *truth*, or *love*, for example.

Part 2 Common Nouns and Proper Nouns

If you call yourself a student, you are giving yourself a name that you share with all the boys and girls in the class. If you call yourself a boy or a girl, you share that name with about half your classmates. *Student*, *boy*, and *girl* are names common to whole groups of people. They are common nouns.

Playground, *town*, and *lake* are words that name members of whole groups or places. They are common nouns. Many nouns name whole groups of things, like *book*, *tool*, or *animal*. These are all common nouns.

A **common noun** is the name of a whole class of persons, places, or things. It is a name that is common to the whole class.

You are not simply any person. You have a name that is specifically yours. Margaret Thatcher, Judy Blume, and Captain James T. Kirk are specific people. These names of specific people are called **proper nouns.**

Proper nouns can also name specific places, like Houston and Lake Erie. They may name specific things, like the *Mayflower* and a Big Mac.

A **proper noun** is the name of a particular person, place, or thing. A proper noun always starts with a capital letter.

Common Nouns	**Proper Nouns**
Groups of Persons	Particular Persons
doctor	Dr. Jonas Salk
children	Jane Banks, Michael Banks
lawmaker	Barbara Jordan
Groups of Places	Particular Places
street	Jefferson Street
park	Yosemite National Park
city	Richmond
Groups of Things	Particular Things
bridge	George Washington Bridge
country	Canada
religion	Christianity

You can see that a proper noun may also be a group of words.

Capitalize all words in a proper noun. Do not capitalize the words *a*, *an*, or *the* before a proper noun.

Exercises Find common and proper nouns.

A. Label two columns *Common Noun* and *Proper Noun.* List the numbers from 1 to 20 down the left-hand margin of your paper. Opposite each number, write its noun in the proper column. Be sure to capitalize proper nouns.

1. chair
2. geraldo
3. colorado
4. mountain
5. the rocky mountains
6. ms. parsons
7. school
8. woolworth's
9. the hudson river
10. actor
11. country
12. lake erie
13. elizabeth
14. daughter
15. cowboy
16. atlantic ocean
17. green river
18. martin luther king
19. elmwood elementary school
20. harbor

B. Follow the directions for Exercise A.

1. bridge
2. france
3. cleveland
4. man
5. the chicago black hawks
6. europe
7. philadelphia
8. the white house
9. the new york stock exchange
10. high school
11. world war II
12. detective
13. south america
14. crossword puzzle
15. coca cola
16. saint theresa
17. the jefferson memorial
18. horse
19. monopoly
20. fort

C. Copy these sentences. Capitalize the first word in the sentence and each proper noun.

1. bob mackey drove his car to florida last winter.
2. ms. moore told us about islands in the pacific ocean.
3. a great many potatoes are grown in the state of idaho.
4. my uncle once met the comedian jimmie walker.
5. brenda's birthday is in january.

Part 3 Singular and Plural Nouns

Look at these two nouns: player—players. They are exactly the same except for the last letter.

The noun *player* refers to one person. It is called a singular noun. A **singular** noun names just one person, place, or thing.

The noun *players* ends in *s*. It refers to several persons. It is called a **plural** noun. The word *plural* means *more than one*.

A singular noun names one person, place, or thing.

A plural noun names more than one person, place, or thing.

Here are seven rules for forming the plurals of nouns:

1. To form the plural of most nouns, just add *s*.

hat**s** street**s** hamburger**s** animal**s**
table**s** mile**s** shake**s** movie**s**

2. When the singular ends in *s, sh, ch, x,* or *z,* add *es*.

gas**es** brush**es** box**es**
dress**es** match**es** buzz**es**

3. When the singular ends in *o,* add *s*.

radio**s** solo**s** banjo**s** Eskimo**s**

Exceptions: For the following nouns ending in **o**, add **es:**

echo**es** hero**es** potato**es** tomato**es**

4. When the singular noun ends in *y* with a consonant before it, change the *y* to *i* and add *es*.

pony→pon**ies** baby→bab**ies**
lady→lad**ies** daisy→dais**ies**

5. For most nouns ending in *f* or *ff,* add *s*. For some nouns ending in *f* or *fe,* however, change the *f* to *v* and add *es* or *s*.

belief**s** thief → thie**ves** leaf → lea**ves**
roof**s** knife → kni**ves** half → hal**ves**
dwarf**s** wife → wi**ves** shelf → shel**ves**

6. Some nouns are the same for both singular and plural.

deer sheep trout salmon bass

7. Some nouns form their plurals in special ways.

child → children man → men tooth → teeth
mouse → mice woman → women foot → feet

Using a Dictionary To Find Plurals

Here is a dictionary entry for the word *echo*. Notice that the entry shows the plural ending *-oes*. The plural form is *echoes*. Most dictionaries show the plurals or plural endings of nouns, if the plurals are formed in an irregular way.

Dictionary Entry for *Echo*

ech•o (ek′ō) *n., pl.,* **-oes** [< L. < Gr. *ēchō*] **1.** *a*) the repetition of a sound that occurs when sound waves are reflected from a surface *b*) a sound so made **2.** *a*) any repetition or imitation of the words, ideas, etc. of another *b*) a person who repeats or imitates in this way **3.** sympathetic response **4.** a radar wave reflected from an object, appearing as a spot of light on a radarscope —[**E-**] *Gr. Myth.* a nymph who pined away for Narcissus until only her voice remained —**vi. o-ed -o.ing** **1.** to be filled with echoes [the long hall *echoed* with their laughter] **2.** to be repeated as an echo [his words *echoed* in the valley] —**vt.** **1.** to repeat (the words, ideas, etc.) of (another) **2.** to repeat or reflect (sound) from a surface

When you are in doubt about plurals, consult a dictionary.

Exercises Form plurals of nouns.

A. Number your paper from 1 to 10. Write every plural noun in each sentence. After each noun, write the number of the rule that tells how the plural was formed.

Example: Representatives from three countries signed the treaty.

Representatives—1, countries—4

1. The children heard echoes in the cave.
2. The flies were killed by the sprays.
3. On the fishing trip, I caught two bass and several trout.
4. In come countries even adults believe in witches and elves.
5. There are rushes and bushes in the marshes.
6. The farmer set the potatoes and tomatoes on the tables.
7. If I help you win the prize, will you go halves with me?
8. Three deer and some foxes followed the sheep.
9. Do mice and geese have teeth?
10. The dairies in the cities suffered losses.

B. Write the plural form of these nouns.

1. watch	4. foot	7. leaf	10. company
2. guppy	5. candy	8. hero	11. wife
3. wish	6. porch	9. life	12. woman

Part 4 How Nouns Show Possession

When you speak of something that belongs to someone, you want a short way of expressing that relationship. You do not want to say, for example, "the dog that belongs to Tom" every time you refer to it. In English, the shortcut is the *possessive form* of the noun. The possessive form of *Tom* is *Tom's;* the simple way to refer to the dog he owns is *Tom's dog.*

Possessive nouns show possession, or ownership, of the noun that follows.

Forming Possessives of Singular Nouns

The difference between *Tom* and the possessive form *Tom's* is the ending. *Tom's* has an apostrophe and an *s.*

To form the possessive of a singular noun, add an apostrophe and *s.*

Singular Noun	Possessive Form
baby	baby's
Charles	Charles's
Ms. Wills	Ms. Wills's

Forming Possessives of Plural Nouns

There are two rules to remember for forming the possessive of a plural noun.

1. If the plural noun ends in *s*, simply add an apostrophe after the *s*.

Plural Noun	Possessive Form
flowers	flowers'
pirates	pirates'
cats	cats'
doctors	doctors'
students	students'

2. If the plural noun does not end in *s*, add an apostrophe and an *s* after the apostrophe.

Plural Noun	Possessive Form
men	men's
women	women's
children	children's

Be especially careful when you are adding possessive endings. Notice how the position of the apostrophe affects the meaning of the possesive.

The *student's* pencils means pencils belonging to *one* student.
The *students'* pencils means pencils belonging to *two or more* students.

If you are not sure how to write the possessive form of a noun, do this:

1. Write the noun first.
2. Then follow the rules.

Exercises **Write the possessive form.**

A. Write the word in italics in each sentence so that it shows possession.

1. The doctor took the *runner* pulse.
2. Is that the *manager* phone number?
3. The new *girl* hair was long and curly.
4. Follow your *mother* advice.

5. A parade honored the *astronauts* homecoming.
6. We could see the *raccoon* tracks.
7. The *sailors* raincoats protected them from the spray.
8. The *statue* smile looked real.
9. My *dog* ears perked up.
10. *Tess* butterfly collection has two dozen specimens.

B. Copy these sentences. Underline the person, place, or thing in each sentence that belongs to someone or something else. Then place the apostrophe where it belongs to show who or what possesses the noun you underlined.

1. The childrens presents are in the hall closet.
2. Jims store sells maps.
3. The golf bags are in my fathers car.
4. That architects design won two awards.
5. Many campers tents were destroyed in the forest fire.
6. We used Megans scarf as a bandage.
7. Andreas painting was sold.
8. The mices whiskers twitched nervously.
9. The governors mansion was lit by floodlights.
10. On Ms. Conways desk is a no-smoking sign.

C. Follow the directions for Exercise B.

1. The kings charger reared, his eyes flashing.
2. Ma Barretts pies are known all over Grimsby County.
3. The boys faces looked stunned.
4. Mr. Whites garden always had sunflowers.
5. Jills car has reclining seats.
6. Both wrestlers muscles bulged and strained.
7. Those look like Anitas earmuffs.
8. Suddenly the referees whistle stopped the game.
9. Barneys cats were yowling again.
10. A horned owls feathers make points like ears.

Sentence Patterns The N V Pattern

In an English sentence, the words are put together in a certain order to make sense. The word order of most sentences follows a pattern. In this book, you will study four **sentence patterns.**

Every sentence has a subject and a verb. The subject is usually a noun. In this chart, *N* stands for the noun in the complete subject. *V* stands for the verb in the complete predicate.

N	V
Margie	cheered.
Carl	ate quickly.
The baby	smiled.
The red balloon	popped.
Our puppy	snores.

The word order in these sentences follows a pattern. That pattern is noun-verb, or N V. This pattern is called the **N V pattern.**

Exercises The N V Pattern

A. Make a chart like the one above. Label one column *N* and the other *V*. Write these sentences on the chart.

1. Clouds formed.
2. Jenny skates every day.
3. The teams struggled.
4. Strong winds howled.
5. The dogs barked loudly.
6. Alex whistled.

B. Make a chart of your own for the N V pattern. Write five sentences in the N V pattern.

REVIEW Using Nouns

Recognizing Nouns There are common nouns and proper nouns in each of the following sentences. For each sentence, list the nouns. Capitalize every proper noun you list.

1. Pélé played soccer as a boy in brazil.
2. Rhode island is the smallest state in the nation.
3. In the fog, we could barely see the lighthouse at portland.
4. During class, andrew told a very funny joke.
5. Dr. alexander treated her patients at the hospital.
6. Tracey found beautiful seashells on the beaches of sanibel island.
7. Robert fulton designed the earliest steamboats.
8. People wonder about life on other planets, especially mars.
9. Charlie chaplin was an actor and director for early movies.
10. Alison and todd climbed the sandy dunes on cape cod.

Forming Plurals Write the plural form of each *italicized* noun.

11. *Paper* lined the floor of the hallway.
12. Rita ate the *sandwich*.
13. We picked the *tomato* and *strawberry* from our garden.
14. The *knife* lay on the shelf.
15. The child petted the *deer* and the *goose*.

Forming Possessives Write the possessive form of each italicized noun.

16. The *sightseers* tour took them through the museum.
17. Our *family* van sleeps six people.
18. *Russ* pony trotted around the track.
19. The *robot* chores were cooking and cleaning.
20. The politician wanted the *people* trust.

Using Verbs

Becky ________ the dog.

The words above almost express a message. You can complete the message by putting various words in the blank.

Becky *fed* the dog.
Becky *washed* the dog.
Becky *owned* the dog.

This time the words express a clear message. The words *fed, washed,* and *owned* say what Becky did.

The words *fed, washed,* and *owned* all belong to a group of words called **verbs.** No sentence is complete without a verb. This section will tell you about verbs. It will also show you how to use them.

Part 1 Kinds of Verbs

There are two kinds of verbs.

Some verbs tell about action. They are **action verbs.**

Sue *hit* the ball. Bill *ran* to the window.

Some verbs name action that you cannot see. That is, there is no actual movement taking place.

Barbara *thought* about pets. She *wanted* a puppy.

Some verbs are not action verbs. They simply state that something *is*. They express a state of being. They are **state-of-being verbs.**

Your book *is* on the table The slacks *were* too big.

The most common state-of-being verbs are these:

is	are	were	being
am	was	be	been

Exercises Find action verbs and state-of-being verbs.

A. Copy these sentences. Underline the verb in each sentence.

1. Our school held an art fair.
2. Students displayed their artwork.
3. Colorful ceramic pots lined the tables.
4. A band played music in the gym.
5. The mood at the party was joyful.
6. I took my dog to obedience school.
7. We reward Scamp with dog biscuits.
8. Sharon remembered her umbrella.
9. Last Sunday the weather was hot and humid.
10. Rosario missed the bus this morning.

B. Make two columns on your paper. Head one column *Action Verbs* and the other *State-of-Being Verbs.* Find the verb in each sentence and place it in the right column.

Example: That is Kevin's music stand.
Beth drank the lemonade.

Action Verbs	State-of-Being Verbs
	is
drank	

1. The rabbit's cage was empty.
2. This old dress is still in style.
3. Judy loves dill pickles.
4. We rode our bikes down to the canal.
5. The fourth question on the test was tricky.
6. Suddenly Syd's dark eyes lit up.
7. I know the names of all the lifeguards.
8. Valentina Tereshkova was the first woman in space.
9. The kingfisher swallowed a frog and two fish.
10. Richard's bike accident happened last June.

C. Follow the directions for Exercise B.

1. In 1927, Charles A. Lindbergh flew from New York to Paris.
2. He was alone.
3. He faced many hardships.
4. After many hours in flight, he was successful.
5. The French people welcomed him.
6. He came home on a United States cruiser.
7. The American nation gave him many honors.
8. His solo flight was a great event.
9. It aided the development of aviation.
10. Lindbergh is an important aviation hero.

Part 2 Main Verbs and Helping Verbs

Many verbs are made of more than one word. They are made up of the main verb and helping verbs.
Read these examples:

I *am going* to the concert tonight.
Molly *is going* deep sea fishing.
The children *can go* to the movie by themselves.
Bea and Jessie *will go* to North Carolina.
Mary Casey *has gone* to New York on business.
The snow *has been gone* for a week.
Sam *could have gone* to Mexico.

Helping Verbs +	Main Verb =	Verb
am	going	am going
is	going	is going
can	go	can go
will	go	will go
has	gone	has gone
has been	gone	has been gone
could have	gone	could have gone

The most common of the helping verbs are these forms of *be*, *have*, and *do*:

be	am, are, is, was, were
have	has, have, had
do	does, do, did

These words can also be used by themselves as main verbs.

Used as Helping Verb	Used as Main Verb
Bob *is going*.	Bob *is* the pitcher.
Sally *has gone*.	Sally *has* a moped.
They *did go*.	They *did* a duet.

There are several other helping verbs that you will often use with main verbs:

be	been	can	would	shall	might
being	may	could	should	will	must

A verb tells about action or expresses a state of being. It may be a single word or a group of words, made up of a **main verb** and one or more **helping verbs.**

Separated Parts of the Verb

The main verb and helping verbs are not always together. They may be separated by other parts of the sentence.

The batter **was** not **watching** for signals.
Frankenstein **could**n't **control** his monster.
Andrea **has** never **missed** a band practice.
Max **had** completely **recovered** from the flu.
Did the boys **make** spaghetti?

Notice that *not* and the ending *n't* in the contraction are not verbs, although they do change the meaning of the verbs.

Exercises **Find main verbs and helping verbs.**

A. Number your paper from 1 to 10. Make two columns. Label the first column *Helping Verbs.* Label the second *Main Verb.* Write the verbs for each of these sentences in the right column. (Watch out for separated parts of the verb.)

Example: The books could not be found anywhere.

Helping Verbs	Main Verb
could be	found

1. I was expecting a phone call.
2. The old chestnut tree was hit by lightning.
3. Where can we find a book about marine life?
4. You should have seen the flames.

5. This contest entry might be too late.
6. The beachball had completely collapsed.
7. Skip has never had the measles.
8. That bottle could have floated here from Greenland.
9. We have already eaten our sandwiches.
10. The team had been hoping for a sunny day.

B. Follow the directions for Exercise A.

1. The red wolf is becoming extinct.
2. Coach Perez had called a timeout.
3. The Bears are beating the Vikings, 7–0.
4. People should always eat a nutritious breakfast.
5. Cartoons can sometimes be violent.
6. Did Momoko bring her skateboard?
7. Have you ever written a poem?
8. Curt might be joining the hockey team.
9. Computers will soon be performing many household tasks.
10. A President can't be elected more than twice.

Part 3 Verbs and Direct Objects

In many sentences the thought is complete when there are just a verb and its subject:

Subject	Verb
The audience	applauded.
Mary Ann	coughed.
Donald	worked.

In other sentences the thought is not complete until other words have been added.

Paul dried ____________.
Lucy liked ____________.

So far, you don't know *what* Paul dried or *whom* Lucy liked. We need to complete the sentences.

Paul dried the *dishes*. Lucy liked the new *coach*.

In the first sentence, the word *dishes* receives the action of the verb *dried*. It completes the meaning of the verb. It is the **direct object** of the verb.

In the second sentence, *coach* receives the action of *liked*. It completes the meaning of the verb. It is the **direct object** of the verb.

The direct object tells what receives the action of the verb.

Recognizing Direct Objects

To find the direct object in a sentence, first find the verb. Then ask *what?* or *whom?*

Examples: Christy likes math.
Christy likes *what?* math
The direct object is *math*.

Mrs. McKenna hired Kim.
Mrs. McKenna hired *whom?* Kim
The direct object is *Kim*.

Direct objects only answer *what?* or *whom?* after the verb. They do not tell *when* or *where* or *how*. You will see there are no direct objects in the following sentences.

Liz studies in the morning.
They drove to the beach.
Julio reads quickly.

Exercises **Add direct objects.**

A. Write direct objects that will complete these sentences.

1. The reporter wrote a good ________.

2. The Cardinals scored a __________.
3. Newspapers littered the __________.
4. Jolita rode the __________ with ease.
5. Leroy planted __________ in his front yard.
6. Nicky read a __________ yesterday.
7. Harvey wore a bright yellow __________.
8. Kristin put the __________ in her wallet.
9. My favorite radio station plays good __________.
10. Did you close the __________?

B. Write sentences using these verbs. Put a direct object in each sentence. Draw a circle around the direct object.

1. have caught
2. filled
3. would have stopped
4. was twisting
5. painted
6. will open
7. has invented
8. ruined
9. should limit
10. might use

Exercises Find direct objects.

A. Copy the following sentences. Underline the verb twice. Draw a circle around the direct object.

Example: The policeman stopped all traffic.

1. The scuba diver found a shipwreck.
2. Bruce won the race.
3. The pilot steered his craft onto the airfield.
4. I am studying science now.
5. The children have built a huge snowman.
6. The Bureau of the Mint manufactures all coins.
7. Katy will repair the brakes on her bike.
8. Dolores likes brownies with ice cream on top.
9. On Thanksgiving Day we eat turkey with gravy.
10. The United States exports grains to the Far East.

B. Number your paper from 1 to 10. Find and write the direct objects in these sentences.

1. Janet Guthrie drove the Corvette.
2. Jody will answer the telephone.
3. Our basketball team won its first game.
4. In 1785, Jean Pierre Blanchard invented the parachute.
5. Sonia made pizzas for the party.
6. The sailors unfurled the mainsail.
7. The teacher wrote the assignment on the blackboard.
8. The zookeeper fed raw meat to the lions.
9. Did you drop the carton of eggs?
10. Beth placed the saddle on the horse's back.

Part 4 Linking Verbs

State-of-being verbs are often called **linking verbs.** Here are some examples.

The sky *was* blue.
The omelet *smells* delicious.
The table *looked* unsteady.

Linking verbs connect the subject with a word in the predicate. In the examples, they connect *sky* with *blue, omelet* with *delicious*, and *table* with *unsteady*.

The words *is, am, are, was, were, be, become* are often used as linking verbs. The words *seem, look, appear, smell, taste, feel,* and *sound* are sometimes linking verbs.

The words that follow linking verbs and tell something about the subject are either nouns or adjectives. These words complete the meaning of the linking verbs.

Here are some examples of nouns that follow linking verbs. These nouns are called **predicate nouns.** See how each predicate noun is connected to the subject.

My mother *is* a coach.

The Beatles *were* a very popular group.

He *will be* the pitcher.

Here are some examples of adjectives that follow linking verbs. These adjectives are called **predicate adjectives.** See how each predicate adjective describes the subject.

Leslie *looked* unhappy.

The roads *were* very slippery.

Greg *is being* stubborn.

Exercises **Find the linking verbs.**

A. At the top of three columns write *Subject, Linking Verb,* and *Word Linked to Subject.* Find the three parts in each sentence. Write them in the proper columns.

Example: The contestants in the marathon appeared weary.

Subject	Linking Verb	Word Linked to Subject
contestants	appeared	weary

1. Jane Fonda is an actress.
2. That clown's hat looks ridiculous.
3. The fresh bread smells delicious.
4. A young kangaroo is a joey.
5. Don't bullfights seem brutal?
6. Samuel's story sounds unbelieveable.
7. That mask looks scary.
8. Underwater, straight lines will appear wavy.
9. Ebenezer Scrooge is a character in "A Christmas Carol."
10. We should be quiet during the rehearsal.

B. Follow the directions for Exercise A.

1. The edge of this knife is dull.
2. My skates are becoming rusty.
3. The chili tastes fiery.
4. The fastest animal is the cheetah.
5. I don't feel sleepy.
6. The huge trees are sequoias.
7. Our country's oldest national park is Yellowstone.
8. The Vikings may have been Scandinavian pirates.
9. Mother must be very angry.
10. The most popular breed of dog is the poodle.

Direct Objects or Predicate Words?

What are the differences between these two sentences?

Kate played the piano.
Kate is a musician.

You have learned about two kinds of verbs. There are action verbs and linking verbs. You have also learned about two kinds of words that follow verbs and complete their meaning. There are direct objects. There are also predicate nouns or predicate adjectives.

How can you tell which words are direct objects and which words are predicate words?

First, find the verb in a sentence. Is the verb an action verb or a linking verb?

1. If an **action verb** is followed by a word, a noun, that tells *what* or *whom*, that word is a **direct object.**

   Examples: Bob *is studying* his **math.**
   We *had* **pizza** for lunch.

2. If a **linking verb** is followed by a word that tells about the the subject, that word is a **predicate noun** or a **predicate adjective.**

Examples: Julie *is* a **student.**
We *are* **hungry.**

Now compare these two examples:

Kate played the piano.

Played is an action verb.
Piano is the direct object.

Kate is a musician.

Is is a linking verb.
Musician is the predicate noun.

Exercises **Find direct objects and predicate words.**

A. Some of the verbs in the following sentences are linking verbs followed by predicate words. Others are action verbs followed by direct objects. Copy the sentences. Draw circles around the linking verbs and predicate words. Underline the action verbs and direct objects.

Examples: Emmett Kelly (is) a famous (clown.)
Congress approved the treaty.

1. The campers carried firewood to the campsite.
2. Marina is a good athlete.
3. Vacations always seem too short.
4. The police detective felt the damp earth.
5. A down quilt feels very cozy.
6. The golfer had hit the ball into the water.
7. According to legend, Betsy Ross made the first flag.
8. The bill may soon become a law.
9. Mopeds use gas efficiently.
10. Mopeds are efficient vehicles.

B. Follow the directions for Exercise A.

1. The cashier added the figures.

2. The Soviet Union is the largest country in the world.
3. Kim has been a crossing guard.
4. The floor of the gym seems sticky.
5. Jason smelled smoke down the hall.
6. Chris angrily closed her locker.
7. Cheryl's story was good.
8. The auditorium quickly became noisy.
9. The goalie stopped the puck just in time.
10. Some Eskimos use snowmobiles instead of dog sleds.

Part 5 Verb Tenses

Verbs are time-telling words. They not only tell of an action or a state of being. They also tell *when* something takes place. By changing their forms, they tell whether the action or state of being is past, present, or future. These changes in form to show time are called **tenses.**

The **present tense** indicates an action or state of being happening now.

I *work* at school. I *am* a student.

The **past tense** indicates an action or state of being completed in the past.

I *worked* all last summer. I *was* a library aide.

The **future tense** indicates an action or state of being happening in the future.

I *will work* at the pool next year. I *will be* a lifeguard.

Tense changes are made in three ways:

1. by a change in spelling: *know, knew, known*
2. by a change in ending: *look, looked*
3. by a change in helping verbs: *did work, will work*

Forming Tenses

Present Tense

In general, the present tense of the verb is the same as the name of the verb: *call, do, race*. An *-s* or *-es* is added to the verb when it is used with *he, she,* or *it* or a singular noun.

I	call	we	call
you	call	you	call
he, she, it	call*s*	they	call

I	do	we	do
you	do	you	do
he, she, it	do*es*	they	do

Past Tense

The past tense of most verbs is formed by adding *-d* or *-ed* to the present tense:

race—race*d* call—call*ed*

These verbs are called **regular verbs.**

The past tense of other verbs, called **irregular verbs,** is usually shown by a change of spelling:

do—*did* think—*thought*

Future Tense

The future tense is formed by using the helping words *will* or *shall* with the present tense:

will race shall think

Exercises Recognize and use verb tenses.

A. Number your paper from 1 to 10. Write the verb in each of the following sentences. Name the tense of each verb.

1. Alison does crossword puzzles.

2. Sir Edmund Hillary climbed Mount Everest.
3. Our class will plan a school carnival.
4. We saw a porpoise show.
5. The fans cheered Peter Frampton.
6. "Mork and Mindy" is hilarious.
7. Students will take a bus home from school.
8. Tracy Austin plays fine tennis.
9. I will return this book to the library.
10. Indians first explored this wilderness.

B. Number your paper from 1 to 10. Write the form of the verb asked for in each of the following sentences.

Example: The runner (past of *cross*) the finish line.

crossed

1. I (future of *read*) all of the Hardy Boys mysteries.
2. The lawyer (past of *argue*) her case.
3. We (present of *roast*) chestnuts in the fireplace.
4. Tyrone (past of *make*) a lamp for his room.
5. The airplane (future of *land*) in a few minutes.
6. Scott O'Dell (past of *write*) *Island of the Blue Dolphins*.
7. Eric and Teresa (past of *pick*) raspberries.
8. A cricket game (present of *confuse*) most American spectators.
9. Sponges (present of *live*) in the deep seas.
10. The track team (future of *run*) in a meet tomorrow.

C. Write a sentence for each of the verbs below. Use the verb in the tense indicated.

1. hurry (future)
2. think (past)
3. enjoy (present)
4. call (past)
5. remove (past)
6. finish (future)

Sentence Patterns The N V N Pattern

The **N V N pattern** describes a sentence with three parts. The first *N* stands for the subject noun. The *V* stands for the verb. The second *N* stands for the direct object noun. Each of the sentences in the following chart is in the N V N pattern.

N	V	N
Rosa	ordered	waffles.
Henry	plays	chess.
The carpenter	pounded	the nails.
The class	presented	a play.

Exercises The N V N Pattern

A. Make a chart like the one above. Label the three columns *N, V,* and *N.* Write these sentences on the chart.

1. Diana collects seashells.
2. Plants need sunlight.
3. My brother likes toffee.
4. Yuri climbed that peak.
5. The judges awarded prizes.
6. Eric bakes tasty bread.
7. NASA launched a rocket.
8. Our team won the game.

B. Copy this chart. Complete each sentence in the N V N pattern.

N	V	N
1. ____________	shook	the house.
2. King Kong	grabbed	____________.
3. ____________	saw	____________.
4. Tony	________________	two hamburgers.
5. ____________	called	Lou Ann.
6. The goat	rammed	____________.

Sentence Patterns The N LV N Pattern

The **N LV N pattern** describes a sentence with three parts. The first *N* stands for the subject noun. *LV* stands for a linking verb. The second *N* stands for the noun that follows the linking verb.

N	LV	N
Chimpanzees	are	mammals.
Allen	is	my friend.
My favorite dessert	is	pudding.
The blizzard	was	a disaster.

Exercises The N LV N Pattern

A. Make a chart like the one above. Label the three columns *N, LV,* and *N.* Write these sentences on the chart.

1. Dee is my sister.
2. Pumpkins are vegetables.
3. This chair is an antique.
4. The Tortugas are islands.
5. Pete is an artist.
6. Mushrooms are parasites.
7. The sun is a star.
8. My aunt is a jogger.

B. Make a chart like the one below. Complete each sentence in the N LV N pattern.

N	LV	N
1. ________	is	a useful tool.
2. My best friend	was	________.
3. ________	are	reptiles.
4. The Riveras	________	my neighbors.
5. ________	are	________.

C. Make a chart of your own. Label the columns *N, LV,* and *N.* Write five sentences in the N LV N pattern.

Sentence Patterns The N LV Adj Pattern

There are three parts to sentences that have the **N LV Adj pattern.** The *N* stands for the subject noun. *LV* stands for a linking verb. *Adj* stands for the predicate adjective. Each of the sentences in the following chart is in the N LV Adj pattern.

N	LV	Adj
Peter	is	friendly.
The water	looks	murky.
Your voice	sounds	hoarse.
This melon	tastes	sweet.

Exercises The N LV Adj Pattern

A. Make a chart like the one above. Label the three columns *N, LV,* and *Adj.* Write these sentences on the chart.

1. Lottie seems cautious.
2. This ice is slippery.
3. Cherry pie is delicious.
4. Skydivers are adventurous.
5. Jeff seemed lucky.
6. The Cubs were victorious.
7. The sky looked gloomy.
8. My father will be late.

B. Make a chart like the one below. Complete each sentence in the N LV Adj pattern.

	N	LV	Adj
1.	________	is	cheerful.
2.	The snow	became	________.
3.	Clowns	look	________.
4.	The Soos	________	busy.
5.	________	was	________.

C. Make a chart of your own. Label the columns *N, LV,* and *Adj.* Write five sentences in the N LV Adj pattern.

REVIEW Using Verbs

Action Verbs and Linking Verbs Write each verb. Beside the verb, write *Action* or *Linking* to show what the verb is. If an action verb has a direct object, write the direct object. Or, write the predicate word that completes a linking verb.

1. An arsonist sets fires.
2. Our youth club elected officers last night.
3. The team seems ready for the big game.
4. Deena borrowed my basketball.
5. The patient's condition has become critical.
6. After a rain, the air feels heavy.
7. Mangos are tropical fruits.
8. Steve carefully crossed the footbridge.
9. The gymnast practiced on the ropes.
10. Jeopardy is a game for three or more players.

Parts of the Verb The verbs in the following sentences are made of helping verbs and main verbs. Find the verb in each sentence, and write the complete verb.

11. Dry ice is sometimes used in ice cream makers.
12. Bears at Yellowstone will come up to the car.
13. The rescue party must have searched the woods.
14. Ms. Andretti has not assigned homework.
15. Have you ever ridden on a motorcycle?

Verb Tenses Write each verb and its tense.

16. Carlotta saw the eclipse.
17. Mr. and Mrs. Lewis train seeing-eye dogs.
18. Sportswriters will name the all-star team.
19. Admiral Peary explored the North Pole.
20. Brian expects an apology.

Using Irregular Verbs

Part 1 Principal Parts of Verbs

Depending on how a verb is used, it can take many forms. For the verb *talk*, for example, these are some of the variations:

We **talked** until midnight.
The lawyer **had talked** to the judge.
David and Todd **will talk** on the phone.
We **would have talked** longer.

While *talk* can be used in many ways, the verb has three main forms. These three are known as the **principal parts.** Every verb has three principal parts:

1. Present	2. Past	3. Past participle
talk	talked	talked

Here are some examples:

Present	Past	Past Participle
call	called	called
look	looked	looked
hurry	hurried	hurried
race	raced	raced
stop	stopped	stopped

The *present* part of the verb is its present tense. (Add *-s* or *-es* when it is used with a singular noun or *he, she,* or *it.*) The present part used with *will* or *shall* forms the future tense.

The *past* part of the verb is its past tense.

The *past participle* is used with helping verbs to make other forms of the verb. Here are some examples of these other forms:

has called	was being called
have called	shall be called
had called	has been called
was called	will have called
were called	should have been called

Part 2 Regular Verbs

In the list of principal parts given above, the verbs are **regular verbs.** Every verb that is *regular* forms its past tense by adding **-ed** (*called*) or **-d** (*raced*) to the present form. The past participle is the same as the past form and is always used with a helping verb. Most verbs in English are regular.

Exercise **Form principal parts.**

Number your paper from 1 to 10. Write the verb form indicated for each of the following regular verbs. Use one or more helping verbs with each past participle.

1. print (past)
2. ask (present)
3. dream (past participle)
4. want (past)
5. use (past participle)
6. help (past participle)
7. confuse (present)
8. list (past)
9. cover (past participle)
10. like (future)

Part 3 Irregular Verbs

Some verbs do not form their second and third parts in a regular way. These five verbs are examples:

Present	Past	Past Participle
feel	felt	felt
go	went	gone
know	knew	known
see	saw	seen
think	thought	thought

These verbs are not regular verbs. They are called **irregular verbs.**

There are about sixty of these irregular verbs in English. The best way to learn about them is to memorize their three principal parts. A list of the most commonly used irregular verbs is given on page 275.

When you are using irregular verbs, you should remember these two rules:

1. The past form is always used by itself, **without** a helping verb.
   We *went* to the library.
2. The past participle is always used **with** a helping verb.
   We *have gone* to the library.

Helping Verbs

The words most often used with the third principal part of all verbs are the forms of *be* and *have*. Here they are, so that you can refer to them when you need to.

Be

I	am	*or*	was	we	are	*or*	were
you	are		were	you	are		were
he, she, it	is		was	they	are		were

Be, been, and *being* must be used with helping verbs.

Janice *will be* the manager.
My father *has been* very sick.
You *are being* stubborn.

Have

I	have	*or*	had	we	have	*or*	had
you	have		had	you	have		had
he, she, it	has		had	they	have		had

Using a Dictionary To Find Principal Parts

If you are not sure about a verb form, look it up in a dictionary. If the verb is regular, only one form will usually be listed.

If the verb is irregular, the dictionary will give the irregular forms. It will give two forms if the past and past participle are the same: *say, said.* It will give all three principal parts if they are all different: *sing, sang, sung.*

Dictionary Entry for *Begin*

present

be·gin (bi gin′), **v.** to start being, doing, acting, etc.; get under way [Work *begins* at 8:00 A.M. His cold *began* with a sore throat.] —**be·gan′**, *p.;* **be·gun′**, *p.p.*

past participle

past

Principal Parts of Common Irregular Verbs

Present	Past	Past Participle
begin	began	(have) begun
break	broke	(have) broken
bring	brought	(have) brought
choose	chose	(have) chosen
come	came	(have) come
do	did	(have) done
drink	drank	(have) drunk
eat	ate	(have) eaten
fall	fell	(have) fallen
freeze	froze	(have) frozen
give	gave	(have) given
go	went	(have) gone
grow	grew	(have) grown
have	had	(have) had
know	knew	(have) known
ride	rode	(have) ridden
ring	rang	(have) rung
rise	rose	(have) risen
run	ran	(have) run
say	said	(have) said
see	saw	(have) seen
sing	sang	(have) sung
sit	sat	(have) sat
speak	spoke	(have) spoken
steal	stole	(have) stolen
swim	swam	(have) swum
take	took	(have) taken
teach	taught	(have) taught
throw	threw	(have) thrown
wear	wore	(have) worn
write	wrote	(have) written

Part 4 Practice Pages on Irregular Verbs

Regular verbs have the same form for the past and past participle. Using helping verbs with the past participle is no problem.

Irregular verbs, however, often have different forms for the past and past participle. Since you can use helping verbs only with the past participle, you must know which form is the past participle.

The exercise below will help you find which irregular verbs give you problems. Following this exercise, there is a page of exercises for each verb tested. When you know which verbs give you difficulty, you can then turn to the exercise pages on those verbs.

Exercise Use irregular verbs.

Number your paper from 1 to 15. For each sentence, write the correct word from the two given in the parentheses.

1. We (drank, drunk) the juice after football practice.
2. Jesse's notebook has (fell, fallen) off the desk.
3. Last month, sixty visitors (came, come) to the school.
4. The doctor (did, done) all she could.
5. Andrew has (did, done) all his assignments.
6. The puppy has (ran, run) into the flower garden.
7. Mr. Lee (spoke, spoken) to us about the teen center.
8. All this loud music has (gave, given) me a headache.
9. My father has (went, gone) to the store.
10. Our team has (swam, swum) in the state meets.
11. Have you ever (ran, run) in a relay race?
12. My father (saw, seen) me in the class play.
13. Somebody has (took, taken) my lunch.
14. We have (drank, drunk) the lemonade.
15. Morgan has already (wrote, written) to his friend.

Say It Right   Hear It Right

Say these sentences until they sound correct and natural to you.

1. *Have*n't the Lombardis *come* home from their trip?
2. Yes, they *came* home last night.
3. The traffic *had come* to a standstill.
4. Why *have* so many people *come* to the park?
5. They *came* to see the fireworks.
6. *Has* the mail *come* yet?
7. It *came* early this morning.
8. We *had come* to the end of the road.
9. The gift *came* in a huge cardboard box.
10. New members *should have come* to the first meeting.

Write It Right

Write the correct verb from the two forms given in parentheses. Check your answer by reading the sentence to yourself.

1. You should have (came, come) to the basketball game.
2. The President had (came, come) to give a speech.
3. Who (came, come) to the door?
4. A messenger had (came, come) with a note.
5. John (came, come) to school late again.
6. Lisa has (came, come) to visit you.
7. The presents (came, come) yesterday afternoon.
8. Have you (came, come) from Denver?
9. Philip (came, come) early to help with the refreshments.
10. Has Jeannette (came, come) in yet?
11. The deliverymen (came, come) with the packages.
12. The fire chief (came, come) to the Boy Scout meeting.
13. He had (came, come) to discuss fire safety.
14. Wendy (came, come) to the variety show last week.
15. Our puppy (came, come) home from the vet's office yesterday.

Say It Right Hear It Right

Say these sentences until they sound correct and natural to you.

1. Jeff *did* the wrong math problems.
2. What *have* you *done* with my gym shoes?
3. Tell me what you *did* on your vacation.
4. Sally *had done* two extra credit projects.
5. What *was done* about the broken window?
6. Wendy *did* more than her share.
7. Robert *did* everything he could to help, too.
8. Didn't you think they *had done* an excellent job?
9. The acrobats *did* tricks on the high wire.
10. These card tricks *are done* with ordinary cards.

Write It Right

Write the correct verb from the two forms given in parentheses. Check your answer by reading the sentence to yourself.

1. Who (did, done) the dishes last night?
2. Peggy certainly (did, done) a good job on the painting.
3. Haven't you (did, done) your homework?
4. Nothing has been (did, done) about the gutted building.
5. Who (did, done) that drawing of Rod Carew?
6. Midge had never (did, done) a cartwheel before.
7. Our dog (did, done) every trick we taught him.
8. Has Roberto (did, done) all of the questions?
9. I could have (did, done) another lap around the track.
10. What was (did, done) with the extra cookies?
11. The diver (did, done) a back flip off the high dive.
12. Have you (did, done) oral book reports this year?
13. Myra (did, done) a tap dance for the talent show.
14. Who (did, done) the paint job on that car?
15. Those paintings were (did, done) by Andrew Wyeth.

Drink
Drank
Drunk

Say It Right Hear It Right

Say these sentences until they sound correct and natural to you.

1. No one *drank* the warm milk.
2. *Have* you *drunk* your lemonade?
3. I *drank* two glasses.
4. My cat *has* always *drunk* apple juice.
5. The knights *drank* a toast to their king.
6. Dad left before he *had drunk* his coffee.
7. Who *drank* my milkshake?
8. The dog *has drunk* all of its water.
9. Tony *must have drunk* the rest of my soda.
10. On the farm we *drank* water from the well.

Write It Right

Write the correct verb from the two forms given. Check your answer by saying the complete sentence to yourself.

1. The hot chocolate we had (drank, drunk) warmed us up.
2. The sparrows (drank, drunk) from the bird bath.
3. In England tea is (drank, drunk) more than coffee.
4. Why haven't you (drank, drunk) your orange juice?
5. My dog Peppy (drank, drunk) from the garden hose.
6. The parched land (drank, drunk) up the rain.
7. Matt couldn't have (drank, drunk) all of the punch.
8. Pam has never (drank, drunk) buttermilk.
9. I could have (drank, drunk) a gallon of water.
10. After exercising, Jean (drank, drunk) a cup of water.
11. The elephants (drank, drunk) from the stream.
12. Our kittens (drank, drunk) all the milk from the saucer.
13. Could Milly have (drank, drunk) all the cola?
14. The camels (drank, drunk) from the pond in the oasis.
15. Formula is (drank, drunk) by small babies.

Say It Right Hear It Right

Say these sentences until they sound correct and natural to you.

1. The vase *fell* from the shelf.
2. I *have fallen* over your shoes three times now.
3. Sherry tripped and *fell* on the stairs.
4. Rain *had* not *fallen* for several weeks.
5. *Has* that picture *fallen* off the wall again?
6. My grades *fell* when I stopped doing my homework.
7. The temperature *fell* sharply last night.
8. All the leaves *had fallen* by late September.
9. The show's ratings *have fallen* sharply.
10. A potted plant *fell* from the windowsill.

Write It Right

Write the correct verb from the two forms given. Check your answer by saying the complete sentence to yourself.

1. The satellite must have (fell, fallen) to the earth.
2. The shirts have (fell, fallen) from the hangers.
3. Some ashes had (fell, fallen) from the grill.
4. Amy has (fell, fallen) in love again.
5. Chuck (fell, fallen) into the pool by accident.
6. Six inches of snow have (fell, fallen) since this morning.
7. The dictionary has (fell, fallen) to the floor.
8. The horse slipped on a rock and (fell, fallen).
9. Stock market prices have (fell, fallen) again today.
10. Those keys must have (fell, fallen) out of his pocket.
11. Dad slipped on the ice and (fell, fallen).
12. When the chef opened the oven door, the cake (fell, fallen).
13. All the leaves have (fell, fallen) from the trees.
14. Lois Lane (fell, fallen) in love with Superman.
15. The price of soybeans should have (fell, fallen) this season.

Say It Right Hear It Right

Say these sentences until they sound correct and natural to you.

1. The doctor *gave* me a flu shot.
2. *Have* you ever *given* a dog a bath?
3. Judy *has*n't *given* her speech.
4. Raymond *gave* me a puzzle for my birthday.
5. I *have given* Mary all of her assignments.
6. Who *gave* you the new record?
7. The princess *was given* a gold ring.
8. My older sister *had given* me a ride on her motorcycle.
9. Ms. Reynolds' piano students *have given* concerts.
10. The sudden crash *gave* me a scare.

Write It Right

Write the correct verb from the two forms given in parentheses. Check your answer by reading the sentence to yourself.

1. I have (gave, given) her directions to the theater.
2. The Drama Club (gave, given) the play last night.
3. All the actors have (gave, given) excellent performances.
4. Hasn't Michael (gave, given) your pen back?
5. Uncle Dave (gave, given) me two passes to the hockey game.
6. This award is (gave, given) to the best students.
7. Rick has (gave, given) away all his old comic books.
8. I (gave, given) my sister the keys.
9. Mr. Fabri has (gave, given) us our band uniforms.
10. The President (gave, given) a speech to Congress.
11. Our club (gave, given) a going-away party for Louise.
12. The millionaire has (gave, given) thousands to charity.
13. Has Jill (gave, given) you the directions?
14. She (gave, given) them to me today.
15. Dad must have (gave, given) Mom those flowers.

Use the Right Word

Say It Right Hear It Right

Say these sentences until they sound correct and natural to you.

1. *Have* you ever *gone* trout fishing?
2. I *went* once with my family.
3. An hour *had gone* by.
4. My grades *went* from bad to worse.
5. The cheesecake *was gone* in no time.
6. *Has* Roxanna *gone* camping?
7. She *went* with her family this morning.
8. We *should have gone* to the water show.
9. Marla *went* through the fun house.
10. The art classes *have gone* on a field trip.

Write It Right

Write the correct verb from the two forms given in parentheses. Check your answer by reading the sentence to yourself.

1. Jo and Beth (went, gone) to the meeting.
2. We (went, gone) to the park for a picnic.
3. Allen (went, gone) to Missouri last summer.
4. Have you ever (went, gone) camping in the mountains?
5. After everyone had (went, gone), Victor did the dishes.
6. Have you (went, gone) to a professional hockey game?
7. Karen (went, gone) on the hiking trip.
8. Have you (went, gone) jogging lately?
9. I (went, gone) just this morning.
10. We (went, gone) to do the laundry after dinner.
11. Joel has (went, gone) to the library.
12. Rita (went, gone) to a soccer clinic today.
13. The children have (went, gone) to sleep already.
14. We (went, gone) to Six Flags, an amusement park.
15. The rain clouds have finally (went, gone) away.

Run
Ran
Run

Say It Right   Hear It Right

Say these sentences until they sound correct and natural to you.

1. Jane's dog *ran* after my cat.
2. Which way *have* the boys *run?*
3. We *ran* all the way home.
4. The Kentucky Derby *is* always *run* in May.
5. *Has* Sandy ever *run* a movie projector?
6. She *ran* it the last time we saw a movie in class.
7. The grandfather clock *had* finally *run* down.
8. The trains *ran* on time.
9. The police *must have run* out of clues.
10. The parents' association *ran* the school fair.

Write It Right

Write the correct verb from the two forms given in parentheses. Check your answer by reading the sentence to yourself.

1. The batteries in your calculator may have (ran, run) down.
2. Bill Rodgers has (ran, run) in the Boston Marathon.
3. He also (ran, run) marathons in two Olympics.
4. Our bus had (ran, run) out of gas.
5. Have you ever (ran, run) that fast before?
6. My digital watch has always (ran, run) well.
7. I (ran, run) two miles before school this morning.
8. Who (ran, run) against Lyndon Johnson in 1964?
9. The Indianapolis 500 wasn't (ran, run) because of rain.
10. Raise your hand if you haven't (ran, run) the fifty-yard dash.
11. Which trains (ran, run) late today?
12. The twins (ran, run) in the sack race.
13. Bonny had (ran, run) the hurdles and the relay.
14. Lewis (ran, run) a fever of 102° all night.
15. The secretary has (ran, run) off seven copies of the report.

Say It Right   Hear It Right

Say these sentences until they sound correct and natural to you.

1. *Has* Mrs. Levy's class *seen* the crafts show?
2. We *saw* a great dolphin show at Marineland.
3. A tall, bearded man *was seen* leaving the bank.
4. No one ever *saw* him again.
5. *Have* you ever *seen* a triple play?
6. No, but I once *saw* a grand slam homerun.
7. Mona *saw* the All-Star game.
8. Giant Pandas *are* seldom *seen* outside of China.
9. Randy *saw* the finish line just ahead of her.
10. The divers *had seen* a sunken ship.

Write It Right

Write the correct verb from the two forms given in parentheses. Check your answer by reading the sentence to yourself.

1. Lee (saw, seen) the variety show last night.
2. He could have (saw, seen) it with us tonight.
3. Our class (saw, seen) the Cousteau special about Atlantis.
4. I haven't (saw, seen) Maria all day.
5. Have you ever (saw, seen) the Olympic Games on television?
6. You look as if you had (saw, seen) a ghost.
7. Has anybody (saw, seen) my sweatshirt?
8. We (saw, seen) a filmstrip about the Civil War.
9. Betty (saw, seen) an accident on her way downtown.
10. Have you ever (saw, seen) any ducks in this pond?
11. Has your class (saw, seen) the movie *The Red Pony?*
12. Bill (saw, seen) a spider catch a fly in its web.
13. I may have (saw, seen) that segment of "M*A*S*H" before.
14. Jerry (saw, seen) a moped parked outside the store.
15. Have you ever (saw, seen) a twenty-dollar gold piece?

Say It Right Hear It Right

Say these sentences until they sound correct and natural to you.

1. The actor *spoke* in a deep voice.
2. Carlotta *has* always *spoken* Italian at home.
3. Raymond *spoke* with a Southern accent.
4. Ms. Weber *has spoken* to me about my project.
5. The greeting *was spoken* by the President.
6. Wendy *should have spoken* sooner.
7. The lecturer *spoke* about schools in France.
8. The pledge *was spoken* solemnly.
9. Kelly *spoke* to Ms. Evans on the phone.
10. The foreign student *spoke* Portuguese.

Write It Right

Write the correct verb from the two forms given. Check your answer by saying the complete sentence to yourself.

1. Carol (spoke, spoken) into the microphone.
2. Spanish is (spoke, spoken) at this store.
3. When the boss (spoke, spoken), we listened.
4. The coach (spoke, spoken) in an even, calm voice.
5. The lawyer has (spoke, spoken) to the judge.
6. Darren's lines were (spoke, spoken) with great force.
7. Dr. Taylor (spoke, spoken) at my sister's graduation.
8. The girls (spoke, spoken) in Chinese.
9. We should have (spoke, spoken) to the mayor.
10. Kris has (spoke, spoken) to the neighbors about babysitting.
11. The first word the baby (spoke, spoken) was "Mama."
12. Angry words were (spoke, spoken) between the two men.
13. French is (spoke, spoken) in many places in Canada.
14. Dirk has (spoke, spoken) to his boss about a raise.
15. Dad (spoke, spoken) to Lisa about her report card.

Say It Right Hear It Right

Say these sentences until they sound correct and natural to you.

1. The girls *swam* to the deep end of the pool.
2. Barry *has swum* across the lake.
3. The counselors *swam* with the campers.
4. The relay race *was swum* first.
5. That child *should have swum* closer to shore.
6. Snorkelers *swam* in the clear waters.
7. *Have* you ever *swum* in salt water?
8. The trained porpoises *swam* in formation.
9. Several whales almost *swam* ashore.
10. Deena *had swum* faster than Laura.

Write It Right

Write the correct verb from the two forms given. Check your answer by saying the complete sentence to yourself.

1. Diana Nyad has (swam, swum) long distances.
2. We (swam, swum) in a man-made lake.
3. Curt has (swam, swum) on the team for two years.
4. A scuba diver (swam, swum) to the ship's wreckage.
5. The trout (swam, swum) right to my hook.
6. These rapids have never been (swam, swum).
7. The shark (swam, swum) in circles.
8. Some of the crew members (swam, swum) ashore.
9. The water ballet group (swam, swum) to music.
10. The marathon swimmer (swam, swum) alongside a boat.
11. The minnows (swam, swum) into my net.
12. Mark Spitz has (swam, swum) in the Olympics.
13. Paul and Sean have (swam, swum) out to the sand bar.
14. Our dog Molly (swam, swum) in the lake.
15. That race was (swam, swum) in record time.

Say It Right Hear It Right

Say these sentences until they sound correct and natural to you.

1. What *took* you so long?
2. You must *have taken* a wrong turn at the stoplight.
3. My brother *has taken* my bike to Hill Park.
4. He *took* it early this morning.
5. The second graders *were taken* to the circus.
6. *Have* you ever *taken* a boat ride?
7. We *took* one when we went to New York.
8. Who *took* my pencil?
9. Jenny *took* her sister's advice.
10. The photographer *has taken* pictures of each student.

Write It Right

Write the correct verb from the two forms given in parentheses. Check your answer by reading the sentence to yourself.

1. Ted's family (took, taken) a plane to San Diego.
2. Have you (took, taken) your medicine?
3. Who (took, taken) the Ping-Pong paddles?
4. It has (took, taken) Brad an hour to get ready.
5. Leona (took, taken) the science test this morning.
6. I had already (took, taken) mine.
7. It (took, taken) us two hours to get through the traffic.
8. Bonita (took, taken) her brother to the movies.
9. We should have (took, taken) the shortcut home.
10. Julie was (took, taken) to the nurse's office.
11. We should have (took, taken) the train.
12. Have you (took, taken) your vitamins?
13. The secretary (took, taken) notes during the meeting.
14. Leroy has (took, taken) his skateboard to the park.
15. Anita (took, taken) two aspirin and went to bed.

Say It Right Hear It Right

Say these sentences until they sound correct and natural to you.

1. Kevin *wrote* Mother another letter.
2. He *has written* to her every week.
3. Who *wrote* that song?
4. This book *was written* by Robert Louis Stevenson.
5. Louise *wrote* a very funny story.
6. Raoul *had written* the letter in both Spanish and English.
7. Carole King *has written* many popular songs.
8. Ms. Novak *wrote* our assignments on the chalkboard.
9. Rick *has written* a script for a TV show.
10. Jan *wrote* the message beside the phone.

Write It Right

Write the correct verb from the two forms given in parentheses. Check your answer by reading the sentence to yourself.

1. Have you (wrote, written) your report yet?
2. I (wrote, written) half of it.
3. Mark Twain (wrote, written) *Tom Sawyer*.
4. Stacy has (wrote, written) a letter to the newspaper.
5. Lennon and McCartney (wrote, written) many Beatles' songs.
6. George Harrison (wrote, written) some of their material.
7. Was *The Pigman* (write, written) by Paul Zindel?
8. Yes, it was Paul Zindel who (wrote, written) that novel.
9. Has anyone (wrote, written) to Darren?
10. Was the note (wrote, written) or typed?
11. Mom (wrote, written) a letter to Aunt Marion.
12. It was (wrote, written) on the stationery I gave her.
13. Who (wrote, written) the book *Crazy Eights?*
14. Marti has (wrote, written) a report about telephones.
15. Bob and Jed both have (wrote, written) their paragraphs.

REVIEW Using Irregular Verbs

Irregular Verbs Write the correct verb from the two forms given in parentheses. Check your answer by reading the sentence to yourself.

1. We (saw, seen) the model plane in an open field.
2. The birds (drank, drunk) from the fountain in the park.
3. We haven't (swam, swum) much this year.
4. The bull (came, come) close to the matador.
5. Trish (did, done) a handspring on the mat.
6. Have you ever (saw, seen) a polar bear?
7. Each student had (did, done) a good job.
8. The fortune teller (gave, given) his predictions.
9. A rock (went, gone) through the window.
10. George has (gave, given) me a message for them.
11. Judy has (fell, fallen) behind in her work this week.
12. Jason has (went, gone) ten miles on his bike.
13. Blaine has never (saw, seen) a marathon.
14. Davis dodged the tackle and (ran, run) toward the goal line.
15. Roberto (saw, seen) his relatives on holidays.
16. Lindsay has (took, taken) weekly guitar lessons.
17. The troops (took, taken) orders from the captain.
18. I have (spoke, spoken) to my parents about my plans.
19. Mr. Kaminski (wrote, written) a riddle on the board.
20. You should have (saw, seen) that movie!

Using Troublesome Verbs Correctly

Section 5 showed you how to use many irregular verbs. Besides these, there are other verbs that are troublesome. Some are pairs of verbs that are often confused. Others are verbs that are often misused.

This section will help you to sort out the confusion so that you can use all these verbs correctly.

Part 1 Pairs of Verbs That Are Often Confused

See how the following pairs of verbs are used. Study the difference in the meanings. Avoid making mistakes when you use these words.

Can and *May*

Use **can** when you are talking about being able to do something. *Can* is always used as a helping verb. It has no principal parts.

Use **may** when you are asking or giving permission. *May* is also used only as a helping verb. It has no principal parts.

Can you *see* me?
Tina *can swim* like a fish.

May I *go* with you?
You *may go* to the party.

Exercise Use *can* and *may* correctly.

Number your paper from 1 to 10. Write the correct verb from the two given in parentheses.

1. (May, Can) you write backwards?
2. (May, Can) I help you with anything for the party?
3. You (can, may) turn the pancakes now.
4. (Can, May) that little stove heat this whole room?
5. (May, Can) Melinda and I go out in the canoe?
6. (May, Can) you read the bottom line without glasses?
7. A catbird (can, may) imitate other birds.
8. (May, Can) I please be excused?
9. (Can, May) Eduardo go to the park with us?
10. Stevie (may, can) count up to forty-nine.

Leave and *Let*

Leave means to go away from a person, place, or thing. The principal parts are **leave, left, left.**

Let means to permit or allow. The principal parts are **let, let, let.**

Leave the room.
Jim *left* his hat here.
Sue *has left* for Mexico.

Let me see your ring.
I *let* go of the reins.
Has Dad *let* you drive?

Exercise Use *leave* and *let* correctly.

Number your paper from 1 to 10. Write the correct verb from the two given in parentheses.

1. Betty (let, left) me see her stamp collection.
2. (Let, Leave) Jim have the last piece of the cake.
3. (Leave, Let) the dog alone.
4. The fishing net had (let, left) all the minnows through.
5. Don't (let, leave) the baby fall backwards.
6. Who (let, left) the lid off the paint can?
7. (Leave, Let) your umbrella on the porch.
8. That licorice has (let, left) a bad taste in my mouth.
9. (Leave, Let) me take your coat.
10. Somebody must have (let, left) the cat out.

Lie and *Lay*

Lie means "to rest in a reclining position." The principal parts are **lie, lay, lain.**

Lay means "to put or place." The principal parts are **lay, laid, laid.**

Lie still and rest.
The cat *lay* on the porch.
How long *has* he *lain* there?

Lay your books here.
Max *laid* the brush down.
Pam *has laid* aside her work.

Exercise Use *lie* and *lay* correctly.

Number your paper from 1 to 10. Write the correct verb from the two given in parentheses.

1. The dog likes to (lay, lie) on the rug.
2. My dad (lay, laid) his ties over the doorknob.
3. (Lay, Lie) your cards face up.
4. The trainer can make the lions (lie, lay) still.
5. Where did you (lie, lay) the newspaper?
6. (Lay, Lie) on the deck and take a nap.
7. The boy's cowlick wouldn't (lie, lay) down.
8. Don't ever (lie, lay) plastic dishes on the hot stove.
9. Mr. Ware had (lain, laid) on the sofa.
10. Papers (laid, lay) all over the ball diamond.

Review Exercises Use the right verb.

A. Write the correct verb from the two given.

1. Don't (lay, lie) on my towel.
2. (May, Can) Marcia and Fred really read that fast?
3. Certainly Jean (may, can) leave her bike in our garage.
4. (Leave, Let) the needle of the compass settle.
5. A sea turtle will (lie, lay) her eggs in the sand.
6. (May, Can) we ask Trudy to stay for supper?
7. Cindy always (lets, leaves) the icing till last.
8. Bricklayers never (lie, lay) bricks without a trowel.
9. The bus (lets, leaves) from Fountain Square every half-hour.
10. (May, Can) you hold all the groceries?

B. Follow the directions for Exercise A.

1. The explorers had (left, let) their camp during the snowstorm.
2. (May, Can) we try shooting Green River Rapids?

3. Have you (lain, laid) the spoons on the right side of the plates?

4. (Can, May) you figure out what's inside the box?

5. The brake will not (leave, let) the wheels spin freely.

6. You and she (may, can) take a copy of the play.

7. My cat (lay, laid) near the heater.

8. You (can, may) often see forty miles from this lookout.

9. (Leave, Let) Grandpa help you.

10. Have you (lain, laid) in the sun?

Rise and *Raise*

Rise means "to get up or go up." The principal parts are **rise, rose, risen.**

Raise means "to lift." It also means "to grow something." The principal parts are **raise, raised, raised.**

The dough *rises* slowly.
The sun *rose* later today.
Has the curtain *risen* yet?

Raise your hands.
Brad *raised* the flag.
Have they *raised* the price?

Exercise **Use *rise* and *raise* correctly.**

Number your paper from 1 to 10. Write the correct verb from the two given in parentheses.

1. All the ducks (raised, rose) into the air at once.

2. (Raise, Rise) your foot while I straighten the rug.

3. In this vampire movie, Count Dracula (raises, rises) from the dead.

4. Has the temperature in the engine room (raised, risen)?

5. The Kellogg boys (raise, rise) rabbits.

6. Turn off the burner when steam (rises, raises) from the kettle.

7. Marcy and Clare will (raise, rise) the curtain at eight sharp.

8. Did the moon (rise, raise) earlier or later?
9. It's not so hard to (raise, rise) tomatoes.
10. Did the drum major (raise, rise) his baton?

Sit and *Set*

Sit means "to rest." The principal parts are **sit, sat, sat.**

Set means "to place or put." The principal parts are **set, set, set.**

Sit and rest awhile.	*Set* the groceries here.
Our guests *sat* down.	Jill *set* the camera on the tripod.
Have you *sat* on stage?	*Have* they *set* the plane down safely?

Exercise **Use *sit* and *set* correctly.**

Write the correct verb from the two given.

1. Muffer barked suddenly and (sat, set) up.
2. Elizabeth (sat, set) out the milk for the cats.
3. Jud had (sat, set) in the waiting room.
4. (Set, Sit) the baby in his high chair, Jan.
5. The baby (set, sat) there chewing his spoon.
6. Mary climbed up the rock and (sat, set) down.
7. They had (set, sat) out lanterns for the festival.
8. Come in and (set, sit) down for a while.
9. (Set, Sit) down the groceries and help me.
10. (Set, Sit) the fudge in the refrigerator to cool.

Teach and *Learn*

You **teach** somebody to do something. The principal parts are **teach, taught, taught.**

You **learn** to do something with practice. The principal parts are **learn, learned, learned.**

Mr. Adams *teaches* history.
He once *taught* science.
Have you *taught* dancing?

Learn this part.
Nina *learned* to ski.
Have you *learned* to swim?

Exercise **Use *teach* and *learn* correctly.**

Write the correct verb from the two given in parentheses.

1. Can you (learn, teach) me to swim?
2. Fay has (taught, learned) her parakeet to talk.
3. My little brother has (learned, taught) the alphabet.
4. Marilyn will (learn, teach) her nephew about traffic rules.
5. I just (learned, taught) to play chess.
6. Will you (learn, teach) me to braid my hair?
7. Juanita (learned, taught) us Spanish.
8. Patty would like to (teach, learn) to fly.
9. The pioneers (taught, learned) their children to be independent.
10. I can't (learn, teach) my puppy any tricks.

Review Exercises **Use the right verb.**

A. Number your paper from 1 to 10. Write the correct verb from the two given in parentheses.

1. (Teach, Learn) me how to make a cake.
2. Jeff (sat, set) the alarm for 5 A.M.
3. Kathy should (rise, raise) next and take her place on stage.
4. (Set, Sit) still while I measure your arm.
5. I (learned, taught) the basic strokes at the Y swimming lessons.
6. Do they (raise, rise) corn in Kansas?
7. (Learn, Teach) Jessica and me how to throw a lasso.
8. The box had (set, sat) right where I left it.
9. He had (taught, learned) us to eat with chopsticks.
10. Did Jill (raise, rise) the flag this morning?

B. Follow the directions for Exercise A.

1. In a standing ovation, the audience (raises, rises) up and applauds.
2. You have to (sit, set) still to fish.
3. (Set, Sit) the balance beam along this side of the gym.
4. The cardinal had (taught, learned) its baby bird to fly.
5. Louise didn't even (rise, raise) her voice.
6. (Learn, Teach) the beginners how to hold their rackets.
7. The barometer is (raising, rising).
8. My Uncle Frank (set, sat) up waiting for me.
9. (Raise, Rise) the hood and look at the engine.
10. Please (teach, learn) me how to play the guitar.

Part 2 Using Negatives Correctly

Negatives are words that say "no." *Not, none, nobody, nowhere, nothing,* and *never* are negatives. Contractions such as *can't, don't, doesn't, wouldn't, won't, isn't,* and *aren't* are negatives. Each contains a shortened form of the word *not.*

Two "no" words used in the same sentence make what is called a **double negative.** Avoid double negatives in talking and writing. Using double negatives is always incorrect.

Read the following sentences. Notice that there are two ways to correct a double negative. Both correct ways use only one negative in a sentence.

Wrong: Dan doesn't have no paper.
Right: Dan doesn't have any paper.
or
Dan has no paper.

Wrong: He doesn't have none.
Right: He doesn't have any.
or
He has none.

Wrong: Can't nobody solve this puzzle?
Right: Can't anybody solve this puzzle?
or
Can nobody solve this puzzle?

Exercises **Use one negative.**

A. Write the following conversation, or take turns reading it aloud. Choose the right word from the parentheses.

RUTH: Thank you, I can't eat (no, any) more pie.

JACK: Didn't you have (none, any)?

RUTH: Oh, yes. I couldn't eat (any, no) more

PETER: Isn't it (no, any) good?

RUTH: Yes, it's good, but I (ever, never) eat more than one piece.

PAUL: I don't know (nothing, anything) I like better than pie. I never heard (nobody, anybody) refuse pie before.

JANE: Can't (anybody, nobody) eat Ruth's pie?

PAUL: I wouldn't (never, ever) want to see any pie wasted. I'll eat it.

B. Number your paper from 1 to 10. Write the correct word from the two given in parentheses.

1. Gary can think of (nobody, anybody) else.
2. Don't you want (any, no) pop?
3. Sandra wouldn't have taken the album (nowhere, anywhere).
4. Albert won't climb (any, no) ladder more than three feet tall.
5. We aren't going (nowhere, anywhere) this summer.
6. I don't (never, ever) want to eat doughnuts again.
7. Sara doesn't go (anywhere, nowhere) without her bike.

8. I haven't heard (nothing, anything).
9. We have (no more, any more) string.
10. Wouldn't you like (no, any) cake?

Part 3 Good Speech Habits

Don't say *ain't.* Use *am not, isn't,* or *aren't,* or *haven't* or *hasn't.*

Say: I *am not* going fishing.
Kevin *isn't* here.
Those *aren't* my fishing poles.
We *haven't* seen her.
Lynn *hasn't* come home yet.

Never use *don't* with the pronouns *he, she,* and *it,* or with a singular noun. Use *doesn't.*

Say: *She doesn't* fish often.
He doesn't like fishing.
It doesn't appeal to him.

Don't use *was* or *wasn't* with the pronouns *we, you,* and *they,* or with a plural noun. Use *were* and *weren't.*

Say: *We weren't* swimming.
Were you fishing?
They were catching big fish.

Exercises Form good speech habits.

A. Number your paper from 1 to 10. Read each sentence. Choose the correct word from the two given. Then read the completed sentence to yourself.

1. These books (ain't, aren't) Ginger's.
2. Why (was, were) the seals in the cage?
3. The weather (don't, doesn't) look that bad.

4. (Was, Were) you at the circus last week?
5. There (ain't, isn't) (nothing, anything) I'd rather do.
6. What (was, were) you thinking about?
7. She (doesn't, don't) ever say (anything, nothing).
8. (Ain't, Aren't) you glad you're you?
9. You (ain't, aren't) going to fall.
10. This card trick (don't, doesn't) (ever, never) fail.

B. Here are ten questions and answers. Write the correct word from the two given in parentheses. Then read the completed pair of sentences to yourself.

1. (Was, Were) you fishing last week?
   No, I (ain't, am not) a fisherman.
2. (Isn't, Ain't) Eric a friend of yours?
   No, he (don't, doesn't) even know me.
3. (Were, Was) your cousins at the class picnic?
   Yes, they (was, were) at the picnic.
4. We (was, were) invited, (weren't, wasn't) we?
   Yes, we (were, was) invited.
5. (Doesn't, Don't) he know the answer?
   No, he (don't, doesn't) know (nothing, anything).
6. It (doesn't, don't) matter to me, but (wasn't, weren't) you using my pen?
   No, I (ain't, haven't) used it, but the twins (was, were) using it.
7. (Don't, Doesn't) Sandra's friends smile (no, any) more?
   Yes, they (was, were) on a hike last Saturday.
8. You (ain't, haven't) seen my jacket, have you?
   No, I (haven't, ain't) seen it (nowhere, anywhere).
9. (Wasn't, Weren't) you and your brothers on a trip?
   Yes, we (was, were) gone six weeks.
10. Why (was, were) you three girls the ones chosen?
    We (were, was) the first volunteers.

REVIEW Using Troublesome Verbs Correctly

Troublesome Verbs Write the correct word from the two given in parentheses. Check your answer by reading the completed sentence to yourself.

1. (Can, May) you read this messy writing?
2. (Can, May) we please use the earphones?
3. Amanda has (left, let) the cash box open.
4. Someone (left, let) the air out of these tires.
5. Baby seals (lay, laid) on the ice.
6. Hunters (lay, laid) moss and grass over the trap.
7. The hot-air balloons (rose, raised) smoothly.
8. (Sit, Set) the colored stones in the aquarium.
9. The three friends (sat, set) on the steps and talked.
10. My brother has (taught, learned) me the game of rugby.

Using Negatives Correctly Write the correct word from the two given in parentheses.

11. The shorter players couldn't get (no, any) rebounds.
12. Don't whales (never, ever) swim close to shore?
13. Hasn't (anybody, nobody) heard this album?
14. The ambulance didn't stop for (anything, nothing).
15. I can't see the Big Dipper (anywhere, nowhere).

Good Speech Habits Write the correct word from the two given in parentheses.

16. Carlos (ain't, isn't) the boss here.
17. She (don't, doesn't) swim the backstroke.
18. Seth (doesn't, don't) win at cards.
19. We (was, were) playing badminton.
20. You (wasn't, weren't) looking at the camera.

Using Pronouns

Part 1 What Are Pronouns?

Read the two paragraphs below. Which paragraph sounds better?

> Mary gets up at seven-thirty each morning. Mary eats breakfast. Mary goes to school. Mary opens Mary's English book and reads from Mary's book.
>
> Mary gets up at seven-thirty each morning. She eats breakfast. She goes to school. She opens her English book and reads from it.

Probably you decided that the second paragraph sounded better. Why did you think so? Perhaps you felt that using the name Mary over and over again became boring or irritating.

How did the second paragraph avoid repetition? Did you notice how it used the pronouns *she* and *her* in place of the name *Mary* and *it* in place of *book?* Use of the pronouns didn't change the meaning of the paragraph, but it improved the sound of it.

A pronoun is a word used in place of a noun.

You learned to use pronouns as soon as you learned to talk. You learned to use certain pronouns to do three things.

1. To refer to yourself:
   I invited *my* cousin to visit *me.*
2. To refer to the person you are talking to:
   You forgot *your* umbrella.
3. To refer to other persons, places, or things:
   The cat blinked *its* eyes.
   The Red Sox won *their* game, 5–3.

Like nouns, pronouns can be singular or plural. Usually, the whole word changes to make different forms. Study this chart of all the forms of pronouns.

Singular Pronouns

Person Speaking:	I	me	my, mine
Person Spoken To:	you	you	your, yours
Other Persons, Places and Things:	he she it	him her it	his her, hers its

Plural Pronouns

Persons Speaking:	we	us	our, ours
Persons Spoken To:	you	you	your, yours
Other Persons, Places and Things:	they	them	their, theirs

Exercises Recognize pronouns.

A. Number your paper from 1 to 10. List the pronouns used in each sentence.

1. The bottle popped its cork.
2. Donna promised she would give me her old bike.
3. Take us to the boat show, please.
4. Your locker is much cleaner than mine.
5. We told them all about the walkathon.
6. You should find Ramon's books and return them to him.
7. He coaxed the chickens out of their coop.
8. I saw the birds as they flew over my yard.
9. A swan cleaned its snowy feathers.
10. We ran past her house.

B. In the following story, the pronouns are in italics. Read the story. Write all the pronouns in a list. After each pronoun, write the word it stands for.

Since Ted is old enough this year, *he* **(1)** can enter the Soap Box Derby. Mr. Williams gave *him* **(2)** a copy of the rules for the race. Ted is building the racer in the garage. Ted's parents are proud that Ted wants to build *it* **(3)** himself. *They* **(4)** often give *him* **(5)** advice. Ted paid $29.95 for the wheel and axle set, but the steering gear cost *him* **(6)** only $5.75. Ted hopes to win the race. *He* **(7)** thinks *he* **(8)** can win *it* **(9)** easily.

C. Write the pronoun or pronouns you would use to refer to each of the following nouns.

1. lake
2. father
3. cats
4. teachers
5. Ms. Howard
6. friends
7. sister
8. brother
9. pencils
10. doctors

Part 2 Pronouns in Subjects

Which of these sentences sounds right to you?

Her went to the party.
She went to the party.

You probably had no trouble in picking the second sentence. Now supose we add the name of someone else who went to the party.

Her and David went to the party.
She and David went to the party.

The second sentence is right. *She and David* is a compound subject. To figure out what pronoun to use in a compound subject, try each part separately.

David went to the party.
She went to the party.

Then put the two subjects together, using the same pronoun.

Follow the same plan when there are two pronouns in the subject. Read these sentences to yourself:

(He, Him) and (I, me) built a radio.
He built a radio. I built a radio.
He and I built a radio.

Here is another simple problem with pronouns. Which would you say: *We had a picnic* or *Us had a picnic?* As you probably know, the first sentence is right.

Now, which of these sentences is correct?

We girls organized a field trip.	(Right. *We* is correct.)
Us girls organized a field trip.	(*Us* is not a subject pronoun. It should never be used in the subject.)

Only these pronouns may be used as **subject pronouns.**

I	**we**
you	**you**
he, she, it	**they**

Exercises Use pronouns in the subject.

A. Write the correct pronoun for each sentence.

1. (We, Us) boys planted a four-foot pine tree.
2. Ms. Tandy and (we, us) came on the bus.
3. The other players and (me, I) got drenched.
4. Did you find two blue mittens? (Them, They) are mine.
5. (They, Them) and the other gloves were behind the bookcase.
6. The raft and (us, we) girls got stuck under Daw's Bridge.
7. My dog and (me, I) went out to take a look.
8. (He, Him) and (us, we) clocked the runners.
9. Brian and (she, her) saw the Little Dipper.
10. (We, Us) are in a hurry.

B. Follow the directions for Exercise A.

1. Susie and (I, me) ran the cold drink stand.
2. The adults and (us, we) use the pool together.
3. (Us, We) girls won the raffle.
4. (Him, He) and (her, she) both come from Louisville.
5. Those boots can't be the ones I lost. (They, Them) don't look like mine.
6. (We, Us) three got all the blame.
7. In the picture, Carla and (he, him) had no heads.
8. (He, Him) and (me, I) were talking to the prison guard.
9. Randy and (me, I) finished the cornflakes.
10. Kitty and (they, them) went up in the ski lift.

Part 3 Pronouns After Linking Verbs

Read these two sentences.

> The captain is *he*.
> *He* is the captain.

These sentences mean the same thing. As you can see, the pronoun following the linking verb *is* can be made the subject without changing the meaning of the sentence.

Pronouns used after linking verbs are called **predicate pronouns.** Predicate pronouns are the same as pronouns used as subjects. You can see this in the following pairs of sentences.

> Our new doctor is she.
> She is our new doctor.
>
> The winners were Ralph and I.
> Ralph and I were the winners.
>
> The teams in the playoffs will be the Bruins and we.
> The Bruins and we will be the teams in the playoffs.

Remember to use these pronouns after linking verbs:

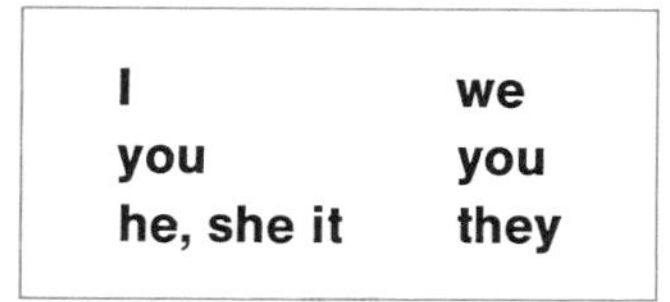

I	**we**
you	**you**
he, she it	**they**

Exercises Use pronouns after linking verbs.

A. Write the correct pronoun for each sentence.

1. The leaders are Valerie and (he, him).
2. It was (he, him) at the counter.
3. The guests of honor will be (we, us) girls.
4. Our club sponsors are Miss Martin and (he, him).
5. The runners-up were (we, us) boys.

6. The directors for the talent show were Maria and (her, she).
7. The only people in the pool were Wayne and (me, I).
8. The earliest arrivals were (him, he) and Ron.
9. Was it (her, she) at the door?
10. The stage managers for our play are Paul and (them, they).

B. Follow the directions for Exercise A.

1. There were several adults and (we, us) girls waiting at the bus stop.
2. Our dinner guests were John and (she, her).
3. That's (he, him) on the pier by the submarine.
4. The fastest outfielders are George and (her, she).
5. The soloists are Wendy and (I, me).
6. My teammates were Isabella and (they, them).
7. The speakers at the assembly will be you and (he, him).
8. The funniest actress in our room is (her, she).
9. Faith's back-up singers were Jenny and (he, him).
10. The only person with new skates was (he, him).

Part 4 Pronouns as Objects

A noun does not change its form when it is used as an object in a sentence. Pronouns, however, have special forms to be used when they are objects. These forms are called the **object pronouns.**

Here are the object pronouns for you to study:

me	**us**
you	**you**
him, her, it	**them**

These sentences will sound natural to you.

Dad drove *us* to the party.
We met *him* later.

Be on guard when one or more pronouns are parts of a compound object.

Dad drove Jane and *us* to the party.
We met *him* and *her* later.

If you are not sure which pronoun to use, say each part separately.

Kay stopped (he, him) and (I, me).
Kay stopped *him*.
Kay stopped *me*.
Kay stopped *him* and *me*.

Exercises **Use pronouns as objects.**

A. Number your paper from 1 to 10. Write the verb. Then write the correct pronoun to be used as the object of the verb.

1. Please call Jim and (I, me) in the morning.
2. The principal asked (them, they) and their parents for suggestions.
3. Mom dropped Matt and (me, I) off at City Hall.
4. The Kiwanis Club sponsored (he, him) in the tournament.
5. Judy's dog bit Pat and (she, her).
6. Ms. Talbot complimented the class and (he, him) on their photos.
7. That owl scared Doug and (I, me) out of our wits.
8. The coach trusted (them, they) and (we, us).
9. Help Brenda and (I, me), please.
10. Will you give Roger and (they, them) a hand?

B. Follow the directions for Exercise A.

1. Snowballs hit David and (we, us).
2. The fire marshall questioned Doug and (he, him).
3. Will you pull (she, her) on this sled?
4. Hold (them, they) at the ten-yard line.
5. Didn't the waitress bill Todd and (I, me) correctly?
6. We left Shelley and (she, her) at the park.
7. A raft carried Tammy and (I, me) downstream.
8. Call Michelle and (me, I) later tonight.
9. That joke embarrassed Wes and (him, he).
10. The ice cream vendor gave Tony and (I, me) the newest flavor.

Part 5 Possessive Pronouns

To make the possessive form of a noun, you add an apostrophe or an apostrophe and an *s* to the noun. Pronouns have special possessive forms. These do not use apostrophes at all.

The possessive pronouns are the following:

my, mine	**our, ours**
your, yours	**your, yours**
his, her, hers, its	**their, theirs**

Now read these sentences that use possessive pronouns:

This is **my** locker.
This locker is **mine.**

Is that **your** ticket?
Is that **yours?**

Here is **his** coat.
The coat is **his.**

Where is **her** lunch?
This lunch is **hers.**

We have **our** friends.
These friends are **ours.**

Are those **your** skis?
Are those **yours?**

Do you know **their** plans?
The plans are **theirs.**

Some people confuse the possessive **its** with the contraction **it's.** *Its* (without an apostrophe) is the possessive form of *it*. *It's* (with an apostrophe) means *it is* or *it has*.

The museum opened *its* new wing.
(The wing belongs to the museum.)

It's almost noon and I'm hungry.
(*It is* almost noon and I'm hungry.)

Exercises **Use possessive pronouns.**

A. Copy the following sentences. Where there is a blank, write the appropriate possessive pronoun.

1. That lunchbag is ______. (The lunchbag belongs to me.)
2. The dog lost ______ bone. (The bone belongs to it.)
3. That glove must be ______. (The glove belongs to you.)
4. Kate took ______ advice. (The advice belongs to him.)
5. This house is ______. (The house belongs to us.)
6. The best part is ______. (The part belongs to her.)
7. The helmets are ______. (The helmets belong to them.)
8. Jim made ______ bed. (The bed belongs to him.)
9. We watered ______ plants. (The plants belong to us.)
10. The wolf showed ______ teeth. (The teeth belong to it.)

B. Copy these sentences. Insert apostrophes correctly.

1. The rat lost its way in the maze.
2. Its snowing throughout the Northeast.
3. Change the thermostat if its set too low.
4. That stuffed dog lost a lot of its stuffing.
5. Scoop up that ground ball while its fair.
6. K-Mart ends its sale on school supplies next week.
7. Leave the puzzle in its box.
8. I hate gum when its stuck on my chair.
9. The school started its basketball season last week.
10. Its too late to go swimming now.

REVIEW Using Pronouns

Subject Pronouns Write the correct pronoun for each sentence. Check by reading the sentence to yourself.

1. (He, Him) and Sue Ellen worked with stained glass.
2. Colleen and (me, I) timed the swimmers.
3. (We, Us) older kids were blamed.
4. Watch those plates. (They, Them) break.
5. (She, Her) and her sister often trade clothes.

Pronouns After Linking Verbs Write the correct pronouns.

6. The top scorers were Joshua and (me, I).
7. The silliest people at the party were (we, us) three.
8. The sports reporters are Kevin and (she, her).
9. My favorite groups are (them, they) and the Bee Gees.
10. Two "Trekkies" are Wendy and (him, he).

Object Pronouns Write the correct pronouns.

11. The pitcher hit (she, her) with a wild pitch.
12. The lifeguard rescued Curt and (he, him).
13. Mom quizzed Jeff and (me, I) on the math.
14. Do you remember Kristen and (we, us)?
15. Do the experts favor (her, she) or Chris Evert?

Possessive Pronouns Copy the following sentences. Where there is a blank, write the appropriate pronoun.

16. These skis are ______. (The skis belong to us.)

17. They gave us ______ autographs. (The autographs belong to them.)

18. Tim cleaned ______ desk. (The desk belongs to him.)

19. The snake shed ______ skin. (The skin belongs to it.)

20. The drawings are ______. (The drawings belong to you.)

Using Adjectives

Part 1 What Are Adjectives?

Does the sentence below tell you very much about what Mr. Rafael drives?

Mr. Rafael drives a van.

Can you tell more about what Mr. Rafael drives when you read the following sentence?

Mr. Rafael drive a small, black van.

What words are added in the second sentence to tell you which kind of van Mr. Rafael drives? *Small* and *black* make the meaning more exact. They are **adjectives.**

Adjectives are words that are used with nouns and pronouns. They are called **modifiers** because they change, or modify, the meaning of the word they go with.

Only the adjectives are different in the following sentences. Read each sentence. Does each adjective change, or modify, the picture you have in your mind?

Kathy drove along the *crowded* highway.
Kathy drove along the *deserted* highway.
Kathy drove along the *narrow* highway.
Kathy drove along the *bumpy* highway.
Kathy drove along the *dusty* highway.

An adjective is a word that modifies a noun or pronoun.

One or more adjectives may be used before the noun or pronoun being modified. When you use two or more adjectives together, separate them with commas.

The *hot, thick, sticky* topping smothered the ice cream.

Adjectives may also follow the noun or pronoun being modified.

I met him, *dirty, tired,* and *hungry,* at the end of the trail.

Some Adjectives Tell *What Kind*

We use adjectives to describe what we are talking about. They tell *what kind* of thing we have in mind.

Henry wore *furry* gloves and a *colorful* scarf.

The alligator's *sharp* teeth are *dangerous* weapons.

Lately we have had *warm, rainy* weather.

The *long, white, woolen* cap is mine.

These are *comfortable* seats.

Many adjectives that tell *what kind* are formed by adding an adjective ending to a noun. Here are some examples:

Noun		Adjective Ending		Adjective
rain	+	-y	=	rainy
color	+	-ful	=	colorful
danger	+	-ous	=	dangerous
wool	+	-en	=	woolen
comfortable	+	-able	=	comfortable

Some Adjectives Tell *How Many*

You use adjectives to tell *how many* of any thing you are talking about. The adjectives in the following sentences appear in italics. They all tell *how many*.

Mr. and Mrs. Ellsworth own *twenty* trucks.

Their trucks travel across *several* states.

Some trucks have *many* license plates.

They have *frequent* repairs but *few* accidents.

Some Adjectives Tell *Which Ones*

Some adjectives tell *which one* or *which ones* we are talking about.

These trucks hold nine rooms of furniture.

Those trucks transport new automobiles.

This truck is used for hauling coal or dirt.

That truck is used to tow away wrecks.

Exercises Use adjectives.

A. Copy these sentences. Draw an arrow from each adjective that tells *what kind* to the noun it modifies.

1. The boys looked for small starfish.
2. Ronnie scraped sticky gum from her shoe.
3. Do you know how to give artificial respiration?
4. An unearthly howl made Rich tremble.
5. These green darts are for Tim.
6. Peculiar noises came from the closet.
7. The sky was filled with white, puffy clouds.
8. Tina complained of stiff knees.
9. Mary's new camera has special gadgets.
10. Did you find a brown wallet?

B. Number your paper from 1 to 10. Make two columns. Head one column *Which Ones.* Head the other *How Many.* Find the adjectives in these sentences and place them in the appropriate column.

Example: Those trees have grown two feet this year.

Which Ones	How Many
those	two

1. That light flashed a signal to some men on the shore.
2. Many people prefer this brand of cereal.
3. Look at this altimeter now.
4. Mr. Harvey had six boxes of cartridges.
5. Is this saddle for Sara?
6. These cards belong to that game.
7. Janet has used this saw many times.
8. We have ordered several cakes from that bakery.
9. That voice doesn't sound like yours.
10. It took four hours to sand those desks.

Part 2 The Articles

The words *a, an,* and *the* are called **articles.** Since they always modify nouns, they are also adjectives.

Use **a** before words beginning with consonant sounds:

a box *a* hat *a* horse *a* moth

Use **an** before words beginning with vowel sounds:

an apple *an* engineer *an* island *an* uncle

Some words begin with a silent *h.* In these words, you do not say the *h* sound. Instead, you begin the word with the sound of the vowel after the *h.* Therefore, you follow the rule given above, and use *an:*

an honor *an* hour *an* honest person

Exercises Use articles.

A. Read the following sentences carefully. Copy the sentences. Fill in the blanks with the articles *a* or *an,* whichever is correct.

1. I just peeled ________ onion.
2. ________ acrobat could do that.
3. Carlos was riding ________ bicycle.
4. Is that ________ iceberg near the horizon?
5. Can you ride ________ horse?
6. Dennis is known as ________ honest person.
7. Mom's gone to ________ important meeting.
8. Does the car have ________ undercoating to prevent rust?
9. Our national bird is ________ eagle.
10. The boat drifted in ________ aimless pattern.

B. There are ten nouns below. Choose five nouns. Write a sentence using each noun you choose. Place an article and an adjective before each noun.

1. person	6. vacation
2. mountains	7. animal
3. friend	8. books
4. meal	9. family
5. clothes	10. house

Part 3 Predicate Adjectives

When an adjective follows a linking verb like *is* or *seemed,* it is part of the predicate. But it often modifies a noun or pronoun in the subject. Look at these examples.

The trees are *tall.*

Donna will be *happy.*

He is *right.*

The patient seemed *dazed.*

When an adjective following a linking verb modifies the subject, it is called a **predicate adjective.**

Exercises Use predicate adjectives.

A. Copy these sentences, putting a predicate adjective in the blank. Draw an arrow from the predicate adjective to the word it modifies.

1. Lemons are __________.
2. Before a test, we are very __________.
3. The boys were __________ after their victory.
4. Every day at noon, I am __________.

5. The sky was __________ this morning.
6. With the new addition, the house will be __________.
7. You are __________ than any other student here.
8. This rose is __________.
9. Rhonda will be __________ when she sees your present.
10. From far away, the bell sounded __________.

B. Follow the directions for Exercise A.

1. The plane to Omaha will be __________.
2. The early settlers were very __________.
3. Your new suit looks __________.
4. That book was __________.
5. The loaves of fresh bread smell __________.
6. Without water, the plants will become __________.
7. Vincent's violin sounds __________.
8. This apple tastes __________.
9. After several days, the leftovers became __________.
10. This movie is too __________.

Part 4 Proper Adjectives

In this section, you have already used many adjectives formed from common nouns, for example, *rainy, comfortable, woolen.* **Proper adjectives** are adjectives formed from proper nouns.

You know that a proper noun names a particular person, place, or thing. By adding adjective endings to some proper nouns, we change them into proper adjectives. Here are some examples:

Proper Noun	Proper Adjective + Noun Modified
Britain	British royalty
Japan	Japanese yen
Mexico	Mexican jewelry
Bible	Biblical quotation

Very often a proper name is used as an adjective without the addition of an adjective ending. Here are some examples of the second kind of proper adjective:

Hitchcock thriller	Cinderella story
Ford engine	Beethoven symphony

A **proper adjective** is an adjective that has been made from a proper noun. A proper adjective begins with a capital letter.

Exercises Use proper adjectives.

A. Write each proper adjective. Capitalize correctly.

1. Is that an irish sheep dog?
2. The austrian ski team won the downhill competition.
3. My sister bought a japanese stereo set.
4. This delicatessen sells polish sausages.
5. When was the alaskan pipeline started?
6. The jewish community is celebrating Rosh Hoshana.
7. We had kentucky fried chicken.
8. The canadian Rockies are higher than the american.
9. Napoleon's army was defeated by the russian winter.
10. The museum just purchased a french painting.

B. Follow the directions for Exercise A.

1. When was the gregorian calendar developed?
2. Valerie had a siamese kitten and a persian cat.
3. Cleopatra ruled the egyptian people.
4. I like italian dressing better than blue cheese or french.
5. Lawrence is taking german lessons.
6. My aunt bought some real indian turquoise.
7. Mrs. Haas was a dutch immigrant.
8. It is hard to add roman numerals.
9. The bantu chief greeted the travelers with dignity.
10. Eduardo drove an italian car across the swiss border.

Part 5 Demonstrative Adjectives

Four adjectives that tell which one, or which ones, are *this, that, these,* and *those.* When they modify nouns or pronouns, they point out specific things.

This cake tastes sweeter than *that* one.
These notebooks cost a quarter each. *Those* notebooks cost a dollar each.

This, that, these and *those* are called **demonstrative adjectives.**

We use *this* and *that* with singular nouns. We use *these* and *those* with plural nouns.

this Frisbee	these Frisbees
that field	those fields

The nouns *kind* and *sort* are singular. Therefore, we say *this kind* and *this sort.* We use *these* and *those* only with the plurals: *these kinds* or *those sorts.*

this kind of pizza	these kinds of sweaters
that sort of movie	those sorts of candies

Using *Those* and *Them*

Those is a word with many uses. It may be used as an adjective:

Where did you find *those* skates?

Those may also be used as a pronoun. As a pronoun it can be the subject of a verb or it can be a direct object.

Those are my sisters. (subject)
Paint *those* tomorrow. (direct object)

Them is always an object pronoun. It is never used as an adjective. You would never use *them* in a sentence like this:

My uncle gave me *those* stamps.

As a pronoun, *them* is never used as the subject. You would use *them* only as an object, as in these examples:

> He gave *them* to me.
> I added *them* to my collection.

Exercises Use demonstrative adjectives and *them*.

A. Number your paper from 1 to 10. Write the correct pronoun from the two given in parentheses. Then read the completed sentence to yourself.

1. Robert needs (that, those) kind of car to finish his model train set.
2. (Them, Those) flowers across the street are snapdragons.
3. Do you like (this, these) kind of coat?
4. (These, Them) girls with me are my cousins.
5. (Those, These) swimming lessons last summer taught me a lot.
6. Lois often buys (them, these) sorts of rings.
7. Can you see (those, them) geese flying south?
8. I think (those, them) kinds of cookies are the best.
9. These cookies have chopped walnuts in (those, them).
10. (Them, These) albums are by the Bee Gees.

B. Copy these sentences. Use *them* or *those* in the blanks. Then read the completed sentence to yourself.

1. You can't ask ____________ for all ____________ labels.
2. Are ____________ posters dry yet?
3. Tell ____________ to come back tomorrow.
4. ____________ fit me better than these slacks.
5. Joan took the boxes and painted ____________.
6. Where did you get all ____________ old magazines?
7. ____________ songs were sung in Spanish.
8. I want those posters. How much do you charge for ____________?

9. All of ____________ boys play on Marvin's team.
10. ____________ were the most expensive shoes.

Part 6 Making Comparisons with Adjectives

A bear is big. An elephant is big. A dinosaur was big.

Are all three animals the same size? Certainly, the answer is no. If you want to say the animals are of different sizes, will the word *big* do the job? Again, the answer is no. But you can change the word *big* so that it will show the differences in the group.

You can use the word *bigger* to compare two persons or things.

> An elephant is *bigger* than a bear.
> A dinosaur was *bigger* than an elephant.

Bigger is called the **comparative form** of *big*.

You can use the word *biggest* to compare three or more persons or things.

> A dinosaur was the *biggest* of the three.
> A dinosaur was the *biggest* of all animals.

Biggest is called the **superlative form** of *big*.

Use the comparative form of an adjective to compare *two* things.

> Between the history and spelling tests, the history test was *more difficult*.

Use the superlative form of an adjective when you are concerned with *three or more* things.

> The math exam was the *most difficult* test of all.

Usually, you make the comparative form of a short adjective by adding *-er*. You make the superlative form by adding *-est*.

Adjective	Comparative Form	Superlative Form
long	longer	longest
old	older	oldest
tall	taller	tallest
big	bigger	biggest
funny	funnier	funniest

For longer adjectives, you form the comparative by using the word *more*. You form the superlative by using the word *most*.

Adjective	Comparative Form	Superlative Form
ridiculous	more ridiculous	most ridiculous
noticeable	more noticeable	most noticeable
careful	more careful	most careful
terrible	more terrible	most terrible

Use only one form of comparison at a time. Do not use *more* and *-er*, or *most* and *-est*.

Wrong: This pillow is *more softer* than that one.
Right: This pillow is *softer* than that one.

Wrong: That painting is the *most prettiest* of all.
Right: That painting is the *prettiest* of all.

The Forms of *Good* and *Bad*

A few adjectives change their forms in other ways. Some adjectives have completely new words for the comparative and superlative forms. Here are two important ones to remember:

good	better	best
bad	worse	worst

Donna is my *good* friend.
She is a *better* cook than I am.
Her ice cream pie is the *best* I've tasted.

David suffered a *bad* sprain.
He was in *worse* pain today.
"I have the *worst* luck," he moaned.

Exercises Use adjectives to make comparisons.

A. Number your paper from 1 to 10. Write the correct form of the adjective from the two given in parentheses. Then read the completed sentence to yourself.

1. Claire is the (carefulest, most careful) driver I know.
2. This sausage pizza tastes (better, more better) than cheese pizza.
3. Who is (youngest, most young) in your family?
4. I was wearing my (bestest, best) jeans.
5. The Sky Harbor weather is (badder, worse) than ours.
6. Have you heard the (latest, most late) news?
7. Todd is (stronger, strongest) than I.
8. Cindy has the (most, mostest) beautiful guitar.
9. The snow was (worse, worser) in the parking lot.
10. That is the (best, better) picture in the whole book.

B. Follow the directions for Exercise A.

1. Between Andrea and Luis, Luis is the (taller, tallest).
2. A balanced meal is (gooder, better) for your health than junk food.
3. A new raincoat will be (expensiver, more expensive) than I expected.
4. Superman is (stronger, strongest) than ordinary humans.
5. Doc was the (smarter, smartest) of the Seven Dwarfs.
6. That is the (funnier, funniest) show of the season.
7. Marguerita's briefcase was (heavy, heavier) than her mother's suitcase.
8. Tomorrow will be (colder, more colder) than today.
9. Who is the (most old, oldest) in your family?
10. Jody thinks radishes have the (worst, worstest) taste of all the vegetables.

REVIEW Using Adjectives

Recognizing Adjectives Write the adjectives in each sentence. Beside each adjective, write the noun it modifies. Put the noun in parentheses. Do not include articles.

1. These candles make an eerie glow.
2. Two batters tried the new metal bats.
3. We went to the top floor of the tall building.
4. Those twelve cheerleaders led the crowd.
5. This wild horse tossed the first rider.
6. We picked these juicy red apples.
7. Poor Charlie Brown didn't get any Valentines.
8. Ted covered the ten puppies with a fuzzy blue blanket.
9. We ate many pancakes with butter and syrup.
10. Lynn heard the dry rattle of the poisonous snake.

Predicate Adjectives Write the predicate adjective in each sentence.

11. A koala bear is Australian.
12. That clock must be wrong.
13. The sky was cloudy today.
14. These baseball uniforms are filthy.
15. Are those boots comfortable?

Adjectives in Comparisons Choose the correct form of the adjective from the two given. Write it.

16. This puzzle is (harder, more hard) than that one.
17. Cindy's voice is (higher, highest) than Diane's.
18. This puzzle is the (more complex, most complex) of all.
19. Which of these two lines is (straighter, straightest)?
20. Julio had a (better, more better) time than Connie did.

Using Adverbs

Part 1 What Are Adverbs?

Adjectives modify nouns and pronouns. **Adverbs** modify verbs, adjectives, and other adverbs. Look at these examples.

Jerry worked *quickly*.
We *always* go there.
The cat ran *away*.
It was *very* windy.

Adverbs usually tell *how, when, where,* or *to what extent* about the words they modify. If you are not sure whether a word is an adverb, ask yourself if it answers one of these questions.

Adverbs Modify Verbs

	Joe whistled.
How?	Joe whistled *loudly.*
Where?	Joe whistled *outside.*
When?	Joe whistled *constantly.*

Adverbs Modify Adjectives

	That is a *bright* light.
How bright?	That is a *very* bright light.
	This stunt is *dangerous.*
How dangerous?	This stunt is *too* dangerous.

Adverbs Modify Other Adverbs

	John dances *well.*
How well?	John dances *extremely* well.
	The horse ran *away.*
To what extent?	The horse ran *far* away.

Generally, an adverb that modifies an adjective or another adverb comes before the word it modifies.

very bright
extremely well

An adverb that modifies a verb may often be placed in more than one position in the sentence.

He reads books *often*.
Often he reads books.
He *often* reads books.

Many adverbs are formed by adding *-ly* to an adjective:

bad—badly	slow—slowly
quick—quickly	happy—happily
careful—carefully	suspicious—suspiciously

Adverbs modify verbs, adjectives, and other adverbs.

Exercises **Find and use adverbs.**

A. Number your paper from 1 to 20. Write *How, Where, When* or *To What Extent* to show what each of these adverbs tells.

1. angrily	6. quite	11. well	16. soon
2. here	7. now	12. almost	17. often
3. slowly	8. too	13. always	18. afterward
4. quickly	9. never	14. very	19. meekly
5. outside	10. ever	15. there	20. early

B. Write five sentences in which you use these adverbs.

very	now	here
never	often	

C. Number your paper from 1 to 10. Write every adverb used in each sentence.

1. Roberto was there yesterday.
2. Suddenly Jill looked up.
3. Soon the sun came out.
4. Because of his cold, Dennis can hardly talk.
5. During the fire drill, the class filed outside quickly but quietly.

6. David sanded the table very carefully.
7. Those two boys are never sleepy.
8. The explosion happened suddenly.
9. Did you ever hear Louisa play?
10. Soon afterward the mist cleared.

Part 2 Making Comparisons with Adverbs

Adverbs, like adjectives, can be changed to comparative and superlative forms. You use the **comparative form** when you consider two persons or things:

Jack ran *faster* than the giant.

You use the **superlative form** when you consider three or more persons or things:

The cheetah runs the *fastest* of all animals.

The comparative and superlative forms of adverbs are formed in three different ways.

1. Some short adverbs add *-er* for the comparative and *-est* for the superlative.

Adverb	Comparative Form	Superlative Form
fast	faster	fastest
hard	harder	hardest

2. Most adverbs that end in *-ly* form the comparative with the word *more*. They form the superlative with the word *most*.

Adverb	Comparative Form	Superlative Form
easily	more easily	most easily
carefully	more carefully	most carefully

3. Some adverbs make their comparative and superlative forms by complete word changes.

Adverb	Comparative Form	Superlative Form
well	better	best
much	more	most
little	less	least
badly	worse	worst

Exercises **Make comparisons with adverbs.**

A. Number your paper from 1 to 10. Label three columns: *Adverb, Comparative,* and *Superlative.* List all of the adverbs below in the first column. Then write their comparative and superlative forms.

1. often
2. heavily
3. soon
4. carefully
5. quickly
6. well
7. easily
8. slowly
9. little
10. hard

B. Number your paper from 1 to 10. Write the correct word from the two given in parentheses.

1. Sheila pitches (most fast, fastest) when the pressure is the greatest.
2. Gayle skates (more carefully, most carefully) than Kenneth.
3. That stunt driver is driving (more recklessly, most recklessly) than ever before.
4. This lid came off (more easily, most easily) of all.
5. Push the car (more hard, harder) if you want to get it out of the snowbank.
6. I did (worse, more bad) than you on the quiz.
7. Power brakes will stop a car (more quickly, quicklier).
8. Nora is the (less, least) noisy person in the room.
9. That dog performs (worse, worst) than any other dog in the act.

10. Among the racers in his age group, Ricky skated (more quickly, most quickly).

Part 3 Adjective or Adverb?

You remember that some adverbs are made by adding *-ly* to an adjective. Read these examples:

My sister is a *careful* driver. My sister drives *carefully*.

Patty is *happy*. Patty smiled *happily*.

Because these words are so much alike, it is sometimes hard to know whether to use the adjective or adverb form. Which would you say?

Anita worked very *careful*. *or* Anita worked very *carefully*.

To find the answer, ask what you are trying to say. Are you trying to say:

which one Anita worked?
what kind Anita worked?
how many Anita worked?

Or are you trying to say:

how Anita worked?

You are trying to say *how*. The kind of word that tells how something happened or how something was done is an adverb. This adverb modifies the verb *worked*. You would use the adverb *carefully* in this sentence.

Anita worked very *carefully*.

When you are choosing the correct modifier, ask yourself:

1. Which word does the modifier tell about?
2. What does the modifier tell?

The chart below will help you to answer these questions.

An **Adverb** tells	An **Adjective** tells
* **How**	* **What kind**
* **When**	* **How many**
* **Where**	* **Which one**
* **To What Extent**	
about a Verb, Adjective, or Adverb	**about a Noun or Pronoun**

Exercises **Choose the right modifier.**

A. Copy each sentence, putting in the correct modifier. Then read the sentence to yourself. Underline the modifier. Draw an arrow from the modifier to the word it modifies. Then write *Adjective* or *Adverb* to show how the modifier is used.

Examples: Mike was (tired, tiredly) after the race.

Mike was *tired* after the race. adjective

The choir sang (good, well).

The choir sang *well.* adverb

1. The barn looked (empty, emptily).
2. That cliff is (sure, surely) too steep for me to climb.
3. Karen didn't feel (really, real) sure of her answer.
4. The team felt (bad, badly) about losing the game.
5. Dan pitched (wild, wildly).
6. After the fight, the boxer looked pretty (bad, badly).
7. You print so (neat, neatly).
8. The actor sang too (poor, poorly) to get the role.
9. Those mountains look (beautiful, beautifully).
10. Our test wasn't (real, really) hard.

B. Follow the directions for Exercise A.

1. The edge of the paper was (real, really) crooked.
2. That map was drawn (bad, badly).
3. I go to the library (regularly, regular) on Friday.
4. This vegetable soup tastes (bad, badly).
5. You sang (remarkable, remarkably) well.
6. The sun set (slow, slowly).
7. The price of the car sounded (incredible, incredibly).
8. The teams were matched pretty (even, evenly).
9. The line was drawn (uneven, unevenly) across the field.
10. Our telephone rang (promptly, prompt) at ten.

Using *Good* and *Well*

The words *good* and *well* are often confused. They form their comparative and superlative forms in exactly the same way:

good	better	best
well	better	best

Good is always an adjective that describes a noun or pronoun. It is never used as an adverb.

You are a good student.
(*Good* modifies *student.*)

That cake looks good.
(*Looks* is used as a linking verb, and *good* modifies *cake.*)

Well is an adjective when it describes a noun or pronoun and means "healthy."

If you take your medicine, you will be well.
(*Well* modifies *you.*)

I feel well.
(*Feel* is a linking verb, and *well* modifies *I.*)

Well is an adverb when it modifies a verb, adverb, or adjective, and tells *how* something is done.

You cook well.
(*Well* modifies *cook.*)

This report is well organized.
(*Well* modifies *organized.*)

Exercises Use *good* and *well* correctly.

A. Write *Adjective* or *Adverb* to tell how each word in italics is used. Then write the word or words that it modifies.

1. The witness had a *good* look at the robber.
2. In training camp, the football players eat *well.*
3. Ted takes *good* care of his bicycle.
4. Can you see *better* without sunglasses?
5. Dana gave the *best* answer.
6. These shoes fit me *best.*
7. Kelly is *good* at tennis.
8. You are *better* at soccer.
9. Andy writes *good* reports.
10. These ski boots don't fit *well.*

B. Follow the directions for Exercise A.

1. The map showed a *better* route than Fran's.
2. Did you have a *good* time?
3. The team did *well* in the exhibition games.
4. Your homemade pies are *better* than pies from the bakery.
5. Ford has a *better* idea.
6. Andrea speaks *well* before large groups.
7. Dave is the *best* catcher on our block.
8. Ramona has a *good* recipe for brownies.
9. Anyone plays *better* after some practice.
10. My dad wore his *best* tie.

REVIEW Using Adverbs

Recognizing Adverbs Copy each sentence. Circle each adverb. Draw an arrow from each adverb to the word it modifies.

1. The campers slept outside.
2. Carol hurriedly ate her breakfast.
3. The stage crew looked everywhere for the props.
4. The conductor never collected our tickets.
5. Today a guide showed us the space capsule.
6. Ants completely covered our picnic blanket.
7. Tom works quite slowly.
8. Have we hiked too far?
9. Instantly, the coach jumped up.
10. Sherry almost always makes free throws.

Adverbs in Comparison Choose the correct form of the adverb from the two given.

11. Penny's toss came (closer, closest) than Pam's.
12. Sam scored (higher, more high) on the last test.
13. Andrea practices (less, least) than she should.
14. Of all the planets, Venus can be seen (more clearly, most clearly).
15. Dave and Jerry have been friends (longer, more longer) than you and I.

Adjective or Adverb? Write the correct modifier.

16. The snow fell (steady, steadily).
17. The solution to the crime seemed (plain, plainly).
18. The fencer lunged (graceful, gracefully).
19. This ink is (true, truly) invisible.
20. Marcy performed (good, well) in the meet.

Using Prepositions and Conjunctions

Little words can do big jobs. In this section, you will learn about some little words that join and relate other words in a sentence. These useful words are called **prepositions** and **conjunctions.** Without them, the other words would have little meaning.

Part 1 What Are Prepositions?

Prepositions are words that show relationships. Read these sentences and notice the relationships expressed.

Jill's gloves are *on the table.*
Jill's gloves are *beside the table.*
Jill's gloves are *under the table.*

Ralph studied *before dinner.*
Ralph studied *during dinner.*
Ralph studied *after dinner.*

I took the photo *of my parents.*
I took the photo *without my parents.*
I took the photo *for my parents.*

In the first group of sentences, you can see that the words *on, beside,* and *under* show the relationship of Jill's gloves to the table. The words show location.

In the second group of sentences, *before, during,* and *after* show the relationship of Ralph's studying to dinner. The words show time.

In the third group of sentences, *of, without,* and *for* show the relationship of the photo to the parents. These words show other different relationships.

All these words that show relationships are **prepositions.**

You can also see that prepositions do not show relationships by themselves. They begin a **phrase,** a group of words that belong together but have no subject and verb. *On the table, before dinner,* and *of my parents* are examples of prepositional phrases in the sentences you've just read. What are other prepositional phrases?

A preposition is a word used with a noun or pronoun, called its *object,* to show the relationship between the noun or pronoun and some other word in the sentence.

A prepositional phrase consists of a preposition, its object, and any modifiers of the object.

Here is a list of words often used as prepositions. Most of these prepositions show location. Others show a relationship of time. Still others relate people and things in special relationships. Study these prepositions and see the relationships that each of them expresses.

Words Often Used as Prepositions

about	before	down	of	through
above	behind	during	off	to
across	below	for	on	toward
after	beneath	from	onto	under
against	beside	in	out	until
along	between	inside	outside	up
among	beyond	into	over	upon
around	but (*except*)	like	past	with
at	by	near	since	without

Exercise **Recognize prepositional phrases.**

Number your paper from 1 to 10. Write the prepositional phrase in each sentence.

1. We make ice cream at home.
2. At midnight the power went off.
3. During practice Kendra sprained her ankle.
4. Westerns on TV often use stunt people.
5. Without sunlight the plants will die.
6. Where is the line of scrimmage?
7. The runners sprinted across town.
8. Marshall caught the long pass from Stevenson.
9. Students gathered in the hallway.
10. Why does David always get into trouble?

Using Prepositional Phrases

The group of words that includes a preposition and its object is a **prepositional phrase.** All the words that modify the object are also part of the phrase.

Examples: We rode *in the bus.*
We rode *in an old, broken-down bus.*

If a preposition has more than one object, all the parts of the object are included in the prepositional phrase.

Example: Weeds grow *in the lawn, the flower garden, and the vegetable garden.*

Exercises **Find the prepositional phrases.**

A. Number your paper from 1 to 10. Write the prepositional phrases in each of the following sentences.

1. The stunt planes performed over the lake.
2. We followed a path through the dark forest.
3. Garbage floated on rivers and streams.
4. A tornado swept across the flat land.
5. The murderer confesses in the third act.
6. Have you ever played on a clay court?
7. Up the spiral staircase is a secret room.
8. Mike Douglas had a magician on his show.
9. Two swimmers leaped into the dark, icy waters.
10. I eat ice cream with fudge sauce.

B. Complete these sentences. You may refer to the list on page 339. There are many correct answers.

1. The plane landed __________ 11 P.M.
2. We hiked __________ the lake.
3. A pencil fell __________ the desk.
4. The captain looked __________ us.

5. Carolyn sat ______________ Bob and me.
6. A posse rode ______________ town.
7. Our canary flew ______________ the house.
8. The ball landed ______________ the stands.
9. Jill sang ______________ me.
10. Wait for me ______________ the gate.

Part 2 Objects of Prepositions

Using Nouns as Objects of Prepositions

You have seen that nouns may be used as subjects or objects of verbs. You will now see how nouns are used as objects of prepositions. Here are some examples of objects of prepositions:

The boys pitched their tents *near the* **river.**
Mickey left his books *in his* **locker.**
The winning run was scored *by* **Bonita.**

Exercise Find nouns used as objects of prepositions.

Number your paper from 1 to 10. For each sentence, write the prepositional phrase. Then underline the noun used as the object of the preposition.

1. We ran laps around the gym.
2. The train stopped past the station.
3. We added wood to the huge bonfire.
4. The fans crowded onto the bleachers.
5. In the science room is a real skeleton.
6. Stacey tried out for the lead role.
7. We learned about the metric system.
8. We drove through the scenic park.
9. Sandy repaired her bike with a wrench.
10. Before the final bell, the champ scored a knockout.

Using Pronouns as Objects of Prepositions

When a pronoun is used as the object of a preposition, its object form must be used.

The object forms are these:

me	us
you	you
him, her, it	them

Examples: The prize was awarded *to us*.
Is there a ticket *for me?*

Using Pronouns in Compound Objects of Prepositions

Usually you make few mistakes in using the object form of pronouns as the object of a preposition. But you may become confused when the object of a preposition is compound.

Simple Object	**Compound Object**
Study *with* **her.**	Study *with* **David** *and* **her.**
Give that *to* **me.**	Give that *to* **her** *and* **me.**

If you are not sure which form to use, first say the sentence with the pronoun alone following the preposition.

Example: We're working for Tom and (she, her).
We're working for *her*.
We're working for Tom and *her*.

Using *Between* and *Among*

Often people use the prepositions *between* and *among* as if there were no difference between them. There is a difference that you should know, so that you can use them correctly. Use *between* to speak of two persons or things. Use *among* to speak of three or more. Here are examples:

Choose **between** *these two programs.*
The next game is **between** *the Jefferson High team and us.*

We will divide the jobs **among** *Nancy, you, and me.*
There was a three-way tie **among** *the Yankees, the Red Sox, and the Indians.*

Exercises Use pronouns as objects of prepositions.

A. Choose the correct pronoun from the two given in parentheses. Write the complete prepositional phrase. Check your answer by reading the sentence to yourself.

Example: The villain shot at Sheriff Dodge and (he, him).

at Sheriff Dodge and him

1. Jan did magic tricks for (us, we).
2. A firecracker exploded near (they, them).
3. Mr. Hernandez ate lunch with Bonnie and (I, me).
4. Mom wrote notes for my sister and (me, I).
5. Prizes were awarded to Keith and (she, her).
6. A fight broke out between Andy and (him, he).
7. Will you take a picture of Britt and (I, me).
8. The chores were divided among Tina, Becky, and (she, her).
9. The librarian glared at Shawn and (us, we).
10. The curtain fell behind Danielle and (her, she).

B. Follow the directions for Exercise A.

1. Sing along with (I, me).
2. A jeep bumped toward (they, them).
3. Beneath (we, us) the ground shook.
4. I wrapped presents for (him, he) and his brother.
5. Two snakes slithered past JoAnn and (me, I).
6. The bike beside Lowell and (her, she) is for sale.

7. Coach Wheatley motioned to Carlotta and (she, her).

8. The playoffs will be between Jefferson Junior High and (we, us).

9. There was a rivalry between Pete, and (him, he).

10. Have you practiced the skit with Denise and (her, she)?

Part 3 Preposition or Adverb?

Several words that are used as prepositions are also used as adverbs.

Examples: We looked *up*. (adverb)
We looked *up the chimney*. (preposition)

The chickens ran *around*. (adverb)
The chickens ran *around the yard*. (preposition)

If you aren't sure whether a word is an adverb or a preposition, see how it is used. If it begins a phrase, it is probably a preposition. If it is used alone, it is probably an adverb.

Exercises Find prepositions and adverbs.

A. In each pair of sentences that follows, one word is used both as an adverb and as a preposition. Number your paper from 1 to 10. After each number, write *a.* and *b.* After each letter, write *Preposition* or *Adverb* depending on which you find in that sentence.

Example: a. Look out! b. Look out the window.
a. Adverb b. Preposition

1. a. The dog turned over. b. That ball went over the fence.

2. a. Two children hid behind the bushes. b. One hiker lagged behind.

3. a. Sharks waited below. b. Below deck is the cabin.

4. a. We are going inside. b. Have you been inside a cockpit?

5. a. Ramona's brother tagged along. b. Ants crawled along the floor.

6. a. Our plane flew through the storm. b. Our plans fell through.

7. a. Above, cranes hoisted steel beams. b. Is the temperature above zero?

8. a. My book fell out the window. b. The fire has gone out.

9. a. Let's ski down this slope. b. That battery has run down.

10. a. A police car drove past. b. Our guests stayed past midnight.

B. Follow the directions for Exercise A.

1. a. Dad finally gave in. b. Jessica talks in her sleep.

2. a. The red paint is used up. b. Can you climb up this rope?

3. a. What lies beyond our solar system? b. Beyond, a star fell.

4. a. My pencil rolled under the desk.. b. A swimmer went under.

5. a. We built a fence around our ranch. b. Larry went downtown and looked around.

6. a. Two paramedics raced by. b. The weaving is by Leslie.

7. a. A mob gathered outside city hall. b. We have gym class outside.

8. a. Beneath is a parking garage. b. Beneath the rug is a trapdoor.

9. a. My report is about apes. b. Tourists wandered about.

10. a. Carol waded along the shore. b. A trail guide rode along.

Part 4 Prepositional Phrases as Modifiers

Prepositional phrases do the same work in a sentence as adjectives and adverbs.

A phrase that modifies a noun or pronoun is an adjective phrase. An adjective phrase tells *which one, what kind,* or *how many* about the noun or pronoun it modifies.

Examples: The window *in the garage* is broken. (which one)

A few yards *of silk* are expensive. (what kind)

We saw statues *of several Presidents.* (how many)

A phrase that modifies a verb is an adverb phrase. An adverb phrase tells *where, when,* or *how* about the verb.

Examples: Jason lived *in Utah.* (where)

I had a cake *on my birthday.* (when)

The crowd ate *in shifts.* (how)

Exercises Find adjective and adverb phrases.

A. Make three columns marked *Word Modified, Phrase,* and *Kind of Phrase.* For each prepositional phrase in the following sentences, fill in the information under the three columns. (You may want to review the questions that adjectives and adverbs answer.)

1. Tracey walked across the bridge.
2. The actor rehearsed in costume.
3. The locker by the stairs is mine.
4. Kay and Lee rode on the tandem bike.
5. Vanessa wrote a speech for her friend.

6. ABBA is a rock group from Sweden.
7. Is the first row of the theater full?
8. Ted opened a bag of Cosmic Candy.
9. The skaters jumped over barrels.
10. Cal crawled under the fence.

B. Follow the directions for Exercise A.

1. The book of ghost stories is scary.
2. The runner stopped at third base.
3. The tower radioed to the plane.
4. The movie portrays life on Mars.
5. We basked in the hot sun.
6. Enter through the side door, please.
7. Two fire trucks sped up the street.
8. The reward for our dog is ten dollars.
9. The girl on the bench is my sister.
10. Millions of people watched the Olympics.

Part 5 Using Prepositional Phrases in the Right Places

Some prepositional phrases may be moved from one position in the sentence to another without changing the meaning of the sentence. Here is an example:

> We visited Florida during our vacation.
> During our vacation, we visited Florida.

To give your writing variety, begin a sentence with a prepositional phrase now and then. However, too many prepositional phrases can become boring. Don't use them too often at the beginnings of sentences.

Some prepositional phrases do not move easily from one position in the sentence to another. The position of the phrase can make a great deal of difference in the meaning of the sentence.

Example: The plant with the red flowers is for sale.
The plant is for sale with the red flowers.

The second sentence is confusing. The prepositional phrase *with the red flowers* should not be moved away from *plant*.

Example: Gary called the dog with a loud voice.
With a loud voice, Gary called the dog.

The second sentence puts the prepositional phrase where it belongs, next to *Gary*. This makes the meaning much clearer.

A prepositional phrase should be placed either directly before or directly after the word it modifies.

Exercises Use prepositional phrases correctly.

A. The following sentences are confusing. By changing the position of one phrase in each sentence, you can make the meaning clear. Rewrite each sentence to make it clear.

1. The album is by Steve Martin on that shelf.
2. Annie was praised for her work by the teacher.
3. Blue jeans are popular with straight legs.
4. Buy your tickets as soon as possible for the concert.
5. The handlebars rusted on my bike.
6. The patient needs a blanket with a fever.
7. The book is yours in my locker.
8. The thief was caught after the robbery by the police.
9. On Mr. Pauley the class played a joke.
10. The train neared the station from Miami.

B. Follow the directions for Exercise A.

1. Kate bought some slippers for her mom with tassels.

2. The pictures fell on the wall.
3. This new album is good by Billy Joel.
4. Keith read a book about outer space in the summer.
5. The bird left the cage with yellow feathers.
6. My room is small but comfortable at home.
7. The water won't drain in the sink.
8. The car had to pull over with a flat tire.
9. Tom slipped and sprained his ankle on the ice.
10. The poodle won a prize with the diamond collar.

Part 6 What Are Conjunctions?

You have learned that relationships between people and things or actions are expressed by prepositions. Relationships are also expressed by another kind of word: **conjunctions.**

How is the word *and* used in each of these sentences?

Tom **and** *David* went to the movie.
The plane *circled* **and** *landed.*
Allen's puppy *broke its leash* **and** *ran away.*
Monica hit a *double* **and** two *singles* in the game.

Do you see that in each sentence, *and* connects words or groups of words of the same type? In the first example, *and* joins two subjects. In the second example, *and* joins two verbs. In the third example, *and* joins two predicates. In the last example, *and* connects two direct objects. The word *and* is a conjunction.

A conjunction is a word that connects words or groups of words. Two other conjunctions we use often are *but* and *or*. Like *and*, they may be used to connect sentence parts.

Andy *or* **Gail** will bring the records. (compound subject)
The performers **danced** *and* **sang.** (compound verb)
The forward **shot for the basket** *but* **missed it.** (compound predicate)
Buy some **bread** *or* some **rolls.** (compound direct object)

The package was **bulky** *but* **light.** (compound predicate adjective)

The band performed **for the faculty** *and* **parents.** (compound object of a preposition)

Exercises Use conjunctions correctly.

A. Copy each sentence. Underline the word or words that are connected by a conjunction. Circle the conjunction.

Example: The Celtics survived that season and gradually improved.

The Celtics survived that season (and) gradually improved.

1. The pitcher and the catcher exchanged signals.
2. Canadians speak French or English.
3. This gadget dries and styles my hair.
4. Nancy or Gail will finish first.
5. The cafeteria serves breakfast and lunch.
6. We ate bacon and eggs.
7. Several students made clay pots and wooden boxes.
8. Running shorts and a T-shirt are our uniform.
9. The toboggan hit the wall and rolled over.
10. Do you play soccer or football?

B. Write sentences with compound subjects, predicates, or objects as the directions ask for. Use *and, but,* or *or.*

Example: Compound direct object. Use a noun and a pronoun.

Please take Amy and me to the library.

1. Compound subject. Use two nouns.
2. Compound predicate.
3. Compound direct object. Use two nouns.
4. Compound subject. Use a noun and a pronoun.
5. Compound direct object. Use two pronouns.

REVIEW Using Prepositions and Conjunctions

Prepositional Phrases Write the prepositional phrases.

1. Bonita is the last person in line.
2. Charlie Chaplin starred in silent films.
3. The library has rooms for meetings.
4. We donated a box of old toys to a charity.
5. Grace handed popsicles to Ken and me.

Preposition or Adverb? Write *Adverb* or *Preposition* to tell what each word in italics is.

6. Don't turn *around*.
7. Fish swam *beneath* the ice.
8. Children *under* twelve are admitted free.
9. It is warm *inside* a sleeping bag.
10. The fog rolled *in*.

Prepositional Phrases as Modifiers Write *Adjective* or *Adverb* to tell what each prepositional phrase is.

11. Randy dashed *toward home plate*.
12. Ginny drew a cartoon *of the lunchroom*.
13. The first signs *of spring* are here.
14. Dr. Jekyll turned *into Mr. Hyde*.
15. The wind whistled *through the trees*.

Conjunctions and Compound Sentence Parts Write the compound sentence parts with their conjunctions.

16. The interviewer and her guest discussed movies.
17. We don't have any chalk or erasers.
18. The skater slipped and fell.
19. Football players should wear helmets and shoulder pads.
20. Dinosaurs roamed the land and swam in the sea.

Using the Parts of Speech

Part 1 The Parts of Speech

In previous sections, you have become familiar with these groups of words:

nouns	verbs	adverbs	conjunctions
pronouns	adjectives	prepositions	

You have been learning to recognize each group of words and to use each group correctly. These seven groups of words are called the **parts of speech.**

The eighth part of speech is the **interjection.** In this section, you will find out about interjections. You will also review all eight parts of speech.

What Are Interjections?

In addition to the seven important groups of words you have studied, there is also a group of words called interjections.

An interjection is a word or short group of words used to express strong feeling. It may express surprise, joy, anger, or sadness. An interjection is often followed by an exclamation mark (!).

Look at these examples of interjections:

> *No way!* I'm not singing by myself.
> *Congratulations!*
> *Great!*
> *Ouch!* That hurts.

Now you have learned about all eight parts of speech.

The Parts of Speech			
nouns	**verbs**	**adverbs**	**conjunctions**
pronouns	**adjectives**	**prepositions**	**interjections**

Words fit into these groups because of the way they are used in a sentence.

Exercises Recognize the parts of speech.

A. Number your paper from 1 to 10. Read each sentence. Then write the underlined word. Beside each word, write what part of speech it is.

1. Fireworks lit the sky.
2. Look! It's Superman!
3. The parade came down Maple Avenue.
4. The bride walked down the aisle.
5. The batter has two strikes.
6. Jack speaks very slowly.
7. The rocket zoomed upward.

8. My dogs begs and shakes hands.
9. Will you write to me?
10. Wow! That water is cold.

B. Follow the directions for Exercise A.

1. They tracked the plane on radar.
2. Bill worries too much.
3. Kirsten has a bank account.
4. Duck! Those rocks are loose.
5. These pictures are fuzzy.
6. We always go to Grandma's house on holidays.
7. The group ate lunch near the fountain.
8. The Scouts learned first aid and water safety.
9. Madame Solga looked into her crystal ball.
10. The hikers sang folksongs as they walked.

Part 2 Using Words as Different Parts of Speech

You cannot tell what part of speech a word is until you see how the word is used in a sentence. Many words may be used in different ways.

In **Section 10**, you learned that the same word could be used as either an adverb or a preposition. For example, look at this pair of sentences:

Hang *on*.
(In this sentence, *on* is an adverb.)

My watch is *on* the table.
(Here, *on* is a preposition.)

Other words may be used as different parts of speech. Here are several more examples for you to study.

We left the dishes in the *sink*.
(In this sentence, *sink* is used as a noun).

I can't float; I *sink*.
(Here, *sink* is used as a verb.)

The farmers *plant* wheat in the spring.
(In this sentence, *plant* is used as a verb.)

This *plant* grows best in sandy soil.
(In this sentence, *plant* is used as a noun.)

My father is a *plant* foreman.
(Here, *plant* is used as an adjective.)

I feel *well*.
(Here, *well* is used as an adjective.)

You skate *well*.
(In this sentence, *well* is an adverb.)

There is only one sure way to decide what part of speech a word is. That way is to see how the word is used in a sentence.

Exercises Recognize the parts of speech.

A. In each pair of sentences that follows, one word is used as two different parts of speech. Number your paper from 1 to 10. After each number, write *a.* and *b.* After each letter, write the word that appears in italics. Tell how it is used. It may be a *noun, verb, adjective, adverb,* or *preposition.*

Example: a. Open a *can* of beans. b. My cousins *can* tomatoes.

a. can, noun b. can, verb

1. a. Turn off the *light*, please. b. The store has no *light* bulbs.

2. a. I brought the dog *in*. b. The horse is *in* the stable.

3. a. There are two new *houses* in our neighborhood. b. The university *houses* visiting players in this dormitory.

4. a. Vince went *outside* for a walk. b. We saw several deer *outside* the cabin.

5. a. Ms. Rosen made a *pencil* drawing of the park. b. I sharpened my *pencil.*

6. a. Carla built a roof *over* the patio. b. Those thunderclouds will soon blow *over.*

7. a. My brother usually *drives* to work. b. Nellie enjoys *drives* in the country.

8. a. The class president *chaired* the meeting. b. This *chair* is too hard.

9. a. A lyric soprano sings *high.* b. The team's fortunes have reached a new *high.*

10. a. Look *up!* b. Alice rode her horse *up* the hill.

B. Follow the directions for Exercise A.

1. a. The king had a *fool* to entertain him. b. Magicians often *fool* the audience.

2. a. Gather *around!* b. Ricky tied tape *around* the handle of the bat.

3. a. Please *hand* me my coat. b. Do these gloves fit your *hands?*

4. a. Have you gone *down* the giant slide? b. Isabella fell *down.*

5. a. When our boat ran into rain, we went *below.* b. The captain is *below* deck.

6. a. The Little League game drew a big *crowd.* b. Some people *crowd* into elevators.

7. a. There are diamonds in that *crown.* b. England's *crown* jewels are extremely valuable.

8. a. This book lists all sorts of *records* in sports and contests. b. She *records* her songs on tape.

9. a. Some workers *strike* for more pay. b. The union will call a *strike* tomorrow.

10. a. *Lower* the picture an inch or two. b. The baby grabbed at pans on the *lower* shelves.

REVIEW The Parts of Speech

Parts of Speech Read each sentence. Write the underlined word. Then write what part of speech the word is in that sentence.

1. <u>She</u> has a pet snake.
2. <u>Oops</u>! I spilled the paint.
3. A luscious <u>smell</u> filled the classroom.
4. Don <u>read</u> three books last week.
5. Are you going to the <u>rock</u> concert?
6. Ed and <u>Steve</u> arm-wrestled on the table.
7. <u>Ingrid</u> speaks three languages.
8. What is a <u>platypus</u>?
9. Bonnie wore a mask <u>and</u> disguised her voice.
10. Barry looked <u>hungrily</u> at the pie.
11. Chlorine <u>kills</u> germs in the pool.
12. <u>Everyone</u> loved the movie.
13. Did you <u>or</u> Jeff pay that library fine?
14. <u>Look out</u>! You're close to the edge.
15. <u>Soon</u> Mom will have a realtor's license.
16. Museums display great works of <u>art</u>.
17. Jonathan tripped <u>over</u> the hose.
18. The new <u>center</u> shows old films.
19. Suddenly the fish flipped <u>over</u>.
20. We walked <u>through</u> the high school building.

Making Subjects and Verbs Agree

A clerk sorts the mail.
Two clerks sort the mail.
Many clerks sorts the mail.

In two of the above sentences, the subject and verb agree. In other words, they match. In one sentence the subject and verb do not agree. Which sentence sounds wrong to you?

If you said the third sentence, you are correct. That subject (*clerks*) and verb (*sorts*) do not agree. The result is like trying to jam together two puzzle pieces that don't belong together.

In this section, you will learn how to make subjects and verbs agree.

Part 1 Rules for Making the Subject and Verb Agree

When a noun stands for one thing, it is **singular.**

student car penny

When a noun stands for more than one thing, it is **plural.**

students cars pennies

Verbs, too, have singular and plural forms. In a sentence, the verb must always agree in number with its subject. The word *number* refers to singular and plural.

Notice these examples:

Singular	**Plural**
Ruth **sings** in the next act.	The girls **sing** this part.
My mother **runs** every morning.	We **run** two miles together.
That boy **speaks** German.	Those boys **speak** Spanish.

When we talk about one girl, we say she *sings*. When we talk about more than one girl, we say the girls *sing*. One person *runs*, but many people *run*. One boy *speaks*, but many boys *speak*.

The *s* at the end of verbs like *sings*, *runs*, and *speaks* shows that the verbs are used with singular nouns. In the examples, the singular nouns *Ruth*, *mother*, and *boy* were the subjects. When the subject is plural, the *s* on the verb is dropped. Look again at the sentences above.

Remember these rules:

1. If the subject is **singular,** use the singular form of the verb.
2. If the subject is **plural,** use the plural form of the verb.

Prepositional Phrases After the Subject

Be careful with prepositional phrases that come after the subject and before the verb. Do not let yourself confuse the subject of the verb with the object of the preposition.

Examples: The members of the band (practices, practice) on Friday.

Who practices? *The members* (subject)
Of the band is a prepositional phrase describing *members*.

The verb must agree with the subject.

The *members* of the band *practice* on Friday.

A pair of tickets (were, was) lost.

What was lost? A *pair* (subject)
Of tickets is a prepositional phrase describing *pair*.

The verb must agree with the subject.

A *pair* of tickets *was* lost.

Exercises Recognize singular and plural forms.

A. On your paper, write the subjects listed below. After each subject, write *Singular* or *Plural* to tell whether it will take the singular or the plural form of the verb.

1. the apples
2. a carnival
3. Sheila
4. the wristwatch
5. autumn leaves
6. the mice
7. the passengers
8. a box
9. the men
10. wild geese

B. Number your paper from 1 to 10. Find the subject and the verb in each sentence below. Write the subject and verb and tell whether they are singular or plural.

Example: The dogs in the yard barked at us.

dogs, barked (plural)

1. A set of books is missing.
2. Angela likes the seat near the window.
3. The taste of chocolate sundaes is delicious.
4. We are using clay in this art project.

5. Woody plays shortstop or second base.

6. Those students in the hall will audition for the talent show.

7. I walked two miles today.

8. The brakes on this bike need adjustment.

9. The high winds last weekend blew that trailer over.

10. A long-distance phone call costs less on weekends.

Special Forms of Certain Verbs

A few verbs have special forms that you should keep in mind.

Is, Was, Are, Were. The verb forms *is* and *was* are singular. The forms *are* and *were* are plural.

Singular: Carlos *is* here. Carlos *was* here.
Plural: The Smiths *are* here. The Smiths *were* here.

Has, Have. The verb form *has* is singular. The form *have* is plural.

Singular: Pam *has* a plan.
Plural: They *have* a plan.

Does, Do. The verb form *does* is singular. The form *do* is plural.

Singular: Joe *does* the cooking.
Plural: They *do* the cooking.

Exercises Make the verb agree with the subject.

A. Number your paper from 1 to 10. Write the correct verb from the two given in parentheses. Check your answer by reading the sentence to yourself.

1. Two ski poles (was, were) standing in the drift.
2. Bob's teeth (has, have) never had a cavity.
3. The locker rooms (is, are) newly painted.
4. My cousin (has, have) been singing in the choir.
5. At high tide, those boats (is, are) floating on the water.

6. (Is, Are) the Boy Scouts coming?
7. The noises in this cave (has, have) weird echoes.
8. Tony's swollen knee (is, are) getting better.
9. Rico (doesn't, don't) waste time.
10. The two stores on Central Street (is, are) closed.

B. Follow the directions for Exercise A.

1. Our bus (has, have) a flat tire.
2. My feet (is, are) too big for these shoes.
3. The girls (was, were) diving for oysters.
4. How many people (is, are) in your family?
5. Some friends of my sister (is, are) coming for dinner.
6. (Is, Are) the Boy Scouts coming?
7. All along the street (was, were) Japanese lanterns.
8. (Does, Do) the canary ever sing?
9. The brakes on this bike (is, are) not working properly.
10. In *Peter Pan,* all the children (is, are) lost.

Part 2 Special Problems with Subjects

Sometimes making subjects and verbs agree is more difficult. There are some subjects that are tricky to use. In this part, you will be learning to use these tricky subjects with the correct verbs.

Certain Pronouns

The words listed below are singular. Each is used with a singular verb form.

each	either	everyone	anyone
one	neither	everybody	nobody

Read these examples over until they sound correct and natural to you.

Each of the boats *has* a motor.
One of the stories *was* scary.
Is either of the answers right?
Neither of the dogs *was* friendly.
Everyone does homework.
Everybody is thirsty.
Is anyone home?
Nobody leaves early.

Watch out especially for these words when they are used as subjects and followed by a prepositional phrase. If the object of the preposition is plural, don't make the mistake of using a plural verb form.

Example: Neither of the cars (are, is) new.

What is the complete subject? *Neither of the cars*
What is the prepositional phrase? *of the cars*
What is the subject? *Neither*
Neither is singular, so the verb must be singular.

Neither of the cars *is* new.

Exercises Make the verb agree with the subject.

A. Copy these sentences, leaving a space for the verb. Draw a circle around the prepositional phrase. Then choose the right form of the verb and write it. Check your answer by reading the sentence to yourself.

Example: Neither of the bolts (fit, fits).

Neither (of the bolts) fits.

1. Nobody in our class (swim, swims) in this race.
2. One of the propellers (was, were) broken.
3. Each of you girls (is, are) allowed five minutes for your speech.
4. Neither of the cats (has, have) been fed.

5. One of the faucets (are, is) leaking.
6. Each of the uniforms (has, have) the school's name on it.
7. Either of the digital clocks (tell, tells) perfect time.
8. Everybody from both classes (was, were) invited.
9. Each of the displays (is, are) on a different country.
10. (Has, Have) either of you brought the hammock?

B. Follow the directions for Exercise A.

1. Neither of the teams (has, have) a coach.
2. Either of those games (is, are) easy.
3. One of my keys (are, is) missing.
4. Everybody in the stands (yell, yells) loudly.
5. Each of the vendors (sell, sells) hot dogs.
6. One of my toes (is, are) numb.
7. (Do, Does) anyone in the room want dessert?
8. Nobody with braces (eats, eat) this candy.
9. Neither of the pitchers (throw, throws) curve balls.
10. Each of those elephants (weighs, weigh) six tons.

There Is, Here Is, Where Is

Many sentences begin with *There*, *Here*, or *Where*. These words are never subjects. In sentences beginning with these words, the subject usually comes after the verb.

Before you can choose the right verb form, you have to know what the subject is. You have to know whether it is singular or plural.

There are your books. (*Books* is the subject; the plural form *are* is correct.)

Here is the path. (*Path* is the subject; the singular form *is* is correct.

Where do the pencils belong? (*Pencils* is the subject; the plural form *do belong* is correct.)

Exercises **Make the verb agree with the subject.**

A. Write the correct form of the verb.

1. Where (does, do) this road go?
2. Here (is, are) your pencils.
3. There (was, were) no salt in the salt shaker.
4. Where (was, were) you waiting?
5. Where (is, are) everybody?
6. Here (is, are) four more pieces for the puzzle.
7. Where (are, is) that cushion with the stripes?
8. There (was, were) many reasons for President Roosevelt's action.
9. Here (is, are) one of the oars.
10. Where (does, do) the books on the table belong?

B. Follow the directions for Exercise A.

1. Here (is, are) the dog food.
2. Where (has, have) the time gone?
3. There (is, are) five good shows on TV.
4. Where (is, are) the entrances to the mall?
5. Here (is, are) the prettiest wildflowers.
6. There (was, were) a penalty on that play.
7. Here (is, are) two of your books.
8. (Has, Have) there been any problems?
9. Where (does, do) helicopters land?
10. There (is, are) a light on each video camera.

Compound Subjects

When two or more parts of a compound subject are joined by the conjunction *and*, use the plural form of the verb.

The mayor and the police chief **were** in the parade.
Are my hat and coat upstairs?

When the parts are joined by *or, either-or,* or *neither-nor,* use the form of the verb that agrees with the nearer subject.

Carol or *Janet* **is singing.**
Neither Mathew nor his *brothers* **are** here.
Either six pencils or one *pen* **costs** a quarter.

Exercises Use the right verb form.

A. Number your paper from 1 to 10. Choose the right form of the verb for each sentence and write it. If a conjunction with *or* or *nor* is used in the subject, also write the part of the compound subject nearer the verb.

Example: Neither my dog nor my cats (has, have) been fed.
cats, have

1. Duchess and her pups (sleeps, sleep) on the back porch.
2. Neither Mary nor I (like, likes) fried foods.
3. Ted and Victoria (has, have) Kodak cameras.
4. Either Mrs. Lind or her children (walks, walk) the dog every afternoon.
5. Neither the girls nor the boys (has, have) the right answer.
6. Everyone and his dog (was, were) there.
7. Seven oranges or one melon (weighs, weigh) three pounds.
8. The swimmers and their coach (practices, practice) every day.
9. Neither the lights nor the phone (works, work).
10. Either Vincent or the other orchestra members (is, are) setting up the chairs.

B. Follow the directions for Exercise A.

1. Superman or Spiderman (is, are) on the case.
2. Red and orange (is, are) warm colors.
3. Switzerland and Italy (shares, share) a border.

4. Neither boots nor a raincoat (keeps, keep) me dry.
5. Pancakes or waffles (is, are) tasty for breakfast.
6. Either skates or a skateboard (goes, go) fast.
7. Gary and Wayne (has, have) the flu.
8. Either Lynn or her sisters (has, have) the comic book.
9. Neither the clocks nor my watch (is, are) right.
10. Either chimes or a buzzer (signals, signal) the guard.

Using *I*

Although *I* stands for a single person, it does not usually take a singular verb form. The only singular verb forms used with it are *am* and *was*.

I *am* the goalie. I *was* here yesterday.

Otherwise, the verb form used with *I* is the same as the plural form.

I *do* my work. I *live* on the next block.
I *have* a cold. I *throw* a good fastball.

Using *You*

The word *you* can stand for one person or for several persons. It may be either singular or plural. Whether it is singular or plural, always use the plural verb form with the pronoun *you*.

You **were** the only *person* with a bike.
You **were** the only *students* in the room.

Exercises **Make the verb agree with the subject.**

A. Write the correct verb from the two given in parentheses. Check your answer by reading the sentence to yourself.

1. You (was, were) ready, weren't you?

2. I (am, are) going for a walk.
3. In that closet (is, are) the roller skates.
4. With your new bike, you (rides, ride) faster than before.
5. Among the library aides, I (is, am) the youngest.
6. You (is, are) welcome at the party.
7. (Has, Have) you brought in the flag?
8. I (am, is) the best speller in the class.
9. (Was, Were) you afraid?
10. My mother and I (am, are) going to the supermarket.

B. Follow the directions for Exercise A.

1. You (was, were) in the play.
2. I (was, were) a caddy last summer.
3. (Does, Do) you know sign language?
4. I (am, is, are) afraid of heights.
5. I (knows, know) three chords on the guitar.
6. You (has, have) a great record collection.
7. I (is, am) learning a new song on the guitar.
8. (Was, Were) you going to study in the library?
9. I (were, was) the only swimmer in the pool.
10. At camp you (was, were) our best counselor.

REVIEW Making Subjects and Verbs Agree

Making Subjects and Verbs Agree Write the correct form of the verb for each sentence. Check your answer by reading the completed sentence to yourself.

1. Missiles (blasts, blast) off at Cape Canaveral.
2. A police officer (directs, direct) traffic here.
3. One sport of the Canadians (is, are) curling.
4. The dogs at the dog pound (looks, look) cute.
5. Six winning games of tennis (makes, make) a set.
6. Those horses (is, are) thoroughbreds.
7. Jane (has, have) a cast on her leg.
8. Donna and Craig (does, do) their chores after school.
9. One of the lamps (needs, need) a new bulb.
10. Neither of these buses (stops, stop) near home.
11. Everyone in the fields (is, are) harvesting crops.
12. Where (does, do) the subway line start?
13. There (is, are) raccoons in the attic.
14. Here (is, are) the six ingredients.
15. Samantha and Cara (is, are) sunburned.
16. Either pants or a skirt (is, are) appropriate.
17. Neither the luggage nor the passengers (has, have) arrived.
18. I (sees, see) the Milky Way.
19. You (was, were) the only runner on the track.
20. I (am, is, are) expecting a phone call.

Using Compound Sentences

Part 1 A Review of the Sentence

Sentences, like words, have different purposes. Before you learn about special kinds of sentences, you should understand what makes a sentence a sentence.

In earlier sections, you learned about the sentence. Let's review the basics. The sentence has two essential parts, the subject and the predicate.

Subject	Predicate
The players	rested.
The players	are weary.
Six weary players	rested quietly.
Six weary players	rested in the locker room.

The **subject** of a sentence, as you have learned, names the person or thing about which something is said. The **predicate** then tells something about the subject.

Compound Parts of the Sentence

You have also learned that all parts of the sentence may be **compound.** That is, all the parts of the sentence may have more than one part. Look at these examples.

Compound Subject:
The *President* and the *Prime Minister* met.

Compound Verb:
Dave Cowens *played* and *coached.*

Compound Predicate:
The firefighters *heard the alarm* and *dashed to the trucks.*

A Definition of the Sentence

You can see that all of these sentences express one main idea. These sentences, like all of those you have been studying, are called **simple sentences.**

Now you are ready for a definition of the simple sentence.

A simple sentence contains only one subject and predicate. Both the subject and the predicate may be compound.

Exercises Review simple sentences.

A. Write the subject and verb in each simple sentence. Draw a vertical line between them. (Remember to look for compound sentence parts.)

Example: Chris and Bill cooked dinner.

Chris, Bill | cooked

1. Nancy and Dennis took a shortcut.
2. Greg is practicing the clarinet.
3. Our class uses the metric system.
4. Did the Raiders score a field goal?
5. The troops arrived by ship.
6. West High School has three thousand students.
7. We learned and practiced first aid.
8. Mom and Julie painted the porch.
9. Meg's fingers and toes are frostbitten.
10. The cat clawed and chewed our furniture.

B. Follow the directions for Exercise A.

1. A new Italian restaurant opened downtown.
2. Some people need very little sleep.
3. I like this album and play it often.
4. The store and the theater are closed for remodeling.
5. Fans filled the ballpark and cheered wildly.
6. Mr. Homer poured the chemicals and did the experiment.
7. Ms. Jackson writes in an elegant script.
8. The magician and his assistant rehearsed backstage.
9. In Illinois, a truck and a train collided yesterday.
10. Josh bought a used bike and fixed it himself.

C. Write five simple sentences. Underline the subject and verb in each sentence. Use capital letters and correct punctuation.

Part 2 What Are Compound Sentences?

Sometimes two sentences are so closely related in thought that you join them together. Then you have a different kind of sentence. You have a sentence that has more than one subject and more than one predicate. You have a sentence with more than one main idea. This is called a **compound sentence.**

Read these examples:

> Snow had fallen all night, **and** it buried everything.
> Beth likes all sports, **but** she enjoys swimming the most.
> Study this map of the city, **or** you will get lost.

Now look at the parts of these compound sentences:

Subject	Verb	Conjunction	Subject	Verb
Snow	had fallen	and	it	buried
Beth	likes	but	she	enjoys
(*you*)	Study	or	you	will get

A Definition of the Compound Sentence

A compound sentence consists of two or more simple sentences joined together.

Why would you want to write compound sentences? Why not use only simple sentences? You will know why as soon as you read this paragraph.

> It was a gray, rainy day. We were looking out the classroom window. We saw something blurry. It was funnel-shaped. It looked cloudy. It seemed to bounce toward us. Finally, we realized what we were seeing. We moved back from the window. It was a tornado coming our way.

You can see that a long series of short sentences is boring and dull. Combined into compound sentences, they sound much better.

> It was a gray, rainy day, and we were looking out the classroom window. We saw something blurry. It was funnel-shaped, and it looked cloudy. It seemed to bounce toward us. Finally, we realized what we were seeing, and we moved back from the window. It was a tornado coming our way.

Exercises **Use compound sentences.**

A. Number your paper from 1 to 10. Label three columns *Subject/Verb, Conjunction,* and *Subject/Verb.* For each sentence, fill in the columns.

Example: Diane left for school, but I stayed home.

Subject/Verb	Conjunction	Subject/Verb
Diane/left	but	I/stayed

1. We take the bus, or we walk home.
2. The heart is a muscle, and it pumps blood.
3. Fur traders go to Alaska, and they look for skins.
4. We have a jar of paste, but it is too dry.
5. Patchwork is an old craft, but it is popular again.
6. Seaweed can be eaten, and it is nutritious.
7. The teacher called on Michelle, but she had forgotten the answer.
8. Wear your winter jacket, or you will be cold.
9. Mary saddled her horse first, and then she helped me with my horse.
10. The Winter Olympics have started, and they are spectacular.

B. Follow the directions for Exercise A.

1. Vic owes me two dollars, but he is broke.
2. A bottle washed ashore, and a note was inside.

3. Jennifer felt lonely, and she called a friend.

4. Bradley organized a soccer team, and Mr. Chan coached.

5. Take ski lessons, and you will feel more confident.

6. Handle the eggs carefully, or they will break.

7. The library has many science fiction books, and I have read most of them.

8. Peters is the star center, but he did not play well today.

9. Sarah wanted a new album, but she couldn't decide on one.

10. Clay and Steve must leave now, or they will miss dinner.

Punctuating Compound Sentences

Since compound sentences are made up of two or more simple sentences, they may be long. To help the reader keep the thoughts clear, put a **comma** before the conjunction in a compound sentence. The comma alerts the reader to the end of the first idea, and it prepares the reader for the second idea.

> Emily mowed the lawn, *and* Carl washed the windows.
> Brian enjoys most music, *but* jazz is his favorite.
> Terri must speak more clearly, *or* the audience won't hear her.
> Grapefruits and oranges are citrus fruits, *and* they contain Vitamin C.

You may leave out the comma only when the two sentences that you join are very short.

> Beth danced and Carol watched.
> Silver tarnishes but steel doesn't.

Exercises **Punctuate compound sentences.**

A. Copy the following compound sentences. Add a comma wherever it is needed. Circle the conjunction that joins both parts of the sentence.

1. Ted dusted and Ernestine swept.

2. Steve jumped from the plane and his parachute opened.

3. I read the front page and Don read the comics.

4. Marietta looked at the money but she couldn't believe her eyes.

5. My sister wants a job but she can't find one.

6. We turned on the light and the mouse ran away.

7. A tire burst and we swerved.

8. The TV is broken but Mom will fix it.

9. Have you finished your homework or will you study in the library?

10. I run one mile every day but my brother runs three miles.

B. Follow the directions for Exercise A.

1. The two boys collided but neither was hurt.

2. Jocelyn felt happy and she smiled at everyone.

3. Bells rang and people cheered.

4. Rattlesnakes bite but pythons don't.

5. The bullfighter twirled his cape and the bull charged.

6. Judy rowed to the middle of the lake and then the boat started leaking.

7. Americans use dollar bills but the English use pound notes.

8. Are you left-handed or are you right-handed?

9. New York has the Statue of Liberty and Philadelphia has the Liberty Bell.

10. Would you like a sandwich or would you rather have pizza?

C. Write five compound sentences. Punctuate them correctly. Circle the conjunction that joins both parts of each sentence. Underline the subject once and the verb twice in each part.

REVIEW Using Compound Sentences

Simple Sentences Write the subjects and verbs in these simple sentences.

1. Lifejackets are used for water safety.
2. Boats docked in the harbor.
3. The Governor and Senator spoke at the rally.
4. Chris waited and worried.
5. Jane Goodall went to Africa and studied chimpanzees.

Compound Sentences Copy each sentence. Add the punctuation needed to make the sentence correct. Underline the subject once and the verb twice in each part.

6. Bird hit the basket again and Indiana State won.
7. We washed the car and it looked terrific.
8. A van pulled up and my friends jumped out.
9. The airport closed and many people were stranded there.
10. Use a lock on your bike or it may be stolen.
11. Are you going to camp or will you stay at home?
12. The pool will open soon and we will take swimming lessons.
13. Sue smiled and Tom smiled back.
14. There was a fire but it was quickly put out.
15. Six inches of snow fell and we shoveled the walk.
16. Vacation will begin soon and everyone is ready for it.
17. A light flashed and the police car began a chase.
18. An astronaut talked to us and we learned about the space program.
19. We need a ladder or we will never reach the roof.
20. A thermometer measures temperature and a barometer measures air pressure.

Using Complex Sentences

Simple and compound sentences are not the only kinds of sentences that you use. Another kind of sentence is the **complex sentence.** In this section, you will see how ideas are expressed in a complex sentence.

Part 1 What Are Complex Sentences?

Before you can know what a complex sentence is, you need to know about clauses.

A clause is a group of words that contains a verb and its subject.

According to this definition, a simple sentence is a clause since it has both a verb and subject.

s. v.
This poster glows in the dark.

s. v.
Naomi James is a skilled sailor.

How about compound sentences? Do they contain clauses? Do they contain two or more groups of words that have a subject and a verb? Look at these examples:

s. v. s. v.
Bradley chopped a hole in the ice, and then he fished.

s. v. s. v.
Six of our swimmers made the finals, but only two won.

The answer is clear. Compound sentences do contain groups of words that have their own subjects and verbs. That is, compound sentences do contain clauses.

Main Clauses

A clause that can stand as a sentence by itself is a **main clause.** The clauses in compound sentences are main clauses. They can stand as simple sentences by themselves. That is why main clauses are sometimes called **independent clauses.**

From these definitions, you can see that you have already been working with clauses. A simple sentence is actually a main (independent) clause. A compound sentence is really two or more main (independent) clauses joined together.

It will be easier to understand sentences, however, if you think of a clause as *part of a sentence.* Think of a clause as a *group of words within a sentence.*

Subordinate Clauses

Now look at clauses of a different kind:

s. v.
after he chopped a hole in the ice

s. v.
when I become an electrician

s. v.
who sail around the world

These clauses do have a subject and verb. However, none of them can stand alone as a sentence. Each clause needs to have something added to make a complete thought. Such clauses are called **subordinate,** or **dependent, clauses.** The word *subordinate* means that these clauses depend on something more important to make a complete thought. Read these subordinate clauses. Think of ways to complete the thoughts.

Because I helped my brother . . .
After Dawn missed the bus . . .
Whenever we visit my aunt . . .

A Definition of the Complex Sentence

Now that you know about main clauses and subordinate clauses, you are ready to learn what a complex sentence is.

A complex sentence is a sentence that contains one main clause and one or more subordinate clauses.

Main Clause	Subordinate Clause
Thomas Adams is the person	who invented chewing gum.
The fireworks began	after the parade was over.
Ed says	that he is on a diet.

Subordinate Clause	Main Clause
Before she cut it,	Meg had waist-length hair.
Since the library is closed,	we must study at home.
What Kate needed	was a new bike.

Exercise Recognize main clauses and subordinate clauses.

Number your paper from 1 to 10. Each of the clauses below has been written without punctuation. Read each clause. Then write *Main* or *Subordinate* to tell what kind each clause is.

1. After we washed the car
2. Water sparkled in the sunlight
3. Vinnie likes cereal and toast
4. Whenever Lionel giggles
5. Although it is the right size
6. Someone left the window open
7. Where Madison Avenue is
8. Who makes stained glass
9. The ship sank during the storm
10. While the new house is being built

Part 2 More About Subordinate Clauses

Look at the following groups of words. Are they subordinate clauses?

until tomorrow after the storm since vacation

You can see that these examples are not subordinate clauses because they have no subject and verb. These groups of words are prepositional phrases.

Phrases and Clauses

Can you tell the difference between a phrase and a subordinate clause? Look at these examples.

Phrases	Clauses
until tomorrow	until Mary (s.) arrives (v.)
after the storm	after the painters (s.) have finished (v.) the house

A clause has a subject and a verb. A phrase does not. When you work with subordinate clauses, remember to look for a subject and verb.

Exercise Recognize phrases and clauses.

Read each of the following groups of words. Then write *Phrase* or *Clause* to tell what each group is.

1. Since we all agree
2. Because he was late
3. Since last September
4. Before the bell rings
5. Inside the cave
6. When the tide rises
7. Before class
8. In the alley
9. When we got our report cards
10. Where the judge sits

Words Often Used To Begin Subordinate Clauses

Read these subordinate clauses:

When the door opened *After* the concert is over

Now, cover the first word in each clause, and read the clause again. What happens? Each group of words becomes a complete sentence. You can see, then, that the words *when* and *after* are important.

It is said that these words *subordinate* the group of words they introduce. They introduce subordinate clauses.

Here is a list of words often used to begin subordinate clauses:

after	because	than	when
although	before	though	whenever
as	if	unless	where
as if	since	until	wherever
as long as	so that	whatever	while

Subordinate clauses may also begin with these words:

that	who, whom, whose	which
what	whoever, whomever	how

Caution: All of these words are subordinating words only when they introduce a clause. Some of them can be used in other ways.

Exercises **Recognize subordinate clauses.**

A. Find the subordinate clause in each complex sentence. Write the clause. Then underline the subject once and the verb twice.

1. Since she was six, Donna has played tennis.
2. Robert trembled because he was scared.
3. Find out when the game starts.
4. This is the family that has triplets.
5. The horse fell before the race began.
6. Lincoln Park is the place where we meet.
7. As we talked, the politician smiled.
8. *Summer of Fear* is the book that I liked best.

9. Donny and Marie Osmond, who had their own TV show, just made a movie.
10. Can you study while you listen to music?

B. Follow the directions for Exercise A.

1. Tracy Austin, who is a teenager, plays pro tennis.
2. Their dog barks whenever the doorbell rings.
3. Beth wondered how actors are trained.
4. Alana shopped while Mom and I waited.
5. Jeff imagined that he was a time traveler.
6. After choir practice ended, we went to Laurel's house.
7. A new toy that I saw tosses a football.
8. Although it looks easy, a back flip is difficult.
9. Few people know what makes them happy.
10. Can you babysit after school is out?

C. Write five complex sentences. Underline the main clause once and the subordinate clause twice.

Part 3 More About Sentence Fragments

The sentence fragments that you studied in **Section 2** were easy to spot. They were fragments because they lacked a verb or the subject of a verb.

Now you'll learn about another kind of sentence fragment, the subordinate clause. A subordinate clause has both a verb and a subject. It is still a fragment, however, because its meaning is not complete. Look at the groups of words below.

When he was young
Where young people go
That Dallas would win the Superbowl

A subordinate clause must not be written as a complete sentence. It must always be joined to a main clause.

Fragment: When he was young
Sentence: When he was young, Einstein did poorly in math.

Fragment: Where young people go
Sentence: The drop-in center is a place where young people go.

Fragment: That Dallas would win the Superbowl
Sentence: We were hoping that Dallas would win the Superbowl.

Exercises Recognize sentence fragments.

A. Decide whether the groups of words below are sentences or fragments. Write *S* for *Sentence* or *F* for *Fragment.* Add words to make each fragment a complete sentence.

1. If I need help, I'll call you
2. Since you asked
3. Although the bike is old
4. Where I live
5. Tina told Jack that he was lazy
6. As she shoveled snow
7. When he paints
8. We played basketball until the sun set
9. I saw a man who was juggling oranges
10. As the deadline approached

B. Follow the directions for Exercise A.

1. Because the gates were locked
2. If you work hard
3. The hamster escaped when I opened the cage
4. Although he ran for President
5. Carla thought that she must be dreaming
6. When the storm uprooted a tree

7. We ate popcorn as we watched the movie
8. This station plays the top ten songs
9. Eat breakfast before you leave
10. While the cake cools

Part 4 A Review of Sentences

In this book you have learned about three kinds of sentences that you use.

• You know that a **simple sentence** contains one subject and one predicate. A simple sentence expresses one main idea. You will remember, however, that parts of the simple sentence may be compound.

Examples: The baseball team (s.) and the lacrosse team (s.) won (v.) yesterday.

Dan (s.) and Mary (s.) read (v.) and discussed (v.) the history assignment.

• You have learned that a **compound sentence** consists of two simple sentences. These simple sentences are joined together by a conjunction. A compound sentence expresses two main ideas that are related in thought.

Examples: The baseball team (s.) won (v.) yesterday, *but* the wrestling team (s.) lost (v.).

Dan (s.) studied (v.) history, *and* Mary (s.) did (v.) her math.

• You have also learned that a **complex sentence** contains one main clause and one or more subordinate clauses. A complex sentence expresses one main idea, and one or more ideas that depend on the main idea.

s. v.
Examples: *Although the baseball team won yesterday,*

s. v.
the lacrosse team lost.

s. v. s. v.
Dan studied history *while Mary watched television*

Exercises **Recognize the kinds of sentences.**

A. Number your paper from 1 to 10. For each sentence, write *Simple, Compound,* or *Complex* to tell what kind it is.

1. The dog with the pointed ears is a Doberman.
2. Vacation begins on Friday, and our family is going to the lake.
3. Because Vanessa sensed danger, she left.
4. I helped Mandy with the crossword puzzle.
5. Models paraded in the new spring fashions.
6. Justin hit a single, and then he stole second base.
7. When Tracy serves, she often wins the game.
8. The movie is a space thriller, and a robot is the star.
9. What Megan likes best is art class.
10. Clark made a skateboard that has a motor.

B. Follow the directions for Exercise A.

1. The Amazing Wanda rides a unicycle as she juggles.
2. Many people say that they are shy.
3. Where is the nearest fire extinguisher?
4. Franklin bumped into Diane, and she dropped her books.
5. Our neighbors play volleyball in an empty lot.
6. The next solar eclipse will be in 2017.
7. The comedian told jokes, but no one laughed.
8. Arnold screamed when he opened the box.
9. If the weather is warm, we'll go to the beach.
10. The commercials that I like best are the funny ones.

REVIEW Using Complex Sentences

Complex Sentences Write the subordinate clause in each complex sentence.

1. Although we were tired, we couldn't sleep.
2. Marco, who comes from Italy, speaks no English.
3. I didn't know that your ears were pierced.
4. Before I was six, we had moved four times.
5. When Dad is angry, he becomes quiet.
6. A teller rang the alarm after the robbers had fled.
7. I jog along the lake whenever the weather is good.
8. Tom, who is my oldest brother, works in a bank.
9. Call me if you need a ride.
10. We saw a movie that was terrifying.
11. Pam asked where the best beaches are.
12. We climbed a mountain that was twelve hundred feet high.
13. Julie listened as the chef explained.
14. I disagree with the referee who called that penalty.
15. We met a girl who reminded us of Tatum O'Neal.

Review of Sentences For each sentence, write *Simple, Compound,* or *Complex* to tell what kind it is.

16. Mrs. Adams teaches math at the high school.
17. The President threw out the ball, and the game began.
18. Although the bike chain works, it needs oil.
19. I've heard of a zoo where there are no cages.
20. Some cars were buried for weeks after the blizzard.

Diagraming the Sentence

Part 1 What Is Diagraming?

A street map is a clear picture of the roads in a town. An x-ray is a clear picture of the parts of the body. Like a map or an x-ray, a **diagram** of a sentence is a picture of the sentence and its parts. A diagram of a sentence shows clearly how each word in a sentence relates to every other word. A diagram shows how each word functions in a sentence.

When you make diagrams, you follow patterns. It is important to follow the patterns exactly. You will need to be careful to put words in special places. You will need to be careful to make vertical lines, horizontal lines, straight lines, or slanted lines. Copy words exactly as they appear in a sentence, with capital letters or without them. Do not copy any punctuation marks except the apostrophes within a word.

In this section, you will be learning how to diagram parts of a sentence. You'll see how diagraming can help you to understand sentences.

Part 2 Diagraming Verbs and Their Subjects

A sentence diagram always begins on a horizontal line. The subject is placed at the left side of the line. The verb is placed at the right side of the line. A vertical line cuts the line in two and separates the subject from the verb.

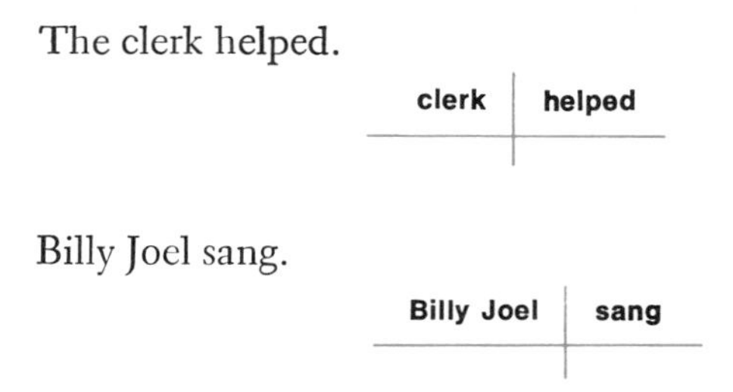

Exercise **Diagram the verbs and their subjects.**

Diagram the verb and its simple subject in each of the following sentences. (Ignore all other words.)

1. Mr. Rosen skis.
2. Marcy sneezed.
3. Bulls charge.
4. Darren laughed at my joke.
5. Horns honked loudly.
6. Tammy Dillon left.
7. The candy melted in the sun.
8. The floors creaked.
9. Mayor Best campaigned.
10. The Falcons will play on Friday.

Part 3 Diagraming Subjects in Unusual Order

Unusual order does not change the positions of subjects and verbs on diagrams.

Above the clouds soared the jet.

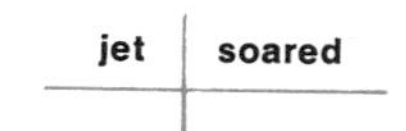

Out from the darkness walked a stranger.

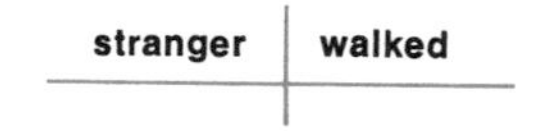

Exercise Diagram subjects in unusual order.

Diagram the subject and verbs in the following sentences. (Ignore all other words.)

1. Down the ice skated Miller.
2. Behind the door lay a wallet.
3. On Casey's pants were patches.
4. From the sky shot a star.
5. Under a blanket rested the cat.
6. Slowly into the water sank the boat.
7. Around my arm wound the snake.
8. Across the pool raced the swimmers.
9. In the back of the desk was a secret drawer.
10. In the distance blared a foghorn.

Part 4 Diagraming Questions

When you diagram a question, put the subject and verb in normal order.

Did Sara ride her bike?

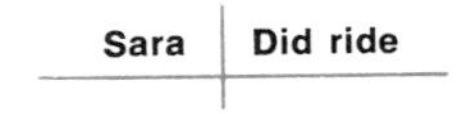

Have you sent for tickets?

Exercise Diagram questions.

Diagram the subject and verb in each of the following questions. (Ignore all other words.)

1. Will Natalie Cole sing?
2. Have you noticed a change?
3. Did the paint dry?
4. Shall we sit in a booth?
5. Has the sherbet melted?
6. Would you like a snack?
7. When will school begin?
8. Did you get a booster shot?
9. Has Jennifer learned her lines?
10. Did you enjoy the movie?

Part 5 Diagraming Imperative Sentences

When the subject of an imperative sentence is understood, show it on your diagram by writing (*you*).

Put air in this tire.

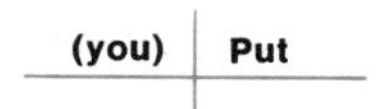

Show your pass to the guard.

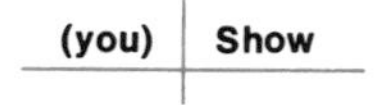

Exercise Diagram imperative sentences.

Diagram the subjects and verbs in the following imperative sentences. (Ignore all other words.)

1. Remember your locker combination.
2. Consider this problem.
3. Throw the ball with your left hand.
4. Find more recent information.
5. Hold your breath underwater.
6. Close all of the windows.
7. Change the radio station.
8. Watch that documentary on TV.
9. Observe this stunt carefully.
10. Store those old toys in the garage.

Part 6 Diagraming Sentences with *There*

There is usually just an "extra" word. It is placed on a separate line above the subject in a sentence diagram.

There were three lifeguards on duty.

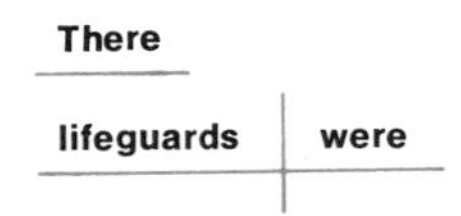

Is there a map of this museum?

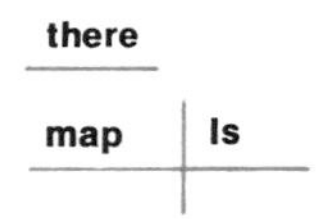

Exercise Diagram sentences with *there.*

Diagram the subjects and verbs and the word *there* in the following sentences.

1. There are eight notes in the scale.
2. There are hundreds of people in line.
3. There are two pounds of apples on the scale.
4. Is there a punchline to this joke?
5. Was there a package on our porch?
6. There is no room at this motel.
7. Were there sand-crabs on the beach?
8. Is there time for another match?
9. There are seventy horses on this ranch.
10. Are there fifty-two cards in a deck?

Part 7 Diagraming Compound Subjects and Verbs

To diagram the two or more parts of a compound subject, it is necessary to split the subject line. Put the conjunction on a connecting dotted line.

Tanya and her brother missed the bus.

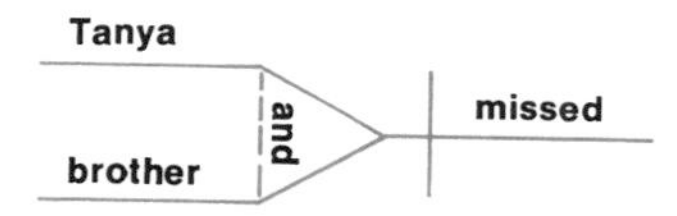

To diagram the two or more parts of a compound predicate, split the predicate line. Put the conjunction on a connecting dotted line.

Sam swept, washed, and waxed the floor.

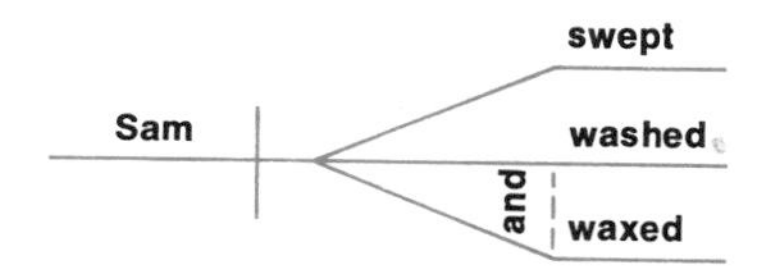

Exercise Diagram compound subjects and verbs.

Diagram the compound subjects and verbs in the following sentences.

1. The captain and crew swam to shore.
2. Margie stayed and helped with decorations.
3. Ron and I rode in a seaplane.
4. Kara and her mother raked the leaves.
5. Staple or clip your papers together.
6. Annie waited and hoped for a chance.
7. The leaders met and discussed a truce.
8. Kevin and Marvin wrestled in the meet.
9. Have Maggie and Lisa planned a party?
10. Inside my pocket were two nails and a thumbtack.

Part 8 Diagraming Sentences Containing Direct Objects

When you diagram a sentence, place a direct object on the horizontal line following the verb. Separate it from the action verb by an upright line that does not cut through the subject-verb line.

My friends buy discount records.

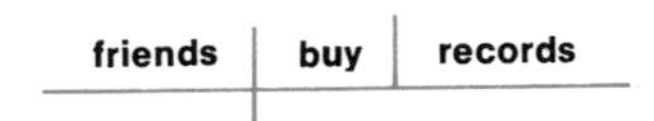

For **compound direct objects,** continue the horizontal line a little way beyond the verb and then split it. Make as many parallel direct object lines as you need. Put the upright line before the split, to show that all the words that follow are direct objects.

I trust Michelle, Steve, and Toby.

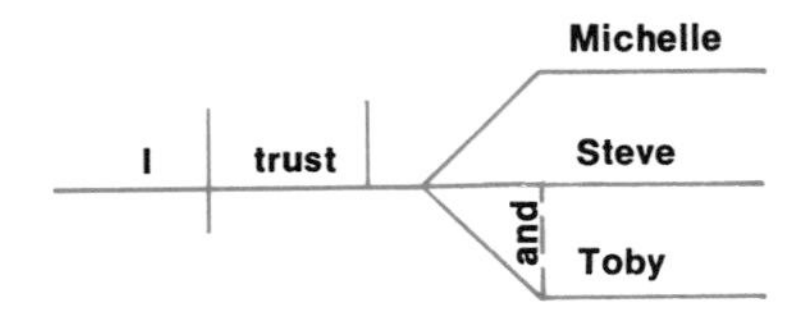

Exercise Diagram sentences containing direct objects.

Diagram the subjects, verbs, and direct objects in the following sentences. (Some direct objects may be compound.)

1. Dawn plays the saxophone.
2. The stars guide sailors at sea.
3. Noel makes jewelry from driftwood.
4. Did you weave this cloth?
5. People built castles and statues in the sand.

6. Is Jamie using the telephone?
7. My family uses a van for camping.
8. Dogs can hear high-pitched sounds.
9. Put your name and address on the application.
10. Mark has played defense and offense.

Part 9 Diagraming Sentences Containing Predicate Nouns

The diagram for a sentence containing a predicate noun is different from the diagram for a sentence containing a direct object.

A Cyclops was a one-eyed monster.

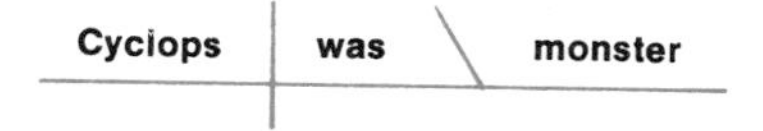

Notice that the predicate noun is on the horizontal line in the same position as the direct object. But the line that separates the predicate noun from the linking verb slants back toward the subject. This is to show its close relationship to the subject.

For sentences containing **compound predicate nouns,** use parallel lines. Put the slanting line before the main line is split.

Duke was a poor pet but a good watchdog.

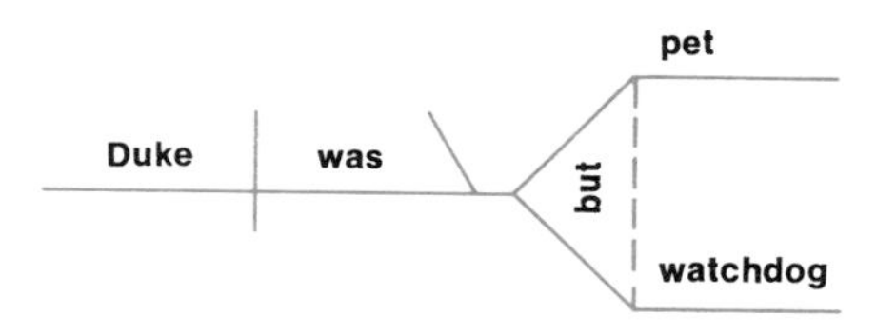

Exercise **Diagram sentences containing predicate nouns.**

Diagram the subjects, linking verbs, and predicate nouns in the following sentences.

1. Those girls are skaters.
2. That boy is a model.
3. Canoes are light, slender boats.
4. Was Tiant the pitcher?
5. Diana and Minerva were Roman goddesses.
6. The Milky Way is a galaxy of stars.
7. Langston Hughes was a poet.
8. The Navajos are a tribe of the Southwest.
9. Danny became a good player and a good sport.
10. Jesse James and Billy the Kid were outlaws.

Part 10 Diagraming Sentences Containing Predicate Adjectives

You show a predicate adjective on a diagram just as you show a predicate noun. Place it on the horizontal line following the linking verb, and separate it from the verb by a line slanting back toward the subject.

Good babysitters are reliable.

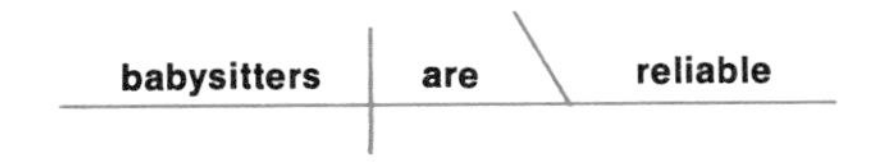

For sentences with **compound predicate adjectives,** use parallel lines. Put the slanting line before the main line is split.

The earth feels damp and spongy.

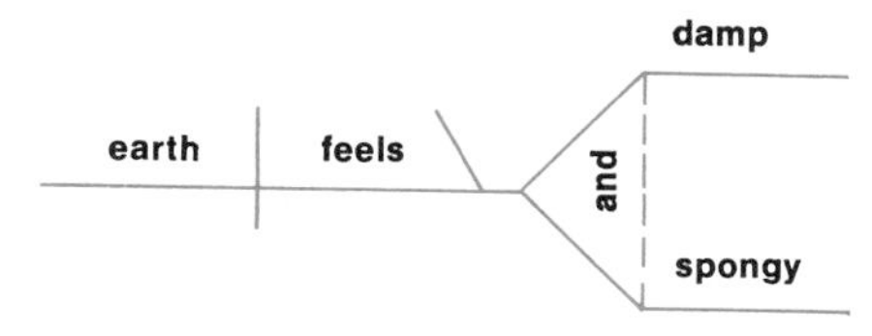

Exercise **Diagram sentences containing predicate adjectives.**

Diagram the subjects, verbs, and predicate adjectives.

1. Inez seems ambitious.
2. That taco smells delicious.
3. Our teacher is patient and enthusiastic.
4. Contact lenses should feel comfortable.
5. Jamaica is lush and lovely.
6. Is Vitamin C good for colds?
7. Be still.
8. Will the photos be ready today?
9. A coral reef feels sharp and brittle.
10. The coach and players are exhausted.

Part 11 Diagraming Sentences Containing Adjectives

On a diagram, an adjective is shown on a line that slants down from the noun or pronoun it modifies. Articles, which are also adjectives, are shown the same way.

The new school has a large, bright gym.

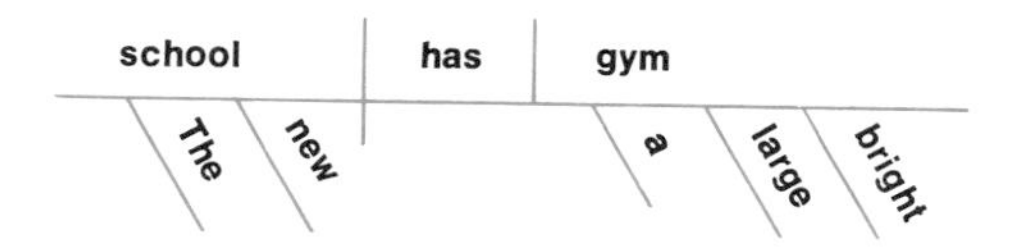

Carol Brown is a strong, steady swimmer.

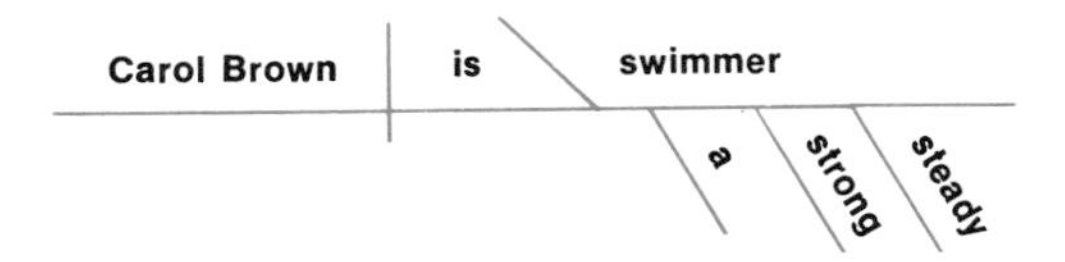

Exercise **Diagram sentences containing adjectives.**

Diagram the subjects, verbs, and adjectives in the following sentences. Also diagram any direct objects, predicate nouns, or predicate adjectives.

1. Mike wears plaid suspenders.
2. A new student entered the classroom.
3. A special squad defused the strange bomb.
4. Forest fires do tremendous damage.
5. A sari is a long Indian dress.
6. Out of the grass slid two green snakes.
7. The boy and his little brother are hungry.
8. Does the track team have a new coach?
9. This reddish plant has poisonous leaves.
10. Mr. Wayne has a pleasant face and a friendly smile.

Part 12 Diagraming Sentences Containing Possessive Nouns

In the diagram, possessive nouns are written on lines slanting down from the nouns with which they are used.

Those are Penny's skis.

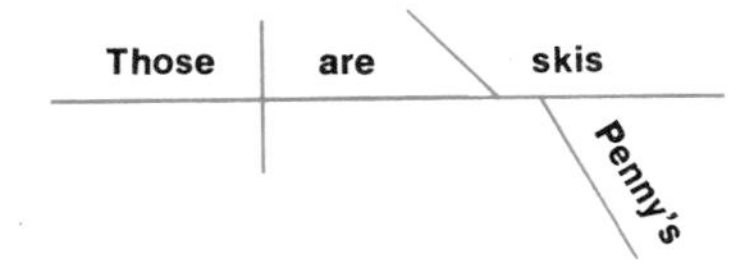

Exercise **Diagram sentences containing possessive nouns.**

Diagram the subjects, verbs, and possessive nouns in the following sentences. Also diagram any direct objects, predicate nouns or predicate adjectives, and adjectives.

1. I washed Bobby's car.
2. Samantha's serve is accurate.
3. Have you heard Eric's joke?
4. Ingrid is the Masons' babysitter.
5. Alex beat Steve's time.
6. Into the lead ran Steve Cauthen's horse.
7. Chicago's weather is windy.
8. My uncle has a pilot's license.
9. Watch the champion's difficult new dive.
10. Jill's mother is a dentist.

Part 13 Diagraming Sentences Containing Adverbs

Adverbs, like adjectives, are shown on diagrams on slanting lines attached to the words they modify. The following diagram shows an adverb modifying a verb.

Finally, the small plane radioed the tower.

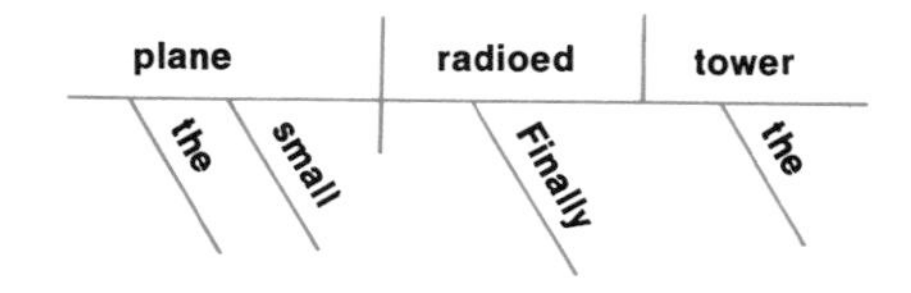

The next diagram shows one adverb modifying an adjective and another modifying an adverb.

Some truly great athletes began competition quite late.

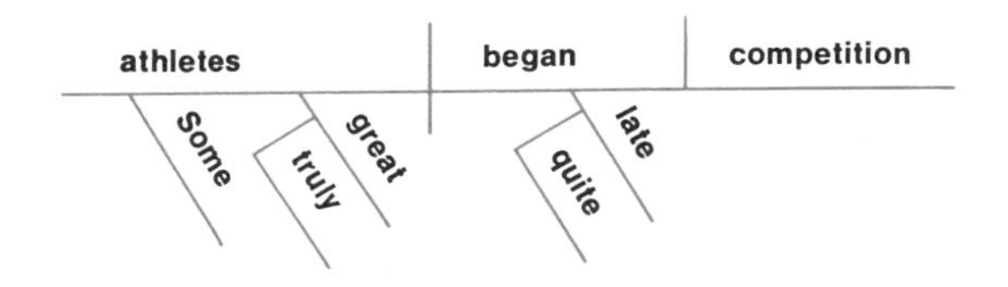

(Notice how *truly* is attached to *great*. Notice how *quite* is attached to *late*.)

Exercise Diagram sentences containing adverbs.

Diagram the subjects, verbs, and adverbs in the following sentences. Also diagram adjectives, predicate adjectives or predicate nouns, and direct objects.

1. JoAnn carefully avoided an argument.
2. This store usually has good bargains.
3. Now Sandy's racer rides smoothly.
4. Lena and Rachel dive well.
5. This stereo's sound is very clear.
6. Dad and Mom jog here daily.
7. Does Ellery Queen always solve the crime?
8. Handle these plates carefully.
9. You must visit me very soon.
10. The doctor sometimes treats really serious injuries.

Part 14 Diagraming Prepositional Phrases

In diagrams, a prepositional phrase is placed below the word it modifies. The preposition is shown on a line slanting down from the modified word. Attached to the slanting line is a horizontal line on which the object of the preposition is written. Any modifiers are shown below the object on a slanted line.

Remember that a prepositional phrase can function as an adjective or as an adverb. A prepositional phrase that modifies a noun or pronoun is an adjective phrase. A prepositional phrase that modifies a verb is an adverb phrase. In the following example, *with red hair* is an adjective phrase. *In our band* is an adverb phrase.

The girl with red hair plays in our band.

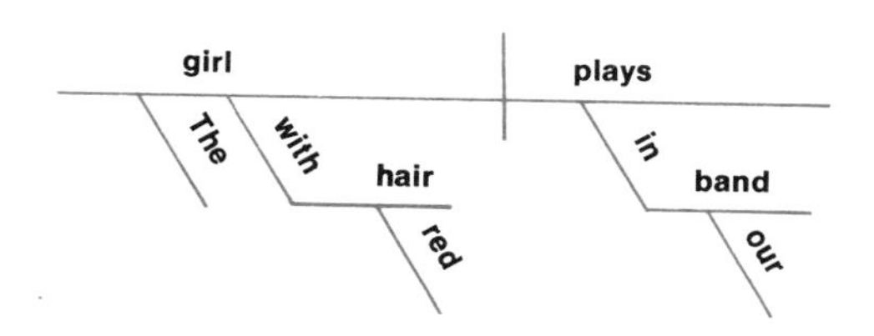

Exercise **Diagram sentences containing prepositional phrases.**

Diagram the subjects, verbs, and prepositional phrases in the following sentences.

1. Marlene sits at that desk.
2. Everyone in the room laughed.
3. Toby wandered down the alley.
4. Several cars had stopped near the corner.
5. Mary Ann waited at the station.
6. Have you walked past the new theater?
7. The owner of that car has been found.
8. Will you sit beside me?
9. The workers inside the mine were rescued.
10. A large tree fell during the storm.

Part 15 Diagraming Compound Sentences

It is not difficult to diagram compound sentences if you can already diagram simple sentences. A compound sentence is really two, or more, simple sentences joined together. Therefore, you draw the diagram for the first half of the sentence, draw a dotted-line "step" for the conjunction, and then draw the diagram for the second half.

Irma is a skillful artist, and she has won many prizes.

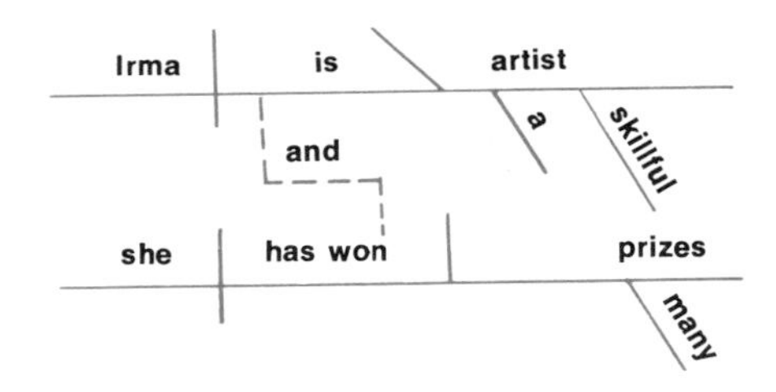

Exercise Diagram compound sentences.

Diagram the following compound sentences. Diagram each part of the sentence. Then join the parts.

1. Terry opened his locker, and he found a frog inside.
2. Natalie was very busy, but she took a break.
3. Sally is blonde, but her sister is brunette.
4. Amy's plan was unusual, but everyone agreed.
5. There are four trophies, but we have five winners.
6. Bring a lunch, or buy one here.
7. Is the movie good, or shall we skip it?
8. Have you started your project, or will you begin soon?
9. Some Indian jewelry is silver, and it is quite beautiful.
10. The Nobel Prize is awarded annually, and it is a great honor.

REVIEW Diagraming the Sentence

Diagraming Sentences Diagram the following sentences.

1. Jody shivered.
2. From the palms hang coconuts.
3. Do truckers drive through the night?
4. Try this paint.
5. There are no stores on the island.
6. Is there a leash for birds?
7. Neal and Scott traded lunches.
8. Maria makes and sells wooden toys.
9. We recycle cans, bottles, and papers.
10. John Glenn is a politician and former astronaut.
11. That cartoon is funny but true.
12. Can you answer that difficult riddle?
13. Some apes have learned a special language.
14. The court's decision is final.
15. Mr. Van talks gruffly but acts gently.
16. Very few people understand highly technical language.
17. Use this penknife carefully.
18. Bears' fans are loyal, but the team is still losing.
19. The principal introduced the graduates, but a student gave the speech.
20. The glacier moved slowly, and it covered the mountainside.

HANDBOOK SECTION 16

Capitalization

Capitalization is the use of capital letters at the beginnings of words. It marks certain words as special. Your name, for example, is more special than the word *girl* or *boy*. Therefore, your name is capitalized in writing.

Capital letters are also used to call attention to certain special words. For instance, words that begin sentences are capitalized. In that way, capital letters make reading easier.

In this section, you will learn when to capitalize words. Study the rules and their examples. You will want to refer to these rules whenever you have a question about capitalization.

Proper Nouns and Adjectives

Capitalize proper nouns and proper adjectives.

A **common noun** is the name of a whole group of persons, places, or things.

man country book

A **proper noun** is the name of a particular person, place, or thing.

Thomas **J**efferson **S**weden **B**ible

A **proper adjective** is an adjective formed from a proper noun.

Jeffersonian ideas **S**wedish meatballs **B**iblical story

There are many different kinds of proper nouns. The following rules will help you recognize many proper nouns which need to be capitalized.

Names and Titles

Capitalize the names of people.

Begin every word in a person's name with a capital letter. An **initial** stands for a name. Write initials as capital letters. Put a period after every initial.

Susan **B.** **A**nthony **A.** **J.** **F**oyt **S.** **F.** **B.** **M**orse

Capitalize a title used with a person's name.

Dr. **M**artin and **C**oach **B**ell discussed exercise.
Have you seen **M**s. **G**ray or **M**r. **T**ownsend?

Capitalize the word *I*.

Mary and **I** planted sunflower seeds.

Exercises Use capital letters correctly.

A. Write the words that should be capitalized, using the necessary capital letters.

1. Bob and i read a mystery by theodore taylor.
2. The name spencer a. marks was on the plaque.
3. Some people think that thomas edison was a genius.
4. The name nadine means "hope."
5. Dr. george washington carver was born a slave.
6. This series was based on books by laura ingalls wilder.
7. Stacy and i played tennis against kenny and maria.
8. We live next door to mr. and mrs. torres.
9. The best teacher i ever had was professor eileen black.
10. Annette made an appointment with our dentist, dr. adams.

B. Follow the directions for Exercise A.

1. The Indians william brant and red jacket signed a treaty with moses cleaveland.
2. Tomorrow i will cut mr. quinlan's lawn.
3. President lincoln met harriet beecher stowe.
4. Sandy and dennis visited their uncle, mr. cage.
5. The leader of althea's group is mrs. hartley.
6. The boxer cassius clay changed his name to muhammed ali.
7. Dr. rosenberg and his family went to italy on vacation.
8. One of the speakers was senator edward kennedy.
9. Either lottie or i can take you to ms. franklin's office.
10. When did marian anderson begin her career?

Months, Days, and Holidays

Capitalize the names of months, days, and holidays.

Do not capitalize the names of the four seasons.

> On **F**riday, **D**ecember 16, our **C**hristmas vacation begins.
> My favorite season is winter.

Particular Places and Things

Capitalize the names of particular places and things.

Capitalize the names of cities, states, and countries.

Which is larger, **P**ortland, **O**regon, or **D**etroit, **M**ichigan?
Brazil is the largest country in **S**outh **A**merica, and **C**anada is the largest country in **N**orth **A**merica.

Capitalize the names of streets, buildings, and bridges.

The **C**hambers **B**uilding is at the corner of **G**reenlawn **A**venue and **H**igh **S**treet.

Capitalize all geographical names.

Also capitalize the words *North, South, East,* and *West* when they refer to a section of a country.

Most of the area between the **R**ocky **M**ountains in the **W**est and the **A**ppalachian **M**ountains in the **E**ast is drained by three rivers, the **M**ississippi, the **O**hio, and the **M**issouri.

Exercises **Use capital letters correctly.**

A. Number your paper from 1 to 10. For each sentence, write the words that should be capitalized. Capitalize them correctly.

1. If you can't come at easter, come next summer.
2. We could see long island and new jersey from the top of the world trade center.
3. Is the amazon river in brazil or in argentina?
4. Dean's dairy bar isn't open on holidays.
5. Doreen was in the west visiting relatives in arizona.
6. We passed by the lazy k ranch just before sunset.
7. The first king of hawaii was king kamehameha.
8. Interstate highway 80 carries heavy traffic.
9. The famous irwin hospital is in the east.
10. Five states border the gulf of mexico.

B. Follow the directions for Exercise A.

1. I have never visited any states in the south except florida.
2. Which are the most powerful tribes in the west?
3. The snowy peaks of the grand tetons are gorgeous.
4. The astronauts will speak in houston on tuesday.
5. The altitude of denver, colorado, is one mile above sea level.
6. The golden gate bridge is in san francisco.
7. We are spending the christmas holidays in colorado.
8. There are special thanksgiving celebrations at plimoth plantation.
9. People gathered on cathedral square in the kremlin in moscow.
10. We will land in puerto rico on thursday, july 12.

Races, Religions, Nationalities, and Languages

Capitalize the names of races, religions, nationalities, and languages.

Modern **A**merican **I**ndian artists often use traditional designs in their work.

Judaism, **C**hristianity, and the **M**uslim religion share a belief in one **G**od.

The **R**ussians and the **C**hinese have frequent arguments about their border.

Does this junior high offer **F**rench?

Clubs, Organizations, and Businesses

Capitalize the names of clubs, organizations, and business firms.

My uncle belongs to the **C**enterville **G**arden **C**lub.

Where is the headquarters of the **B**oy **S**couts of **A**merica?

Don's mother works for **G**eneral **M**otors.

Exercises Use capital letters correctly.

A. Number your paper from 1 to 10. Copy each of the following groups of words. Wherever necessary, change small letters to capitals.

1. a dutch windmill
2. african art
3. german potato salad
4. the cub scouts
5. polish sausage
6. a methodist minister
7. chinese food
8. the campfire girls
9. bell telephone company
10. the arab oil fields

B. Number your paper from 1 to 10. Copy each of the following sentences. Wherever necessary, change small letters to capitals.

1. Our school has language classes in french, italian, and spanish.
2. The olmecs were an ancient indian tribe in mexico.
3. Gabriel joined the united states marine corps.
4. Were those tourists speaking japanese?
5. Many people in india practice hinduism.
6. Dolores's mother is a systems analyst for digital equipment company.
7. The elmwood photography club meets every monday in the carnegie library.
8. Roberto is active in the peoria chamber of commerce.
9. The museum exhibits include an egyptian mummy and several roman statues.
10. The irish writer jonathan swift wrote a great english novel about a man named gulliver.

First Words

Sentences

Capitalize the first word of every sentence.

Workers digging the foundation found an ancient burial ground.
When will the eclipse begin?
Look out!

Poetry

Capitalize the first word in most lines of poetry.

The wind was a torrent of darkness among the gusty trees,
The moon was a ghostly galleon tossed upon cloudy seas,
The road was a ribbon of moonlight over the purple moor,
And the highwayman came riding—
Riding—riding—
The highwayman came riding, up to the old inn-door.

—from "The Highwayman" ALFRED NOYES

Sometimes, especially in modern poetry, the lines of a poem do not begin with a capital letter.

Will I remember
how I looked
and what I did
when I was young
(when I am old)?
Will I remember what I wondered?
When I am old,
who will I be?
Still me?

—RICHARD J. MARGOLIS

Exercises **Use capital letters correctly.**

A. Number your paper from 1 to 10. Find the words in the following sentences that should be capitalized. Copy each sentence or poem, using the necessary capital letters.

1. the third sunday in june is father's day.
2. is cotton still an important crop in the south?
3. listen, my children, and you shall hear
   of the midnight ride of paul revere,
   on the eighteenth of april, in seventy-five;
   hardly a man is now alive
   who remembers that famous day and year.
   —from "Paul Revere's Ride" HENRY WADSWORTH LONGFELLOW
4. last year we had a dry summer and a rainy fall.
5. do you like italian food? we can have pizza at tina's restaurant.
6. there is a program on television tonight about japan.
7. dr. frances gilbert teaches english at carroll university.
8. on tuesday i will celebrate my birthday.
9. this month has five saturdays.
10. have you seen any movies by woody allen?

B. Follow the directions for Exercise A.

1. the orchestra will play two works by wolfgang amadeus mozart.
2. mom is going to dearborn, michigan, on friday.
3. on wednesday i'll be late for dinner. the girl scouts are having a meeting at four o'clock.
4. what is the spanish word for *hello*?
5. our new address is 141 miller avenue.
6. we celebrate flag day on june 14.
7. are you visiting montreal, in quebec? there, many canadians speak french.

8. yesterday rabbi silver spoke at the synagogue in newton.
9. the setting of the book is boston, massachusetts.
10. The Rhinoceros

    the Rhino is a homely beast,
    for human eyes he's not a feast,
    but you and i will never know
    why Nature chose to make him so,
    farewell, farewell, you old rhinoceros,
    i'll stare at something less prepoceros.

    —OGDEN NASH

Direct Quotations

When you write the exact words somebody else said, you are **quoting** that person. The words are a **direct quotation.**

Capitalize the beginning of every direct quotation.

"**T**omorrow we can expect heavy rain," said the forecaster.

Usually, when you are writing what a person said, you add words before or after the direct quotation to tell who said it. If these explaining words come at the beginning of a sentence, use a capital letter there. Use another capital letter at the beginning of the direct quotation.

"**T**he game is starting now," my brother said.
My mother asked, "**D**o you have any homework?"

Letters

Capitalize the greeting and the closing of a letter.

Examples: **D**ear **S**ir:
Sincerely,
Dear **L**inda,
Your friend,

Outlines

Capitalize the first word of each line of an outline.

Capitalization and Punctuation

I. **U**se of capital letters

A. **P**roper nouns and adjectives

B. **F**irst words

1. **S**entences
2. **P**oetry
3. **D**irect quotations
4. **L**etters
5. **O**utlines
6. **T**itles

II. **U**se of periods

Exercises Use capital letters correctly.

A. Copy the following. Use correct capitalization.

1. "try these crutches," the doctor said.
2. she asked, "is a violin a fiddle?"
3. "the pineapple is delicious," Stu said.
4. he asked, "is Gordon a nurse?"
5. "where is my mistake?" Amy asked.
6. the fortune teller said, "pick a card."
7. Ms. Berg asked, "where is your homework?"
8. Rona commented, "you're a good basketball player."
9. "the park is closed," the guard told us.
10. "where is a salesperson?" the customer asked.

B. Follow the directions for Exercise A.

1. indians of the northeast

I. groups

A. lake indians

B. woodland indians

II. important foods

A. lake indians

1. wild rice
2. fish

B. woodland indians

1. corn
2. deer and other game

2. dear kathleen,

thank you for showing me the sights of washington, d.c., last week. nothing here in chicago seems as exciting as the white house, the capitol, or the smithsonian institution.

in one of my classes, i showed my photos of george washington's home. we talked about the design of mount vernon and why it was built on the potomac river. my teacher, ms. reynolds, asked about the small buildings surrounding the main house. for once, i felt like an expert.

i hope that next july you will come to visit me. i'll make sure that you have a good time here in the midwest.

very truly yours,
alison

Titles

Capitalize the first word and all important words in chapter titles, titles of magazine articles, titles of short stories or single poems, titles of television programs, and titles of songs. Use quotation marks for these titles.

Chapter title:	"**T**he **T**roubled **C**ity"
Magazine article:	"**W**inning and **L**osing"
Short story:	"**T**he **M**onkey's **P**aw"
Poem:	"**A**nnabel **L**ee"
Television program:	"60 **M**inutes"
Song:	"**H**ome on the **R**ange"

Capitalize the first word and all important words in titles of books, newspapers, magazines, and movies.

Underline these titles. (When printed, they are *italicized.*)

Book title:	***R**oots*
Newspaper:	***T**he **N**ew **Y**ork **T**imes*
Magazine:	***P**eople*
Movie:	***T**he **B**ad **N**ews **B**ears*

Do not capitalize a little word such as *a, an, by, for, from, in,* or *the* unless it comes first or last.

Exercises Use capital letters correctly.

A. Copy these titles. Capitalize correctly.

1. "making friends and keeping them" (magazine article)
2. *teen* (magazine)
3. "the ransom of red chief" (short story)
4. *star trek* (movie)
5. "the underwater world" (chapter title)
6. *los angeles times* (newspaper)
7. "dust of snow" (poem)
8. "on broadway" (song)
9. "the incredible hulk" (television program)
10. *all creatures great and small* (book)

B. Follow the directions for Exercise A.

1. "battlestar galactica" (television program)
2. *the pigman* (book)
3. *superman* (movie)
4. "the spirit of democracy" (chapter title)
5. *miami herald* (newspaper)
6. "the bat" (poem)
7. "to build a fire" (short story)
8. "born free" (song)
9. *time* (magazine)
10. "what do your dreams mean?" (magazine article)

REVIEW Capitalization

Capital Letters Copy each of the following sentences. Change small letters to capital letters wherever necessary.

1. when is barry manilow's next concert?
2. immediately, judge chase addressed the jury.
3. jack's birthday is during the summer, but mine is november 8.
4. this tuesday will be groundhog day.
5. last winter chicago, illinois, had record snowfalls.
6. people attend bullfights in madrid, spain.
7. the two largest states are texas and alaska.
8. we met mayor minsky at city hall.
9. thornton junior high is on ridge avenue.
10. the snake river runs through a deep gorge.
11. glacier national park and yellowstone national park are in the west.
12. we traveled north to the grand canyon.
13. the japanese welcomed ambassador graf.
14. the catholic priest recited the prayer in latin.
15. did you play in the lakeville little league?
16. ralston-purina company makes different animal foods.
17. "here is the royal gorge bridge," the guide said.
18. bill asked, "have you ever had a greek salad?"
19. i read both *the outsiders* and *that was then, this is now.*
20. "the swan" is a poem by w. r. rodgers.

HANDBOOK SECTION 17

Punctuation

Punctuation is the use of commas, periods, apostrophes and other marks, in writing. The marks, called **punctuation marks,** make the meaning of sentences clear.

Good punctuation is an aid to the reader. It helps the reader to understand whether a sentence is a statement, a question, or an exclamation. Periods and commas keep words and sentences from running together and confusing the reader. Punctuation marks also point out when a word has been abbreviated or shortened. Without punctuation marks, a piece of writing would be as difficult to read as a coded message.

In this section, you will learn how to use punctuation marks. Whenever you write, these rules will help you write correctly. Look at them whenever you need help with punctuation.

End Marks

The signal that shows where a sentence begins is a capital letter. The punctuation marks that show where a sentence ends are called **end marks.**

There are three important end marks: (1) the **period,** (2) the **question mark,** and (3) the **exclamation point.**

The Period

Use a period at the end of a declarative sentence. A declarative sentence tells something.

> This is my poster for the exhibit.
>
> Sarah and Josh are going to the dance.

Use a period at the end of an imperative sentence. An imperative sentence requests, instructs, or orders.

> Put your poster on the bulletin board.
>
> Read the directions carefully.

Use a period after an abbreviation.

Words are often written in a shortened form to save time and space. These shortened forms of words are called **abbreviations.** On calendars, for example, the names of the days are often abbreviated, as in *Mon.* for *Monday.*

You use the abbreviation *A.M.* to stand for the two Latin words, *ante meridiem,* which mean "before noon." The abbreviation *P.M.* stands for *post meridiem,* meaning "after noon."

Here are examples of other common abbreviations. Notice how some abbreviations have two or three parts, with each part standing for one or more words. A period is then used after each part of the abbreviation.

St. = Street or Saint	in. = inch
Mt. = Mount or Mountain	doz. = dozen
R.R. = Railroad	Dr. = Doctor
P.O. = Post Office	Mr. = Mister

U.S.A. = United States of America
D.C. = District of Columbia

Periods are not used after some abbreviations. Here are some examples:

m = meter
g = gram
l = liter
CB = Citizens' Band
ZIP = Zone Improvement Plan

Note: Check with your local post office for the correct state abbreviations used with ZIP codes. All of the two-letter abbreviations are made and approved by the United States Postal Service. These special abbreviations are to be used only for the mail. Here are a few examples of these special abbreviations:

CA = California   OH = Ohio   VT = Vermont

If you are not sure whether an abbreviation should be written with or without periods, look up the abbreviation in a dictionary.

It is important to know the most common abbreviations, but it is also important to use abbreviations correctly.

You should use most abbreviations only in lists, addresses, arithmetic problems, or other special forms of writing. They should not be used in sentences. For example, on an application for a library card, or on an envelope, you may write your address in this way:

152 W. Madison Rd.

In a sentence, you should write this:

I live at 152 West Madison Road.

As a general rule, the only abbreviations you should use in sentences are *A.M.* and *P.M.*, and *B.C.* and *A.D.*, and titles with names, such as *Dr. Brothers*.

Use a period after an initial.

A name is often shortened to its first letter, which is called an **initial.** Always use a period after an initial.

U.S. Grant (Ulysses Simpson Grant)

Robert E. Lee (Robert Edward Lee)

Use a period after each numeral or letter that shows a division of an outline or that precedes an item in a list.

An Outline

Punctuation

I. End marks
   A. The period
      1. Sentences
      2. Abbreviations and initials
      3. Outlines and lists
   B. The question mark
   C. The exclamation point
II. The comma

A List

Shopping list

1. apples
2. eggs
3. bread
4. lettuce

Exercises **Use periods correctly.**

A. Number your paper from 1 to 10. Copy the following phrases, putting periods where necessary.

1. 4 ft 10 in
2. Washington, D C
3. 1 c sugar
4. Bedford Ave
5. Aug 30

6. Butterford Chocolate Co, Inc
7. Dr H M Ritchie
8. Los Angeles CA 90053
9. (list) First five presidents
   1 George Washington
   2 John Adams
   3 Thomas Jefferson
   4 James Madison
   5 James Monroe
10. (outline) Super-8 movie-making
    I Major equipment needed
       A Camera
          1 For silent movies
          2 For sound movies
       B Projector
    II Other materials needed
       A Film
       B Splicer

B. Write abbreviations for the following groups of words.

1. Eastern Standard Time
2. New York, New York
3. Reverend John Marsh
4. 4 gallons
5. Mount Snow
6. Raleigh, North Carolina
7. December 9
8. Benander Game Company
9. 10 square feet
10. Durapools, Incorporated

C. List five abbreviations used in your math book. Beside each abbreviation, write the word it stands for.

The Question Mark

Use a question mark at the end of an interrogative sentence. An interrogative sentence is a sentence that asks a question.

Where are we? Are you going to the game?

The Exclamation Point

Use an exclamation point at the end of an exclamatory sentence. An exclamatory sentence is a sentence that expresses strong feeling, or excitement.

Jackie struck out! Be careful!

Use an exclamation point after an interjection. An interjection is a word or group of words used to express strong feeling. Words often used as other parts of speech may become interjections when they express strong feeling.

Oh! How beautiful! Wow! What an ending!

Exercises Use periods, question marks, and exclamation points correctly.

A. Copy the following sentences. Supply the missing punctuation.

1. Mr and Mrs Gregory go to Miami every winter
2. Ouch This pan is hot
3. Dr Evans will be in his office until 4:30
4. What circus did P T Barnum manage
5. Ms Carol F Kiley will speak at the N H S graduation
6. My new address is 600 W 24 St
7. Don't touch that broken glass
8. We stopped at an L C Carran gas station
9. How many Coke bottles are you returning
10. Help The gearshift is stuck in reverse

B. Follow the directions for Exercise A.

1. Terrific We got the last four tickets
2. How much does that album cost
3. W E B DuBois was a writer and a professor of sociology
4. Jump out of the way of that car
5. Mail the letter to Miss Deborah K Sobol
6. Is Dr Howard your dentist
7. The poet Hilda Dolittle signed her poems H D
8. Oh, no You didn't forget the picnic lunch, did you
9. Did Vanessa try out for the team last night
10. We met Dr Rusnak at her cousin's home

The Comma

Commas in Sentences

Commas tell the reader to pause slightly. The pause keeps the reader from running together words that should be kept apart. Commas are a great help in reading.

Use commas to separate a series of words. Two words are not a series. There are always three or more words in a series.

> The boys entered dogs, cats, and hamsters in the show.
>
> The day was sunny, hot, and humid.

In a series, commas are placed *after* each word but the last.

You can see how important it is to separate the parts of a series by reading these sentences.

> Bob stuffed himself with cheese, pizza, ice cream, sandwiches, chocolate, milk, and peanuts.
>
> Bob stuffed himself with cheese pizza, ice cream sandwiches, chocolate milk, and peanuts.

Both sentences might be right. It depends upon what Bob did eat. The writer has to use commas correctly to tell the reader what Bob ate.

Use a comma after introductory words such as *yes* or *no*.

Yes, I'm going.

No, I can't go out tonight.

Use a comma in a compound sentence. Place the comma at the end of the first complete thought.

Clark Kent disappeared, and Superman arrived.

We ran fast, but we nearly missed the bus.

When a subordinate clause begins a complex sentence, use a comma to separate it from the main clause.

When Clark Kent disappeared, Superman arrived.

Although we ran fast, we missed the bus.

Exercises Use commas correctly.

A. Copy these sentences. Place commas where they are needed.

1. Yes we went to the zoo last summer.
2. You can take a bus to the zoo but we drove there.
3. We took our lunches and we spent the whole day.
4. We saw a hippopotamus a gorilla and an anteater.
5. Since the zoo was built two buildings have been added.
6. After the seals performed they were fed by their trainer.
7. There were monkeys of every size color and shape.
8. Two monkeys started a fight and another watched.
9. We took pictures had a boat ride and saw a movie.
10. The movie was good but it wasn't as much fun as the animals at the zoo.

B. Follow the directions for Exercise A.

1. No it's not raining.
2. Karen aimed fired and just missed the bull's eye.
3. Motels are all right but I like campgrounds better.
4. Robert and Anna weeded the garden and Doug and Nancy repaired the fence.
5. Although it was raining we still went swimming.
6. Denmark Norway and Sweden are called Scandinavian countries.
7. Will you drive us or should we take the bus?
8. The spaghetti tomato sauce and spices are in that cupboard.
9. Because Joe was sick he missed the test.
10. My sisters' names are Linda Donna and Jean.

Use commas to set off the name of a person spoken to. If the name comes at the start or end of the sentence, one comma is enough. If the name comes in the middle of the sentence, place one comma before the name and another comma after it.

Please answer the phone, Jim.

Ginny, may I use your pen?

I believe, Mark, that you are right.

Set off an appositive by commas. An **appositive** is a word or group of words that means the same as the noun just before it. The appositive gives more information about the noun.

The words in italics in the following sentences are appositives. Notice that they tell more about *Mr. Lopez* and *our neighbor*. Notice also that they are set off by commas.

Mr. Lopez, the scoutmaster, moved away.

Our neighbor, Ms. Carl, drives an ambulance.

Separate the parts of a date by commas. If the date appears in the middle of a sentence, place a comma after the last part.

On November 7, 1962, Eleanor Roosevelt died.

We'll expect you on Tuesday, April 4.

Note: Do not place a comma between the month and the number of the day: April 4.

Separate the name of a city from the name of a state or country by a comma. If the two names come in the middle of a sentence, place a comma after the second name.

My grandmother was born in Dublin, Ireland.

We left Concord, New Hampshire, at noon.

Exercises **Use commas correctly.**

A. Copy these sentences. Place commas where they are needed.

1. Last summer we went to Phoenix Arizona.
2. Friday May 5 was our opening night.
3. We all met the new principal Mrs. Gomez.
4. At Kitty Hawk North Carolina the Wright brothers successfully flew three gliders.
5. Dad this is Al Cresco a friend of mine.
6. It was hot in Corpus Christi Texas.
7. Hold the line Gerry and I'll ask her.
8. On Saturday January 25 the excavation was begun.
9. Joey and Sandra lunch is ready.
10. The famous comedian Charlie Chaplin accepted the award.

B. Follow the directions for Exercise A.

1. Rhonda were you born in September 1968?

2. Albany New York is on the Hudson River.

3. Mary Shelley's famous novel *Frankenstein* was published in 1818.

4. Mr. Gray let's have the exhibit on Friday February 19.

5. The candidate Ms. Wingreen made a speech.

6. On October 4 1957 the Soviet Union launched the first satellite.

7. You know Adele I'll be away tomorrow.

8. In Duluth Minnesota there is a statue of Jay Cooke the financier.

9. No Mrs. Lucas I have never lived in Dayton Ohio.

10. On October 7 1943 my father was born.

C. Write your own sentences, using commas as indicated by these directions:

1. Write two sentences using commas to set off the names of persons.

2. Write two sentences using commas to set off appositives.

3. Write two sentences using commas to separate the parts of a date.

4. Write two sentences using commas to separate the name of a city from name of a state.

Commas with Quotations

Use a comma to set off the explanatory words of a direct quotation.

When you use a quotation, you are giving the words of a speaker or writer. You are said to be *quoting* the words of the speaker or writer. If you give *exact* words, you are giving a direct quotation. Usually you include explanatory words of your own, like *Mary Kay said, JoAnne answered,* or *Phil asked.*

Courtney announced, "The movie will begin in ten minutes."

In the above sentence, the explanatory words come *before* the quotation. A comma is then placed after the last explanatory word.

Now look at this quotation:

"I want to go home," moaned Lisa.

In the above sentence, the explanatory words come *after* the quotation. A comma is then placed within the quotation marks after the last word of the quotation.

Sometimes the quotation is separated into two parts.

"One of the people in this room," the detective said, "is the murderer."

The sentence above is an example of a **divided quotation.** It is called "divided" because it is made up of two parts that are separated by the explanatory words. A comma is used after the last word of the first part. Another comma is used after the last explanatory word.

The quotations you have just looked at are all direct quotations. A quotation can be either *direct* or *indirect*. In an **indirect quotation** you change the words of a speaker or writer to your own words. No commas are used.

Clark Kent said that he had to make a phone call.

Mrs. Burnham said that we would have a quiz on Friday.

Commas in Letter Parts

Use a comma after the greeting of a friendly letter and after the complimentary close of any letter.

Dear Alice, Sincerely yours,

The Comma To Avoid Confusion

Some sentences can be confusing if commas are not used in them. Here are two examples of such sentences. Read them aloud.

Going up the elevator lost power.

In the grocery bags were in demand.

Now notice how much clearer these sentences are when commas are used.

Going up, the elevator lost power.

In the grocery, bags were in demand.

Use a comma whenever the reader might otherwise be confused.

Exercises **Use commas correctly.**

A. Copy the following sentences. Add commas where they are needed.

1. Benjamin said "I'd like to visit Boston some day."
2. "This cake is delicious" said my father.
3. When Sheila typed the table shook.
4. "It seems to me" Carol said "that this puzzle is missing some pieces."
5. In the story books were forbidden.
6. After we ate the neighbors came to visit.
7. "Who" the caterpillar asked Alice in Wonderland "are you?"
8. According to the paper cups of coffee will cost a dollar each.
9. In the garden flowers were blooming from May through September.
10. "Come here Midnight" Ned called.

B. Follow the directions for Exercise A.

1. While Vickie painted Eric sanded the table.
2. "Tomorrow's weather" the forecaster said "will be sunny and warm."
3. For dinner Tony had spaghetti a salad and dessert.
4. Ms. Miller announced "The concert begins at seven o'clock."
5. "The radio is too loud" my mother complained.
6. When our team lost the players felt depressed.
7. In the kitchen chairs were rearranged.
8. Yvette asked "What's on TV tonight?"
9. After Mr. Knowles left his puppy whined.
10. "Three weeks ago today" Meg said "I got my new bike."

The Apostrophe

The Apostrophe To Show Possession

A **possessive** is a word that shows that someone or something owns something else.

To form the possessive of a singular noun, add an apostrophe and *s* after the apostrophe.

dog + 's = dog's

man + 's = man's

lady + 's = lady's

James + 's = James's

To form the possessive of a plural noun that does not end in *s*, add an apostrophe and an *s* after the apostrophe.

men + 's = men's

geese + 's = geese's

To form the possessive of a plural noun that ends in *s*, add only an apostrophe.

dogs + ' = dogs'

ladies + ' = ladies'

Exercises **Use apostrophes in possessives.**

A. Copy the groups of words below. Make the italicized word in each group show possession.

1. the *girl* sweater
2. *mechanics* tools
3. *bird* nest
4. *babies* toys
5. *announcer* voice
6. *goalies* saves
7. *Chris* lunch
8. *golfer* shots
9. *children* games
10. *family* vacation

B. Make these words show possession. Write the possessive form.

1. hunters
2. Ms. Smith
3. policemen
4. women
5. Louisa
6. poets
7. painter
8. cats
9. horse
10. cyclist
11. Dr. Bliss
12. partner

The Apostrophe in Contractions

A **contraction** is a word made by combining two words and omitting one or more letters. The apostrophe shows where a letter or letters have been omitted. Here are some contractions used often:

can not	=	can't	we are	=	we're
will not	=	won't	does not	=	doesn't
you will	=	you'll	he had, he would	=	he'd
must not	=	mustn't	she had, she would	=	she'd
they are	=	they're	are not	=	aren't

Be careful with *it's* and *its*. Remember:

It's always means *it is* or *it has*.

It's going to rain today.

Its is the possessive of *it*.

The race horse broke *its* leg in a fall.

Remember that no apostrophe is used with the possessive pronouns *yours, hers, ours* and *theirs*.

The black checkers are *yours*.
The red ones are *hers*.
These drawings are *ours*.
I like *theirs* better.

Here are some contractions and other words that are often confused.

Who's means *who is* or *who has*.

Who's at the door?

Whose is the possessive of *who*.

Whose bike is that?

You're means *you are*.

You're coming to the library now, aren't you?

Your is the possessive of *you*.

Hang *your* coat there.

They're means *they are*.

They're waiting for us at the mall.

Their is the possessive form of *they*.

The girls left *their* towels at the pool.

There means a place, or is used to begin sentences.

There is an elephant over *there*.

Exercises **Use apostrophes in contractions.**

A. Write the contractions of these words.

1. I am
2. are not
3. it is
4. will not
5. has not
6. I will
7. she is
8. we would
9. we will
10. is not
11. that is
12. had not

B. Rewrite the following sentences. In each sentence make a contraction of the words in italics.

1. *It is* your turn, Joy.
2. *We are* waiting for Amy.
3. Darren *can not* come out this afternoon.
4. I *have not* delivered the paper yet.
5. Wanda and Mike said that *they are* coming tomorrow.
6. *Who is* going to the library soon?
7. *I am* ready to go.
8. *It is* too bad your dog hurt its leg.
9. *What is* your name?
10. I wish *I had* been there.

The Hyphen

Use a hyphen to separate the parts of a word at the end of a line.

> Before you choose a career, inves-
> tigate many fields.

Only words of two or more syllables can be divided at the end of a line. Never divide words of one syllable, such as *slight* or *bounce*. If you are in doubt about dividing a word, look it up in a dictionary.

A single letter must not be left at the end of a line. For example, this division would be wrong: *a- mong*. A single letter must not appear at the beginning of a line, either. It would be wrong to divide *inventory* like this: *inventor- y*.

Use a hyphen in compound numbers from twenty-one through ninety-nine.

> seventy-six trombones   Twenty-third Psalm

Exercises **Use hyphens correctly.**

A. Copy the following phrases. Decide whether you can divide the word in italics into two parts, each part having more than one letter. If you can, divide the word as you would at the end of a line. Also, add other necessary hyphens.

Examples: the thirty eight *cannons*

the thirty-eight can-
nons

1. forty five *minutes*
2. the fifty ninth *correction*
3. the Twenty Second *Amendment*
4. thirty four *years*
5. eighty one *trailers*
6. seventy nine years *ago*
7. ninety three *skateboards*
8. twenty nine *cents*
9. the sixty fourth *experiment*
10. forty *clarinets*

B. Follow the directions for Exercise A.

1. the eighty fifth *problem*
2. the forty eighth *state*
3. the seventy first *variation*
4. the twenty two *classrooms*
5. ninety seven *cups*
6. the fifty fourth *contestant*
7. seventy nine *students*
8. the thirty sixth *card*
9. your ninety third *birthday*
10. the twenty ninth *story*

Quotation Marks

Direct Quotations

When you write what someone has said or written, you are using a **quotation.** If you write the person's exact words, you write a **direct quotation.** If you do not write his or her exact words, you have an **indirect quotation.** Study these sentences.

Direct quotation: Steven said, "I don't want to go."

Indirect quotation: Steven said that he didn't want to go.

Put quotation marks before and after the words of a direct quotation.

Quotation marks [" "] consist of two pairs of small marks that resemble apostrophes. They tell a reader that the exact words of another speaker or writer are being given.

Quotation marks are *not* used with indirect quotations.

Direct quotation: Molly said, "I'm leaving."

Indirect quotation: Molly said that she was leaving.

Separate the words of a direct quotation from the rest of the sentence with a comma or end mark, in addition to quotation marks.

Jane said, "The dog is hungry."

"The dog is hungry," Jane said.

Notice that in the first sentence above, the comma comes *before* the quotation marks. The second sentence starts with the quoted words, and the comma falls *inside* the quotation marks.

Now look carefully at these sentences:

Mom asked, "Are you hungry?"

"We're starving!" Bill replied.

You can see that in these sentences the question marks and exclamation points fall *inside* the quotation marks.

Place question marks and exclamation points inside quotation marks if they belong to the quotation itself.

Place question marks and exclamation points outside quotation marks if they do not belong to the quotation.

Did Dad say, "Come home at 7:00"?

The baby said, "I see Mama!"

Remember to capitalize the first word of a direct quotation.

Exercises **Punctuate direct quotations.**

A. Read these sentences to yourself. Copy them. Then add all the punctuation marks that are needed.

1. Drop anchor bellowed the captain.
2. Don't forget your key Jeff said Nina.
3. The cashier asked Will there be anything else?
4. Call me when you finish said Ms. Walters.
5. Kevin replied I am finished now.
6. My parents have already said I can't go Pablo complained.
7. Do you really believe in ESP asked Tammy.
8. Did Lillian say I'll be at the pool soon?
9. Ron asked Where are you going?
10. Two eggs, with bacon shouted the waitress.

B. Follow the directions for Exercise A.

1. What was that noise asked my sister.
2. Last call for dinner announced the Amtrak waiter.
3. How can you eat so much pie Willie Anita inquired.
4. Those ears of corn look too big for that basket Mr. Valdez remarked.
5. What a tackle shouted David.
6. Mary said The roof is leaking.
7. Who's there called Michelle.

8. Kathy's mother said I will help you.
9. Watch the derrick Manny cried.
10. Heavens to Betsy exclaimed Mrs. Mulligan.

Divided Quotations

Sometimes a quotation is divided. Explanatory words, like *she said* or *he asked,* occur in the middle of the quotation.

"My favorite movie," Lewis said, "is the original *King Kong.*"

Divided quotations follow the capitalization and punctuation guidelines presented already. In addition, these rules apply:

1. Two sets of quotation marks are used.
2. The explanatory words are followed by a comma or a period. Use a comma if the second part of the quotation does not begin a new sentence. Use a period if the second part of the quotation is a new sentence.

"I can't go," Frank said. "My homework is not done."

"I believe," said Mona, "that you are wrong."

3. The second part of the quotation begins with a capital if it is the start of a new sentence. Otherwise, the second part begins with a small letter.

Exercises **Punctuate divided quotations.**

A. Read each divided quotation to yourself. Then copy the sentence, using punctuation marks and capitals correctly.

1. Are you ready said Bryan I'll time you.
2. The crawl kick isn't hard Judy assured us just keep your knees straight as you swim.
3. Take the game home Sally said generously you can keep it.
4. How much does this spray cost Bonita inquired is it guaranteed to repel mosquitoes?

5. What would you do Mr. Rocher asked if the rope broke?

6. Before you leave said Ms. Schafer I want you to finish this assignment.

7. Where did you go Juanita asked I couldn't find you.

8. Look at my watch exclaimed Sam it doesn't even have water in it.

9. You can pat Prince said Louise he won't bite.

10. The other way Hector insisted is much shorter.

B. Follow the directions for Exercise A.

1. Be careful shouted John the canoe will hit bottom.

2. Ask Mrs. Mitchell suggested Maureen maybe we can broadcast the announcement.

3. No answered Seth my jacket is blue.

4. If you need more spigots said the farmer they're in this sap bucket.

5. Fortunately piped up Andrea I've got fifty cents.

6. Turn the box over my brother suggested maybe the price is on the back.

7. Saturday Dora said I'll come about 8:30.

8. I'm getting cold shivered Robin let's go in.

9. The most interesting castles Beth said were in Europe.

10. Don't worry said my mother it will wash out.

Dialogue

In writing **dialogue** (conversation), begin a new paragraph every time the speaker changes. Use another set of quotation marks for each new speaker.

> "I want to go ice skating this weekend," Thomas said, "but I can't find my skates."
>
> "Can you rent a pair at the rink?" Rosemary asked.
>
> "Yes, I think so," Thomas replied.

Exercise Punctuate conversation correctly.

Read and then rewrite the following conversation. Make correct paragraph divisions and use the correct punctuation.

Fay and Alan looked at the lists of ice cream flavors at Swenson's Dairy have you made up your mind yet Fay asked yes Alan said I'm getting strawberry you always get strawberry Fay said why don't you ever try something new I'm trying to decide between chocolate fudge and cherry ripple that's why I always get strawberry Alan said it's so much faster

Using Quotation Marks for Titles

Use quotation marks to enclose chapter titles, titles of magazine articles, titles of short stories or single poems, titles of television programs, and titles of songs.

Chapter title:	Chapter 9, "State Government Today"
Magazine article:	"Summer Jobs for Teens"
Short Story:	"A Game of Catch"
Poem:	"Out, Out—"
Television program:	"Roots: The Next Generations"
Song:	"Take Me Out to the Ball Game"

Underlining

Underline the titles of books, newspapers, magazines, and movies.

When you are writing or when you are typing, underline these titles, like this: The Contender.

When these titles are printed, they are printed in *italics*, rather than underlined.

Book title:	*The Contender*
Newspaper:	*Baltimore Sun*
Magazine:	*Reader's Digest*
Movie:	*China Syndrome*

Exercises **Punctuate titles correctly.**

A. Number your paper from 1 to 10. Punctuate each of the following titles correctly.

1. Close Encounters of the Third Kind (movie)
2. The Ark (book)
3. Boston Globe (newspaper)
4. Child on Top of a Greenhouse (poem)
5. Football's Superstars (magazine article)
6. Field and Stream (magazine)
7. M*A*S*H (television program)
8. The Age of the Glaciers (chapter title)
9. You Light Up My Life (song)
10. The Tiger's Heart (short story)

B. Follow the directions for Exercise A.

1. How the West Was Won (movie)
2. The Outcasts of Poker Flat (short story)
3. Call It Courage (book)
4. The Diet That's Right for You (magazine article)
5. I'm Nobody! Who Are You? (poem)
6. The Undersea World of Jacques Cousteau (television program)
7. National Geographic (magazine)
8. St. Louis Post-Dispatch (newspaper)
9. Ease On Down (song)
10. Modern Art (chapter title)

REVIEW Punctuation

The Period and Other End Marks Write these sentences, adding periods and end marks wherever necessary.

1. We will attend S E Grover High School
2. Have you seen Dr J L Pollock
3. Meet me at school at 9 A M
4. Will you read my poem, Mr Krause
5. Wow That's terrific

The Comma Write the following sentences, adding commas where they are needed.

6. Melinda said "I rode on the trail near the lake."
7. Yes I'd like to go to Disney World Vicky.
8. Angie likes Andy Gibb and she has many posters of him.
9. Dan Pierce the manager flew to Miami Florida.
10. The treaty was signed on December 10 1898.

The Apostrophe Write each sentence, adding apostrophes where they are needed.

11. My two brothers bikes are identical.
12. Tinas excuse is better than yours, isnt it?
13. California hasnt had rain in months.
14. The womens club held its weekly meeting.
15. Whos pitching for the Cardinals today?

Quotation Marks Write each sentence, adding quotation marks where they are needed.

16. Carl said, I'll run for office.
17. The man shouted, Get out!
18. Did she say, No one cares?
19. Behind the painting, Dad said, is our wall safe.
20. Gail said that she liked the poem The Harbor.

Spelling

Good spelling skills are valuable. They are important for writing reports in school. They are needed for writing different kinds of letters. They are vital for filling out forms and applications. As you grow older and write more, they will become even more necessary. To show people that you are careful and informed, you will need to be able to spell correctly.

You can become a good speller by learning a few basic rules. These rules will help you to write clearly. In this section, you will be learning the most important rules of good spelling. You will also learn how to develop good spelling habits.

How To Become a Better Speller

1. Make a habit of looking at words carefully. Practice seeing every letter. Store the letters in your memory. Many people see a word again and again but don't really look at it. Then they make mistakes like writing *safty* for *safety* or *sayed* for *said*. When you see a new word or a tricky word, like *necessary*, look at all the letters. To help yourself remember the spelling, write the word several times. You may want to keep a list of the new words for later practice.

2. When you speak, pronounce words carefully. Sometimes people misspell words because they say them wrong. Be sure that you are not blending syllables together. For example, you may write *finely* for *finally* if you are mispronouncing it.

3. Find out your own spelling enemies and attack them. Look over your past papers and make a list of the misspelled words. Study these words until you can spell them correctly.

4. Find memory devices to help with problem spellings. Memory devices link words with their correct spellings. Below are some devices. They may give you ideas for other words.

bel**ie**ve	There is a *lie* in bel*ie*ve.
fr**ie**nd	*I* will be your friend to the *end*.
emba**rrass**	I turned *really red* and felt *so silly*.

5. Proofread what you write. To make sure that you have spelled all words correctly, reread your work. Examine it carefully, word for word. Don't let your eyes race over the page and miss misspellings.

6. Use a dictionary. You don't have to know how to spell every word. No one spells everything correctly all the time. A good dictionary can help you to be a better speller. Use a dictionary whenever you need help with your spelling.

7. Study the few important spelling rules given in this section.

How To Master the Spelling of Particular Words

1. Look at a new or difficult word and say it to yourself. Pronounce it carefully. If it has two or more syllables, say it again, one syllable at a time. Look at each syllable as you say it.

2. Look at the letters and say each one. If the word has two or more syllables, pause between syllables as you say the letters.

3. Without looking at the word, write it.

4. Now look at your book or list and see if you have spelled the word correctly. If you have, write it once more. Compare it with the correct spelling again. For best results, repeat the process once more.

5. If you have misspelled the word, notice where the error was. Then repeat steps 3 and 4 until you have spelled the word correctly three times in a row.

Rules for Spelling

The Final Silent e

When a suffix beginning with a vowel is added to a word ending with a silent e, the e is usually dropped.

make + ing = making
confuse + ion = confusion
expense + ive = expensive
believe + able = believable

When a suffix beginning with a consonant is added to a word ending with a silent e, the e is usually kept.

hate + ful = hateful
bore + dom = boredom
hope + less = hopeless
sure + ly = surely

The following words are **exceptions:**

truly argument ninth wholly judgment

Exercise **Add suffixes correctly.**

Find the misspelled words in these sentences and spell them correctly. (In most of the sentences, more than one word is misspelled.)

1. Some fameous people are lonly.
2. Why are we haveing this silly arguement?
3. I am hopeing that this game won't remain scoreless.
4. A jack is usful for changeing tires.
5. Ms. Moore's statment was truly moveing.
6. Terence is blameing me for the damage to his bike.
7. We ordered a flower arrangment of ninty roses.
8. The blazeing fire severly damaged the house.
9. The performance of the dareing acrobats was exciteing.
10. Good writeing skills are a desirable achievment.

Words Ending in *y*

When a suffix is added to a word that ends with *y* following a consonant, the *y* is usually changed to *i*.

noisy + ly = noisily
happy + est = happiest
try + ed = tried
carry + age = carriage
fifty + eth = fiftieth
heavy + ness = heaviness

Note this **exception:** When *-ing* is added, the *y* remains.

bury + ing = burying
deny + ing = denying
cry + ing = crying
apply + ing = applying

When a suffix is added to a word that ends with *y* following a vowel, the *y* usually is not changed.

joy + ful = joyful
stay + ing = staying
pay + ment = payment
annoy + ed = annoyed

The following words are **exceptions:**

paid said gaily gaiety

Exercise **Write words with suffixes and a final *y*.**

Add the suffixes as shown and write the new word.

1. employ + er	6. sneaky + est	11. hurry + ed
2. enjoy + able	7. destroy + er	12. holy + ness
3. marry + age	8. sixty + eth	13. easy + ly
4. play + ed	9. say + ing	14. ready + ness
5. carry + ing	10. reply + es	15. boy + ish

The Suffixes *-ly* and *-ness*

When the suffix *-ly* is added to a word ending with *l*, both *l's* are kept. When *-ness* is added to a word ending in *n*, both *n's* are kept.

practical + ly = practically	mean + ness = meanness
careful + ly = carefully	open + ness = openness

The Addition of Prefixes

When a prefix is added to a word, the spelling of the word stays the same.

un + named = unnamed	re + enter = reenter
dis + appear = disappear	un + known = unknown
in + formal = informal	il + legible = illegible
im + mature = immature	in + appropriate = inappropriate

Exercise **Write words with prefixes and suffixes.**

Find the misspelled words in these sentences and spell them correctly. (In many of the sentences, more than one word is misspelled.)

1. Luis was imobile in a plaster cast.
2. Carolyn likes this meat for its leaness.
3. Sometimes reporters are missinformed.
4. Many students become awfuly unneasy at test time.

5. Mistreating animals should be ilegal.
6. People who write carefuly don't often mispell words.
7. The unevenness of Ken's handwriting makes it ilegible.
8. Idealy, citizens should not dissobey the law.
9. My mother dissapproves of my stubborness.
10. I realy distrust people who are iresponsible.

Words with the "Seed" Sound

Only one English word ends in *sede: supersede*
Three words end in *ceed: exceed, proceed, succeed*
All other words ending in the sound of *seed* are spelled *cede:*

concede   precede   recede   secede

Words with *ie* or *ei*

When the sound is long *e* (ē), the word is spelled *ie* except after *c*.

I Before *E*:

achieve	brief	field	niece	shield
belief	chief	fierce	relieve	yield

Except After *C*:

ceiling   conceited   perceive   receive   receipt

The following words are **exceptions:**

either	leisure	species
neither	seize	weird

Exercise **Write words with the "seed" sound and *ie/ei* words.**

Find the misspelled words in these sentences and spell them correctly. (In some of the sentences, there is more than one misspelled word.)

1. Anna recieved an award for her painting.

2. Did the trucker excede the speed limit?
3. Álvarez preceeds Sanders in the batting order.
4. The mayor beleived that she had been wrong.
5. We saw a breif film about making leisure time work.
6. The criminal yeilded after a feirce fight.
7. The outfielder proseded to snatch the line drive.
8. Weird shadows danced on the cieling.
9. Many people succede because they beleive in themselves.
10. The police cheif siezed the thief.

Doubling the Final Consonant

With words of one syllable, ending with one consonant following one vowel, you double the final consonant before adding *-ing, -ed,* or *-er.*

sit + ing = sitting
hop + ed = hopped
plan + er = planner
shop + er = shopper
sad + er = sadder
stop + ing = stopping
trot + ed = trotted
drag + ing = dragging

The final consonant is **not** doubled when it is preceded by two vowels.

meet + ing = meeting
break + ing = breaking
seem + ed = seemed
loan + ed = loaned
train + er = trainer
soon + er = sooner

Exercise **Double the final consonant.**

Decide whether or not the final consonant should be doubled. Then add the suffix as shown and write the new word.

1. leap + ed
2. fat + er
3. beat + ing
4. cool + er
5. chop + er
6. hem + ed
7. scream + ing
8. flap + ed
9. hot + er
10. hug + ing
11. hear + ing
12. trip + ed
13. swim + er
14. leap + ing
15. peek + ed

Words Often Confused

Sometimes you make a mistake in spelling simply because of your own carelessness or forgetfulness. Other times, however, your problems are caused by the language itself. In English there are many pairs or trios of words that are easily confused. These words sound the same, or nearly the same, but are spelled differently and have different meanings. Words of this type are called **homonyms.**

Here are some examples of homonyms:

do—dew—due
horse—hoarse
pare—pear—pair
tail—tale

When you have problems with homonyms, general spelling rules won't help you. The only solution is to memorize which spelling goes with which meaning.

Here is a list of words frequently used and frequently confused in writing. Study the sets of words, and try to connect each word with its correct meaning. Refer to the list if you have further difficulties with these words.

accept means "to agree to something or to receive something willingly."

My brother will *accept* the job the grocer offered him.

except means "to keep out" or "leave out." As a preposition, *except* means "but" or "leaving out."

Overdue books returned to the library today are *excepted* from the usual fines.

Michelle likes every flavor of ice cream *except* pistachio.

already means "previously or before."

The airplane had *already* landed.

all ready means "completely prepared."

The paramedics were *all ready* for the emergency.

capital means "important." It also refers to the city or town that is the official seat of government of a state or nation.

The *capital* of Illinois is the city of Springfield.

capitol is the building where a state legislature meets.

The *capitol* of Illinois is a stately building in Springfield.

the Capitol is the building in Washington, D. C. in which the United States Congress meets.

The senators arrived at the *Capitol* in time to vote.

hear means "to listen to."

Every time I *hear* this song, I feel happy.

here means "in this place."

Reference books must stay *here* in the library.

it's is the contraction for *it is* or *it has*.

It's nearly midnight.

its shows ownership or possession.

The boat lost *its* sail during the storm.

knew means "understood" or "was familiar with."

The forest ranger *knew* that the fire was out of control.

new is the opposite of old and means "fresh or recent."

Old shoes feel more comfortable than *new* ones.

know means "to understand" or "to be familiar with."

Scientists do not *know* the cause of cancer.

no is a negative word meaning "not" or "not any."

This theater has *no* popcorn.

lead (lĕd) is a heavy, gray metal.

Those pipes are made of *lead*.

lead (lēd) means "to go first, to guide."

These signs will *lead* us to the hiking trail.

led (lĕd) is the past tense of lead (lēd).

Bloodhounds *led* the detectives to the scene of the crime.

loose means "free" or "not tight."

A rider keeps the horse's reins *loose*.

lose means "to mislay or suffer the loss of something."

If you *lose* your book, report the loss to the library.

peace is calm or stillness or the absence of disagreement.

A sunset over the ocean is my idea of *peace.*

piece means "a portion or part."

Who can stop eating after one *piece* of pie?

plain means "clear or simple." It also refers to an expanse of land.

The judge wanted to know the *plain* truth.

Cattle grazed on the grassy *plain.*

plane refers to a flat surface or a woodworking tool. It is also the short form of *airplane.*

We watched the *plane* take off.

The carpenter used her *plane* to make the door level.

principal means "first or most important." It also refers to the head of a school.

A *principal* export of Brazil is coffee.

Our school *principal* organized a safety council.

principle is a rule, truth, or belief.

One *principle* of science is that all matter occupies space.

quiet means "free from noise or disturbance."

The only time our classroom is *quiet* is when it's empty.

quite means "truly or almost completely."

The aquarium tank is *quite* full.

right means "proper or correct." It also means the opposite of left. It also refers to a just claim.

Emily Post is an expert on the *right* way to act.

Turn *right* at the second intersection.

A trial by jury is every citizen's *right.*

write refers to forming words with a pen or pencil.

I will *write* a letter to the editor.

there means "at that place."

Please take your books over *there.*

their means "belonging to them."

Our neighbors sold *their* house and moved to a farm.

they're is the contraction for *they are.*

My sisters have never skied, but *they're* willing to try.

weather is the state of the atmosphere, referring to wind, moisture, temperature, and other such conditions.

Australia has summer *weather* when the United States has winter.

whether indicates a choice or alternative.

Whether we drive or take the train, we will arrive in three hours.

to means "in the direction of."

The surgeon rushed *to* the operating room.

too means "also or very."

The lights went off, and then the heat went off, *too*.

two is the whole number between one and three.

Only *two* of the four climbers reached the peak.

who's is the contraction for *who is* or *who has*.

Who's been chosen to be a crossing guard?

whose is the possessive form of *who*.

Whose skateboard was left on the sidewalk?

your is the possessive form of *you*.

Please bring *your* sheet music to choir practice.

you're is the contraction for *you are*.

You're going to dance, aren't you.

Exercises Use words often confused.

A. Write the correct word from the words in parentheses.

1. Janie and Alice built (their, there, they're) own treehouse.
2. The Indian (lead, led) his tribesmen to the hunting ground.
3. (Who's, Whose) bicycle has racing stripes?
4. Is the cast (all ready, already) for the first performance?
5. Nobody (knew, new) the answer to the fifth question on the test.
6. If I (loose, lose) this dollar bill, I won't eat lunch.
7. A shark is vicious because of (its, it's) double row of teeth.

8. Not every problem has only one (right, write) solution.
9. Did Dwayne (accept, except) the invitation to your party?
10. I study best in a well-lit, (quiet, quite) room.
11. The (capital, capitol, Capitol) in Washington, D. C. is built on a hill.
12. The patient is (know, no) better today.
13. Are you taller than (your, you're) sister?
14. We will play the game (weather, whether) it rains or not.
15. A (piece, peace) of fabric was caught in the machine.

B. Write the correct word from the words in parentheses.

1. The teacher asked us to (right, write) our assignment.
2. We had to hunt for the gerbil that got (loose, lose).
3. The (principal, principle) actor in "M*A*S*H" is Alan Alda.
4. Carlotta ordered a (plain, plane) hamburger.
5. Jaguars seem fierce, but (their, there, they're) afraid of dogs.
6. A fire engine will (lead, led) the parade.
7. Did you (know, no) that ants have five noses?
8. Although bats don't see at night, they (hear, here) where they are.
9. Does your brother know that (your, you're) planning a surprise party?
10. Ceramics is creative, and it's fun, (to, too, two).
11. Eric is the only batter (who's, whose) left-handed.
12. A few of her friends taught us the (knew, new) dances.
13. The city of Austin is the (capital, capitol, Capitol) of Texas.
14. Examine the new bike to see whether (its, it's) scratched.
15. Everyone (accept, except) Donna went down the giant slide.

REVIEW Spelling

Spelling Look at each sentence carefully. Find the misspelled words. Write each word correctly.

1. The candidate is very hopful.
2. Have you stayed in these citys?
3. I carryed grocerys in my bike basket.
4. This canoe is realy unnsteady.
5. The meaness of that little dog is surpriseing.
6. Hard work will often succede.
7. A mobile hangs from the cieling.
8. Bo's dog usualy retreives sticks.
9. Rita spoted the mispelled word.
10. That shouting is unecessary.

Words Often Confused Write the correct word from the words given in parentheses.

11. Everyone (accept, except) John was at practice.
12. Are you (already, all ready) for the recital?
13. Did you (hear, here) that rumor?
14. The cheerleaders have (knew, new) uniforms.
15. An Indian guide (lead, led) the Pilgrims.
16. That sail is too (loose, lose).
17. I put a monogram on a (plain, plane) red sweater.
18. Will you please (right, write) on the chalkboard?
19. The Johnsons opened (their, there, they're) new store.
20. I hope (your, you're) ready for the time trials.

D

E

M

N

O

P

Q

R

S

T

U

V

W

Y

Z

Acknowledgments

William Collins + World Publishing Company: For entries on pages 176, 179, 180, 181, 246, and 274 from *Webster's New World Dictionary of the American Language,* Students Edition; copyright © 1976 by William Collins + World Publishing Company, Inc.

Photographs

Woodfin Camp: Michal Heron, 86; Timothy Eagan, 116; Jim Anderson, 172, 182.

Magnum: Burk Uzzle, ii; Wayne Miller, xiv; Mark Godfrey, 18, 108; Dennis Stock, 26, 134; Bob Adelman, 38; Ron Benvenisti, 48; Charles Gatewood, 62, 102, 142, 158; Danny Lyon, 68; Paul Fusco, 94, 76; Charles Harbutt, 150.

Illustrations

Jeanne Seabright: all handwritten letters. Ken Izzi: special mechanical art. Synthegraphics Corporation: diagrams. Montagu Design: special mechanical art. Marcia Vecchione: art production.

81 82 83 / 10 9 8 7 6 5 4 3